THE
IMMIGRANTS

THE
IMMIGRANTS

**THE GREAT MIGRATION
FROM BRITAIN TO NEW ZEALAND,
1830—1890**

TONY SIMPSON

For Jonathan Brown

First published 1997 by

Godwit Publishing Ltd
15 Rawene Road, P.O. Box 34-683
Birkenhead, Auckland, New Zealand

Reprinted 1998

Published with the support of Creative New Zealand Toi Aotearoa

Typesetting and production by Kate Greenaway
Cover design by Christine Hansen
Printed in Hong Kong

CONTENTS

INTRODUCTION

We left our native land, and far away
Across the waters, sought a world unknown;
But did not know that we in vain might stray
In search of one so lovely as our own
Alexander Marjoribanks, 1845

Between 1853 and 1876, 4,023,518 outward emigrants are recorded as leaving the British Isles, including Ireland.[1] To these must undoubtedly be added many more whose leaving was, for one reason or another, never recorded. Some writers have suggested a figure more than double that supplied by the official statistics. Few of these emigrants returned. This is an astonishing movement of peoples, ranking historically, for example, with the westward population movements which brought down the Roman Empire in the sixth century. Who these people were, why they left their homelands, and where they went are some of the facts fundamental to an understanding of British history in the nineteenth century.

Over the same period, 804,366 of these emigrants came to Australia and New Zealand. This fact is similarly crucial to our understanding of New Zealand history since that time. Until 1864, migrants to New Zealand from Australia far outnumbered those arriving direct from the United Kingdom. This continued to be largely the case until the 1870s, when there was a burst of mass, direct migration. Between 1861 and 1876 the non-Maori population of New Zealand rose from 99,021 to 399,075. Of this increase over the same period, 207,000 was contributed by net immigration. It was not until nearly 1890 that the natural rate of increase of the New Zealand population (the excess of births over deaths) exceeded the population gain from immigration. Of all those who entered New Zealand as immigrants in the century to 1960, more than half had done so before 1890. It is important for us to know, therefore, who these immigrants were, why they came to New Zealand in particular, what perceptions they carried with them, and how they responded to the emigrant experience.

One of the difficulties of doing this is the problem of establishing anything other than the most basic facts about New Zealand immigration. During the nineteenth century, anyone who got off a ship in New Zealand was counted as an immigrant and anyone who left was counted as an emigrant. This is a fairly rough measure, especially given the laxity of many officials during a time when accurate counting was neither so highly regarded nor so readily attained as it is today (when most incomers arrive by air through a very small number of entry points). Nor do the British statistics help much. These not only fail to distinguish between those leaving for Australia and for New Zealand but also cannot tell us how many of those who left went first to Australia and then to New Zealand. The New Zealand arrival statistics suggest, however, that between 1861 and 1891 the net immigration to New Zealand was 272,990.[2]

Raw aggregates of this sort, however dramatic, are necessarily misleading. The pattern varies from year to year. The years 1863 and 1874, for instance, were high points in which the net immigration flows were respectively 35,120 and 38,106. By 1868 and 1881 these flows had fallen to 860 and 6,376 respectively. In 1888 there was actually a negative outflow of 9,175. What we have in these figures are responses to events and circumstances in New Zealand, and in the countries of origin of the immigrants. It is important to know at the very least what these circumstances and events were, what was happening in Britain, and what it was that was drawing people to New Zealand during the nineteenth century.

But as soon as we attempt to go further into such fields as country of origin there is a difficulty. There are some figures available which show that in 1861 about 35% of the New Zealand population was born in England, 28% was New Zealand born, 16% was from Scotland, 9% from Ireland, 8.5% from Wales, 2.6% from Australia, and the balance from a wide range of other countries. Beyond that it is almost impossible to reach any reliable conclusions, because in 1972 the Department of Statistics, which had been patiently collecting, although not collating, raw data on original birthplaces of the population since the beginning of comprehensive censustaking in 1857, in a breathtaking exercise in official vandalism destroyed all of the nineteenth-century returned questionnaires. So we will never know the answers to some crucial questions concerning the origins of immigrants. Other sources such as shipping lists can partially repair this deficiency, but not completely. Thus, all we are able to say with any certainty is that probably in excess of 90% of our nineteenth-century immigrants came from the British Isles and Ireland.[3]

Even the breakdown of this large lump into its basic ethnic components is problematical. Most historians simply repeat the conclusions of their predecessors that this was made up of about 60% English and the balance evenly divided between the other groups. But when these conclusions are traced to their origins they transpire, as is too often the case, to be simply the reified beliefs of the earliest historians — in this case G. H. Scholefield, who in his entry in the 1933 edition of the *Cambridge History of the British Empire* was pleased to report to his readers that 'the purity of the British race is being well conserved in New Zealand'.[4]

Notwithstanding this paucity of hard data, historians who have dealt with the matter have never hesitated to draw broad conclusions about the nature of New Zealand immigration and its consequences. As a result, two broad historiographical schools have developed.[5] These schools share certain basic presuppositions and beliefs. The major of these is that immigration to New Zealand happened in three stages. There was first a period in which significant immigration was under the auspices of the New Zealand Company and its satellites. This period ended about 1855. There was next a period partially characterised by immigration assisted by provincial governments and, for a short time, encouraged by the discovery of gold in some areas. This period ended about 1870. The third and most significant period of immigration covers the decade and a half to 1885, and was characterised by central government assistance as a crucial component in a comprehensive programme of public works and development. This is usually known as the Vogel period, from its political progenitor.

Those emigrants who were driven from their homeland by social circumstances found in New Zealand a much more open society than that they had left, and one which allowed those who wished to do so and were prepared to work the chance to do well and realise their ambitions. But international trade depression curtailed these opportunities from the late 1870s until, in the 1890s, the cloud began to lift and the New Zealand economy was able to recover. During the so-called Long Depression of a decade or more which ended in 1895, two important developments had occurred.

The first was the application of the technology of refrigeration to agriculture, which enabled New Zealand to become a successful international supplier of certain products, particularly sheepmeats and dairy produce, especially to the British market. The second was what amounted to a political revolution in which the community of immigrants responded to the hardships of their depressed circumstances by electing a series of governments, culminating in that of 1890, committed to certain political agendas the immigrants had brought from their homeland. These agendas were directed to ensuring that the circumstances which had driven them from those homelands were not repeated in the new society.

The two historiographical schools begin to part company on the matter of the forces which drove these events. The first, initiated by W. P. Reeves, has been content to perceive these developments as being natural consequences in a colonial immigrant society in which creative political forces are released by the freer atmosphere of the new land, thereby resolving problems which class or other impediments made intractable in the old. Thus, Reeves says that the Vogel period 'was virtually the beginning of state socialism in New Zealand':[6] that is, the start of a triumphant social march culminating in an interventionist, egalitarian democracy. Historians such as Sinclair and the 'Oxford History of New Zealand' group associated with his writings have tended to follow this interpretation.

The alternative interpretation, represented by the writings of W. B. Sutch and his successors, has seen the matter rather differently. These writers suggest that rather than being driven by a natural process, the events described were the result of struggle by ordinary immigrants who found themselves confronted by the very forces, in the form of a landed gentry and their cohorts, they had fled their homelands to escape. This factor, disguised by the relative openness of New Zealand between 1850 and 1880, was not simply dramatised by the Long Depression: the latter in fact created the objective economic and political circumstances in which it might be overcome. It was this process of struggle which created the political revolution of 1890 rather than any natural process inherent in colonial immigration. Thus Sutch remarks:

> The quarter century before 1890 produced causes and the following quarter century produced effects. However, if it had not been for manhood suffrage and the country quota, the egalitarian, predominantly nonconformist immigrants would not have achieved the small farms which were made possible by refrigeration. This achievement could not have been attained without an alliance between the land hungry and those who represented the depressed wage earning class for they — at least the males among them — had the majority of votes in the country.[7]

Recently the whole basis of this traditional historiography has been challenged from two different directions. The first challenge has come from within the historical establishment. The academic historian Fairburn[8] has suggested that nineteenth-century New Zealand was, in fact, nothing like its depiction by either school. Instead he propounds an immigrant society characterised by social isolation, weak community structures, and bondlessness. This accounts, he argues, for the drunkenness and violence of colonial New Zealand. Thus, from this viewpoint, the political agendas of the 1890s owe little to the responses of immigrant citizens to economic and political impediments. Rather they are responses at a much more private and personal level to the individual distress caused by the atomisation which is part of the colonial experience. Thus their emphasis on family cohesion — the small farm, prohibition, and so on — and their point of reference in arcadian rather than utopian images of the ideal society.

The other challenge has come from those academic and popular historians primarily interested in the bicultural nature of New Zealand society; that is, the fact of the existence of a pre-immigrant culture in Aotearoa, and the history of nineteenth- and twentieth-century New Zealand as driven by the relationship between the immigrant arrivals and the Maori.[9] This approach, although it propounds a historiography at variance with that traditionally adopted, had been accepted within the Reeves/Sutch framework as a cultural conflict which constituted a secondary theme within the primary conflict between immigrant ambition and whatever it was which stood in the way of its achievement. Maori resistance to Pakeha settlement, it was perceived, was one of those impediments. The difference in the alternative historiographical approach lies in the perception of that resistance not as an impediment but as a legitimate response to an illegitimate incursion. In the view of this historical group, this response is still valid and is the basis of contemporary Maori agendas and their associated political debates.

Traditional historiography has responded differently to these two challenges. It has adapted to incorporate the bicultural approach into its canon of orthodoxy, although some of the more perceptive of the proponents of both historiographical approaches have observed that ultimately the two cannot be reconciled. The response to the 'alienation' approach has been, on the other hand, one of scepticism or outright rejection on the part of most orthodox historians.[10] This is understandable given that its characterisation of New Zealand society runs directly counter to some of that society's most deeply cherished beliefs and origin myths. Both challenges have initiated a lively debate among historians, and this has led to the much more open examination of the presuppositions which underlie much history writing in New Zealand.[11]

One of the contributors to this debate has made the significant observation that its successful prosecution entails a much more careful re-examination of the *process* of immigration and its consequences.[12] This book is concerned with the questions which are fundamental to that re-examination. What brought British interest to the south Pacific in general and New Zealand in particular? How did that lead to mass immigration both as a matter of policy and as a response to circumstances in the home country? What were those policies and circumstances? What was the objective experience of immigration? How did the immigrants themselves perceive the immigrant experience? What conclusions did they draw as a result, and what were the points of reference from which they formulated those conclusions? And, above all, this being the purpose of history, what does this tell us about contemporary New Zealand?

CHAPTER ONE

THE COMING OF
THE PAKEHA

The English have been interested in the Pacific Ocean since the seventeenth-century explorations of Francis Drake opened up vast new regions to trade and adventure. But it was only during the latter part of the eighteenth century that this interest became a presence. This was the century of mercantilism in English trade, a doctrine described by the historian Barbara Tuchman as

> holding that the colonial role in trade was to serve as the source of raw materials and market for British manufacture, and never, never, to usurp the manufacturing function. This symbiosis was regarded as unalterable. Transportation both ways in British bottoms* and re-export of colonial produce by way of Britain to foreign markets were aspects of the system, which was regulated by some thirty Navigation Acts and by the Board of Trade, the most organised and professional arm of the British government.[1]

The elegant symmetry of this arrangement was no doubt pleasing to the merchants of the City of London and, as the industrial revolution got into its stride, the burgeoning cohorts of British manufacturers. It was less so to the colonial customers it presupposed, and to the putative commercial competitors it proposed to exclude from the colonial marketplaces. In particular it displeased the French, who by the latter part of the eighteenth century had been virtually driven out of Canada, India and the West Indies. During this period, in an almost continuous series of naval battles with the French, the Spanish and the Dutch, Britain established an international naval hegemony which lasted for nearly two centuries. But this hegemony was fragile, regularly challenged and difficult to maintain.

Today, if we wish to make an international journey, we travel by air or

---

* 'Bottoms' refers to cargo vessels of all and every description.

sea more or less in a straight line. Prior to the invention of steam locomotion it was a different matter. Europeans sailing to India proceeded not south and east but west, to Brazil via the Azores or Cape Verde Islands. They then doubled back to Africa, touched at the Cape of Good Hope and travelled north to India via the archipelagos of the Indian Ocean. On the return journey they skirted Madagascar, touched once more at Capetown, and sailed north along the West African coast to Europe. These apparently eccentric routes take best advantage of the prevailing winds. But they involve long distances and journey times. And if wind power is free, the technologies which permit its use are not. Sailing ships are complex machines. Even the simplest of them have well over 100 spars and lines in the rigging alone. Hulls are at the mercy of woodworm. Sails, subject to continuous wear and tear, have to be constantly replaced. Crews ill with scurvy cannot sail ships. Unless these matters can be attended to sailing ships cannot sail. They require an international nexus of depots and revictualling stations if they are to do so.

The British had very few bases on the international sailing route to India, and could not protect their trade without them because they needed them to refit and reprovision their navy. What this meant in practical terms is illustrated by an incident which occurred in July 1782 while Admiral Hughes was patrolling the Bay of Bengal. Off Negapatam he came up

LONDON – WELLINGTON
AVERAGE LENGTH OF VOYAGE — 110 DAYS.

At over three months, the emigrant journey to New Zealand was the longest. Unlike the route shown on this sketch map most ships touched only at Madeira or Cape Verde before the long haul to New Zealand. (ATL)

against the French and, in preparation for battle, asked his captains to report. The reports made alarming reading: his fleet was barely seaworthy, let alone battleworthy. Nevertheless, he engaged. In a short and inconclusive skirmish he lost 33 masts, 18 yards and four bowsprits. The French were similarly damaged, and both fleets broke off the engagement. The French could fall back on Cuddalore and order up replacement stores from Mauritius, their main base. Hughes, who could not, limped back to Bombay and had to abandon the whole eastern coast of India. Two years later he was still sending anguished pleas to the Admiralty for cable, canvas and spars.[2]

The solution to the problem which confronted Hughes, and all other merchant and naval captains, was to find unclaimed land with suitable resources to set up the bases required. The logic of that solution forced English explorers further and further into the South Pacific region, seeking harbours, sources of spars and cordage, trading opportunities and, ultimately, a destination for surplus British population. This process got fully under way in 1768 with the explorations of James Cook. The twentieth century views Cook as a great cartographer and navigator, and so he was. But his expeditions were intended to serve purposes well beyond these disinterested scientific pursuits.[3]

The eighteenth century drew no fine distinctions between science and trade. Cook's instructions required him not only to mark the transit of Venus but also to test the theories of the geographer Dalrymple who posited a large southern continent. If it existed, he was to report on its trade potential. He found no such continent, and by the time Cook returned from his second voyage the revelation of the Pacific was largely complete, with the way open for the subsequent influx of traders, missionaries and settlers. More particularly, he had reported the presence in commercial quantities of spar timber, the raw material for cordage, and whales and seals. He had also confirmed the existence of at least one large land mass — Australia — and of groups of strategically placed islands. All of these things interested his masters in London, but it was Australia which interested them first and foremost. Here lay the prospect of solving another problem: what to do with the surplus wicked among the British populace.

CONVICTS AND THE COLONIES

We have so far forgotten the criminology of earlier centuries as rarely to remark on its curiosities, although we sometimes remember that men and women could be hanged for over 200 felonies, including poaching, shoplifting, consorting with gypsies, impersonating a Chelsea pensioner, damaging Westminster bridge or using a contraceptive device.[4] The harshness of this jurisprudence was mitigated by the sentence of transportation. This was not an eighteenth-century invention. As early as 1584, Richard Hakluyt had proposed it as a means of colonising the Americas. But by the eighteenth century it was a principal component of the English penal system.

The preamble to the 1718 Transportation Act makes its purpose clear: it was an enactment not only to deter criminals but also to supply the colonies with labour. About 3,000 people were sentenced to death annually in Britain in the eighteenth century, but only a few hundred actually died on the gallows each year. The majority were instead reprieved for indentured service for seven years in the American colonies.[5] In the middle years of the century the contractors licensed to conduct this business were sending more than 1,000 people a year from London alone. We are not inclined to think of colonial America as a convict settlement, but one estimate is that over half of its population in the eighteenth century was from this source: nearly 50,000 people between 1719 and 1772. In 1776, with the outbreak of the war with the American colonists, this traffic came to an abrupt end. This did not, of course, stop judges from continuing to pass sentence. County gaols soon filled to bursting. The expedient of mooring hulks on the Thames helped for a while, but soon they too were overflowing. It was clear that some alternative dumping ground for these convicts would have to be found.

Some of the schemes proposed were wild indeed. A serious proposal to establish a penal settlement in Africa far up the Gambia River was abandoned only when it became apparent that the climate would ensure its failure. Even New Zealand was briefly considered, but rejected as too far away and its inhabitants too fierce. But one suggestion kept recurring: Botany Bay on the coast of New South Wales. This had been described by Cook only 16 years earlier as a good anchorage, teeming with fish and abundant wildlife, with fresh water, good soil, wooded, but not too densely, and a minimal native population. It seemed ideal, and when it received the approbation of Joseph Banks, the decision was as good as made.

On 13 May 1787 eleven ships sailed from Spithead under the command of Captain Arthur Phillip. Aboard his flotilla were four companies of marines, 443 sailors and 800 convicts, a third of them women. This was a long step towards the ultimate declaration of New Zealand as a British colony in 1840, although no one thought so at the time. But New Zealand had not been forgotten in the formulation of the Botany Bay project, nor in the instructions issued to Phillip. In August 1786 Lord Sydney addressed the lords commissioners of the Treasury concerning the proposed new settlement: 'It may not be remiss to remark in favour of this plan that considerable advantage will arise from the cultivation of the New Zealand hemp or flax plant in the new intended settlement, the supply of which would be of great consequence to us as a naval power.'[6]

ROPE AND SPARS, SEALS AND WHALES

It is understandable that this should have been on Sydney's mind. Just a few years earlier, officials in Russia, source of most British hemp for rope, had forced up the price of hemp to high levels. An official of the Board of Trade had memorialised that 'the prospect is dark and the evil without remedy whilst Petersburgh shall remain the almost only market of that necessary commodity for the completion of a maritime equipment'.[7]

Phillip's instructions included a requirement to explore the islands to his south-east as a possible source of naval spars and cordage. A Lieutenant Dawes was particularly charged with the responsibility of developing a flax industry on Norfolk Island, and Roger Morley, a master weaver, was included in the expedition to provide the necessary technical skills. The exigencies of initial survival prevented much time being devoted to the proposal in the first instance, but in 1791 Lieutenant Governor King reported on the potential of New Zealand flax.

He was enthusiastic, although his interest was in cloth rather than rope: 'I much fear that until a native of New Zealand is carried to Norfolk Island that the method of dressing that valuable commodity will not be known; and could that be obtained I have no doubt that Norfolk Island would very soon cloath the inhabitants of New South Wales.'[8] Indeed, he was so enthusiastic that two years later he sent an expedition to New Zealand to kidnap two Maori men for this purpose. This unauthorised expedition — which ended in an unseemly dispute over who was to pay the £37 2s it cost — was a failure. Dressing and weaving flax was women's work, the two men indignantly explained. It was beneath their mana, and they knew nothing of it. An embarrassed King returned them to their own country.

The uses of New Zealand flax regularly crop up in eighteenth- and early nineteenth-century British naval records. In 1807 sails and coarse cloth were being manufactured from it in New South Wales. In 1818 and again in 1821 the dockyard at Chatham carried out tests on rope made from New Zealand hemp. The earlier tests were disappointing, but those conducted three years later gave an excellent result.[9] And a Captain Skinner, commanding *Dromedary*, reported from Sydney that the breaking strain of New Zealand rope was superior to others he had tried, that it took tar well and was cheaper to manufacture than the alternatives.

Nor was it hemp alone which attracted official notice to New Zealand. Both Cook and Banks had reported very favourably on the spar timber they saw during their explorations there. These views would have been quite familiar to James Matra, who prepared the proposal which led to the establishment of the settlement at Botany Bay. He had sailed as an officer with Cook, and was probably personally familiar with the suitability of kauri and other timbers for maritime use. This too was a factor picked up by Sydney in his instructions to Phillip. 'It may also be proper,' he minuted, 'to attend to the possibility of procuring from New Zealand any quantity of masts and ship timber for the use of our fleets in India, as the distance between the two countries is not greater than between Great Britain and America. It grows close to the water's edge, is of size and quality superior to any hitherto known, and may be obtained without difficulty.' In 1793 Captain Raven of the *Britannia* prepared a report on the availability of spruce from New Zealand for the authorities in New South Wales. He was as enthusiastic about this as King had been about flax.

As the authorities were instructing Phillip, vessels were also pressing into the South Pacific in search of seal skins and whale oil. Many of these ships were American. The irritable British response to their defeat by the American colonists was a particularly strict application of the Navigation Acts to their erstwhile countrymen which all but ruined the American shipping industry — a process completed by the blockade of Britain by the French during the Napoleonic Wars. Between 1803 and 1807 Bonaparte's navy seized nearly 400 American merchantmen in the Atlantic. As a result, American vessels began to move out of the European trade. Instead they sailed south around Cape Horn, and took the longer but safer trade route across the Pacific to China and India. American merchants quickly developed a thriving business in Chinese ceramics, textiles and tea. Their difficulty was that they had few commodities the Chinese wanted in exchange. They discovered two in sandalwood and sea otter pelts. After rounding the Horn, the Yankee ships would put into a South American port to rest their crews and make any necessary repairs. They then sailed north up the Pacific coast to Canada, traded with the local inhabitants for a cargo of pelts, carried these to Canton, then came back around the Horn to Boston or New York.

But increasingly they found themselves unwelcome in the South American ports where the Spanish maintained their own form of mercantilism. Captains turned instead to Hawaii where they could pick up a cargo of sandalwood as well as refit. This not only made their journey shorter but led to a useful discovery. If they stopped at the Falkland Islands on the way, they could take on a cargo of seal skins. These were as acceptable to the Chinese as otter. In 1805 United States exports to Canton included 140,297 seal skins.[10]

By this time too the American captains were including Sydney in their trading itinerary. New England manufacturers found a ready market in the now well-developed settlements of New South Wales and Tasmania. Aware from the reports of Cook and, later, Vancouver, of the existence of seals in the south of New Zealand, captains began to explore the prospects there. This was not a trade confined to Americans. In 1792 the *Britannia*, the master of which was to report so favourably on the presence of ships' timber in New Zealand the following year, had arrived at Sydney under charter to Enderby & Son in London, with a party of convicts. Casting about for a return cargo, he decided to try for seal skins for the China trade. In November he landed a gang of men at Dusky Sound, and sailed for the Cape of Good Hope for provisions under charter to the garrison officers at Sydney. His intention was to return to Dusky following this voyage, and to take off the men and whatever seal skins they had collected.

Seven months later Captain Raven found his party in good spirits and well fed, largely from local sources. But best of all, 'I found that my people had collected four thousand and five hundred seals' skins, a quantity though not equal to my former expectations, yet I was well convinced they had used every exertion and had procured as many as possible.'[11] It was not long before the trickle of vessels following Raven turned into a flood. A pattern quickly established itself in which gangs stayed ashore for the summer, killing the seals, skinning them and salting the skins, and returning to Sydney or Hobart with their booty at the end of the season. It was a lucrative business. Good-quality skins could fetch up to a guinea each in London, where they were greatly prized by hatters for their waterproof qualities.

Immense numbers of skins were taken. John Grono, one of the best known of the sealing captains, took 35,000 skins off the New Zealand coast in three seasons. Cargoes of 12,000 were common. It did not take the Americans long to join in. In 1804 Governor King complained to London that three American vessels had taken 160,000 skins off a few small islands in Bass Strait in two years. The next year the *Favourite*, out of Nantucket, arrived in Sydney with an astonishing 60,000 skins, some of which were unloaded there, and the balance taken on to Canton.[12] It is hardly surprising that the seal fisheries were rapidly depleted. But this did not greatly perturb the sealers, for off the New Zealand coast they had already discovered an equally lucrative source of trade in whale oil.

Sperm whale oil burns with a bright, clear light. In the eighteenth century it was used extensively in lighthouse beacons and by the wealthy for superior domestic lighting. In the early nineteenth century an even more compelling use was found for it: as a fine lubricant in the developing industries of Britain and New England. The industrial revolution would not have been impossible without the slaughter of whales, but it would have been slower to develop. Whalebone, particularly the whip-like balleen, was also a valuable commodity, fulfilling many of the functions today performed by plastics. The existence of an extensive fishery between New Zealand and Peru was an important find.

In 1792, 59 London-based whalers, previously active largely in the northern hemisphere, returned from the new southern grounds with cargoes of oil and seal skins valued at nearly £200,000. But like their American counterparts they soon found themselves unwelcome in the Spanish ports of the southern Americas, so they looked increasingly to Sydney and Hobart as their bases of operations. But while this ensured they avoided the coast of Peru, the whalers were disadvantaged by the variability of the weather off Australia when they were making for Hobart to refit after the buffeting they had taken coming around the Horn. New Zealand was a far preferable landfall from that perspective. In May 1802 King quizzed the masters of some whaling vessels on this point and was told by them that 'off New Zealand the weather and sea is as favourable as on the coasts of Peru and Chile'. Reporting this to his friend Joseph Banks — and sending him the preserved body of a duckbilled platypus — King remarked: 'The whale fishing . . . off New Zealand may now be pronounced established. A full whaler takes these letters Home, another is almost ready to follow, and four more are filling with very great success.'[13]

In the 35 years from 1790, the southern whale fishery grew into a large industry. Samuel Enderby calculated in 1825 that each season it employed about 10,000 seamen out of the port of London alone. Allowing for a crew of 25 as usual on a whaler, this gives us a fleet of 400 ships. By that same year New England whaleships at least matched the British in numbers. King had noticed the Yankee presence as early as 1805. At its peak in 1847, the American whaling industry included 722 vessels out of 34 New England and other eastern ports, displaced 230,000 tons and employed an estimated 30,000 men.

These ships, each of about 300 tons, cruised the Pacific from north to south and back, sometimes for as long as three years, cutting up whales

and boiling them down at sea until they had a full cargo. In the north their
pivot was Japan; in the south it was New Zealand. Commodore Charles
Wilkes, who commanded a United States flotilla which made a sweep
around the Pacific between 1838 and 1842, an avowed purpose of which
was to foster and protect the American whaling industry, was not
exaggerating when he wrote: 'Our whaling fleet may be said at this very
day to whiten the Pacific Ocean with its canvas, and the proceeds of this
fishery give comfort and happiness to many thousands of our citizens.'[14]

NEW ZEALAND IN THE EARLY
NINETEENTH-CENTURY WORLD

By the end of the second decade of the nineteenth century New Zealand,
virtually unknown to Europeans 50 years previously, was a key element in
the South Pacific trading nexus which had grown up during that half century. Its timber and flax interested naval strategists and traders alike. It
was well known as a source of seal skins. And as a place to rest and refit it
was important to the thriving international whaling industry. It had even
begun to produce a literature.

The published journals of Cook, his fellow officers and scientists, and
of the navigators who followed in his footsteps were well enough known
to the scientific and curious of Europe and America. But in 1807 there
appeared the first account of life in New Zealand by a European who had
lived there. In 1805 the surgeon John Savage spent September and October
at the Bay of Islands. His account, which runs to nearly 100 pages, gives
us a fascinating glimpse of the country just as it was becoming a part of the
pattern of international trading relationships. The narrative is largely taken
up with a lively description of the Maori inhabitants, their customs and
way of life, as Savage understood them. But it is his conclusions which are
of the greatest interest in this context:

> From the preceding pages I imagine it will be seen that New Zealand is
> a country highly interesting: the part of it which I have attempted to
> describe is of greater importance to Europeans than any other, on account
> of the ocean in its vicinity being frequented by spermaceti whales, and
> the ample supply of refreshment it affords. The harbours are safe and
> capacious, the country beautiful, the soil favourable to cultivation; and
> the natives are in all respects a superior race of Indians. These advantages
> hold out great inducements for colonisation, which may hereafter deserve
> the attention of some European power.[15]

Although no Europeans lived there yet, Savage clearly looked forward to the day when they would do so in significant numbers. And he saw a role for the Maori people in this process:

> The exorbitant price of European labour in new colonies, it is extremely probable would be obviated by the assistance of the natives: their intelligence is such as to render them capable of instruction, and I have no doubt but they would prove as essentially useful to a colony established in their country, as the natives of India prove to our Asiatic dominions.

Closer acquaintance with the Maori might have left John Savage less sanguine about their hoped-for tractability and willingness to co-operate in colonising ventures. But his wish that New Zealand might one day support a significant population of Europeans was to be realised perhaps sooner than he anticipated.

CHAPTER TWO

THE STATE OF BRITAIN IN 1830

By the time Savage's book had been published, Britain had entered the final phase of the eighteenth-century international trade wars with the French which had brought European navigators and explorers into the southern oceans in the first instance. Most people are aware that these wars culminated, successfully for the British and their allies, with the defeat of Napoleon at Waterloo in 1815. It is less generally known that the brunt of the fighting in that crucial battle was borne on the allied side by Germans. This was not only because the principal allied force was commanded on behalf of a confederation of German states by General Blücher, but also because a significant number of the troops fighting under the Duke of Wellington were German mercenaries. Of the 67,000 men under Wellington's command at Waterloo, only 24,000 were British.[1] Most were raw recruits. The army which had fought the Peninsula War was otherwise engaged in holding down its own citizens in the north of England by force of arms against one of those worker uprisings which were to become endemic to the British political scene for the next two decades.

TWO REVOLUTIONS: THE INDUSTRIAL AND AGRICULTURAL

If by the expression 'revolution' is meant a short, sharp happening with cataclysmic results, the notion that there were industrial and agricultural revolutions in Britain in the early nineteenth century has been long exploded. Nevertheless, the 50 years from 1790 constitute a culmination to decades of change which left the social and economic landscape of Britain altered for ever.

It is in the field of industry that the developments were most visually spectacular. In the north of England at least, a landscape which had been rural for centuries became, in the space of a few decades, characterised by the factory chimney and the slum city. But the developments in agriculture were also dramatic and, from the point of view of their effect on emigration to New Zealand, more significant.

In 1801, the year of the first modern English census, four out of five people in a total population of 8,900,000 lived in farms, hamlets and villages. By the middle of the century this balance had equalised. By 1851 almost two-thirds of town dwellers had been born there. By 1901 four out of five people lived in towns or cities. In the 1831 census, 961,100 families identified themselves as engaging in farming. This was 28% of all English families. Of these, 686,000 heads of households identified themselves as labourers, meaning that overall between a million and a million and a half people lived on the land as farm labourers or members of their families.[2] This tells us two things. By no means all of those living in rural or semi-rural England were agricultural workers in 1831; and in three decades there had been a steep fall in the number of men employed on the land.

On the face of things, the rapid changes that began to happen within English agriculture from the last decade of the eighteenth century were changes of technology and technique. They encompass such improvements as the introduction of crop rotation, new methods of selective stock breeding, new grass strains and forms of irrigation, and the application of cost accounting to farm management. None of these would have been possible without a change in the overall pattern of the control of rural land.

For centuries land use had been based upon a balance between those who owned land in the strictly legal sense, and those who used it. Owners were obliged to share their rights with those who exercised use rights to common pasturage, timber gathering, grazing, water and so forth. The novelist Daniel Defoe is known to social historians as the author of a work in three volumes describing his travels throughout Britain in 1722 and 1723. In his description of the hills around Halifax he characterises the pattern of English land use which the balance of traditional rights had created: they were 'spread with enclosures from 2 acres to 6 or 7 each, seldom more, and every three or four pieces of land had a house belonging to them'.[3]

It would be wrong to think of eighteenth-century England as a bucolic utopia from which conflict between classes had been abolished. There was almost continuous social friction between owners of land and those entitled to use rights.[4] Increasingly from the middle of the eighteenth century these use rights were extinguished. As this process could proceed only by private

Act of parliament, it was a process which favoured landowners, and one moreover against which the poor, who mostly possessed the rights of use, were powerless. A recent historian of rural England has remarked:

> By the end of the eighteenth century England had come to possess an agriculture which was selfconsciously innovative, progressive, and attuned to the needs of the growing market in food commodities . . . Taking the longer view we can see that this was neither as sudden nor as straightforward as it has sometimes been assumed, but its historical significance cannot be over-emphasised. The agricultural revolution of the eighteenth century was not only a matter of new husbandry techniques, but also of social reorganisations. A new class structure emerged; relations between these classes were conducted on a new basis; rural society was effectively reconstituted. [5]

The process involved was that of enclosure: the legal owner's effective fencing off of land and its attendant resources from common use. In future, owners would have the right to use their land howsoever they liked and for their purposes alone throughout the year. Not for nothing was this the period of the great landscape garden. But it was also the period of the demise of the small, self-sufficient farmer producing an ample subsistence. The bulk of the rural population was pauperised and proletarianised by what amounted to a profound change in the balance of power within the rural community. This process had been proceeding for two centuries,[6] but in the late eighteenth century it accelerated exponentially. Nor did England suffer alone: this was the time of the notorious Highland clearances, and Ireland was also a victim.

The new food surpluses produced by the rationalisation of agriculture went to feed the burgeoning industrial towns. Manchester, in 1800 one of England's largest at 85,000 inhabitants, and Bradford, little more than a village at 13,000, had by 1850 populations of 400,000 and 104,000 respectively. Other towns had become cities in similar and equally rapid fashion. Much of the initial population growth had resulted from internal migration of the surplus rural population, forced off their smallholdings by the 'improving' landowners with whom they had previously shared their rural space.

In the new cities they were absorbed by the developing factories of a new industrial England. This development too was built upon the application of new capital-intensive techniques to what had been Britain's staple export industry since the middle ages — textiles. The process commenced with the introduction of the flying shuttle in 1733 and was enhanced by the introduction of the water frame and spinning jenny in

1770. A case can, indeed, be made that the latter is of much greater significance to the subsequent history of New Zealand than the charting of the New Zealand coast by James Cook at about the same time.

But it was the application of steam power to these production processes in 1785 which was the catalyst for Britain's emergence as an industrial nation. The weaving process, until then a cottage industry, had by 1830 become primarily an activity carried out by machinery in large factories. In 1806 there were no power looms in Manchester; by 1815 there were more than 2,000. This process is charted by the fall in the price of yarn from nearly 40s a pound in 1798 to less than a sixth of that by 1807.[7] It was a process which also ruined the livelihoods of many thousands of hand-loom weavers.[8] This development was not simply a haphazard consequence of rampant free-market capitalism but a carefully thought through and implemented policy. For example, duties on the import of Indian calico rose from 18% to 71% between 1797 and 1813, and the duty on raw cotton was reduced to almost nothing for the first five decades of the nineteenth century. By 1815 cotton textiles accounted for 40% of British exports, and woollen goods for another 18%. By 1830 cotton alone was accounting for well over 50% of all exports.

Ancillary industries grew alongside these. Pig iron output, 68,000 tons per annum in 1788, had by 1815 grown to 300,000 tons.[9] The 5 million tons of coal mined annually in 1780 had doubled by 1800 and grown to 100 million by 1865.[10] Small wonder that the prime minister, Lord Liverpool, felt able to say in a parliamentary debate in 1820: 'Next to the spirit of her people England is indebted for her commercial power and greatness to her machinery. [Inventors and entrepreneurs] are as useful to their country in their generations as any legislators of old were in theirs.'[11] Not all of England, however, endorsed this opinion.

THE CONSEQUENCES OF CHANGE

Liverpool's remarks were made in a debate on a Bill introduced by Lord Stanhope to solve a growing unemployment problem. One of his proposals was to curb the introduction of machinery into areas where cottage industries were already flourishing. The end of the wars with Napoleon had released over a quarter of a million demobilised servicemen on to a labour market already glutted with displaced agricultural labourers, and had also led to a significant fall in demand.

The new factories could absorb some of this surplus, but by no means all. Besides, these factories were capital, not labour intensive. Even David

Ricardo, one of the formulators of the classical economics which supplied the ideological underpinnings of these industrial developments, was constrained to point out in his *Principles of Political Economy and Taxation* (1817) that if mechanisation of production increased the production of stockings fourfold but purchasing power only doubled, then some people were bound to lose their jobs.[12] He was quite right, and politely ignored.

In such circumstances it is hardly surprising that wages fell sharply, and near starvation became the daily lot of many workers and their families. Hand-loom weavers, whose weekly earnings had exceeded 30s in 1801, found that by 1847 these earnings had fallen to 7s for a longer working week. But it was not only those displaced by new technologies who suffered. Comprehensive statistics on wage rates and on diet were not kept until well into the nineteenth century, so it is impossible to map the effects of industrialisation and a glutted labour market with any certainty. Nevertheless, the broad picture is clear and largely uncontroversial. In 1825 an anonymous pamphlet, *A Voice from the Coal Mines*,[13] described the life of a typical industrial worker. He received £1 a week and a tenement room which was tied to his job. Five shillings of this was deducted for candles to light his way in the mine. From the balance he fed himself, his wife and three children. This stretched to two and half loaves of bread, a small quantity of potatoes, a little oatmeal and some meat. In those weeks in which it became necessary to buy other commodities such as clothing or soap or tea, the meat was foregone. Some years later, Dr James Kay's *Moral and Physical Condition of the Working Classes Employed in the Cotton Manufacture in Manchester* (1832), one of the most informative sources for the period, described the life of a factory labourer. Six days a week he rose at five in the morning and worked from six until eight. He then had a breakfast of bread and tea and returned to his work until noon. Dinner at home comprised potatoes with a little melted lard or, rarely, a little of the fat end of bacon. A further six hours of work ending at seven o'clock was capped off with a supper of tea and bread.

The further one went down the social scale the less likely one was to have access to protein. Writing of the labouring poor in the northern manufacturing towns a little later (1844), Friedrich Engels particularly commented on this in his *Condition of the Working Class in England*. Ironically, it was those called upon to undertake the heaviest work, and thus most in need of it, who were least likely to see meat.

The situation was potentially better in the countryside, where there was at least some access to a fresher and more comprehensive range of foodstuffs. 'The diet of those who live in the country is in general more wholesome than those who live in the towns,' remarked William Kitchener in his *Family Oracle of Health* (1827).[14] 'A large portion of it consists of fresh vegetables and milk which, though not excluded from the food of those who live in towns, are enjoyed in much greater plenty and higher perfection in rural situations.' But Kitchener was speaking of the generality of rural dwellers. Rural labourers did not enjoy these happy circumstances. Between 1800 and 1830 many rural labourers were forced to stop raising their own supplementary foods as landlords began to charge rent for the small plots which had previously gone with their cottage. The 1824 *Report of the Select Committee on the Rate of Agricultural Wages and on the Condition and Morals of Labourers in that Employment*[15] particularly remarked:

> It is one of the chief causes of the agricultural labourers being in a worse state than they ever were. Before the war the average rent of cottages with good gardens was thirty shillings a year; it is now in our own neighbourhood commonly five, seven or even ten pounds per annum, and where cottages are in the hands of farmers they always prohibit the labourers from keeping a pig, and claim the produce of the apple trees and of the vine which usually covers the house.

The same committee instanced the case of 46-year-old labourer Thomas Smart, father of 13 children, seven of them alive, who had never been out of work and who had applied only once to his parish for relief (to bury a dead child). Thomas and his family lived on bread and cheese with a small piece of bacon once a month, and sometimes a little milk. He had no pig but counted himself lucky to have a small garden for potatoes. Apart from his rent (£5 a year), his other major expense was shoes. He earned 8s a week, although the harvest brought him an extra 40s and the work of three of his children another 6s. Interestingly, prior to 1812 his wage had been 12s. From other sources we know that this was only about 1s higher than it would have been 50 years earlier, but what it could purchase by way of staple items had fallen significantly thanks largely to the wars with the French. Bread, which in the 1760s accounted for 44% of the expenditure of poor families, by 1790 accounted for 60%. A loaf of bread which had cost 8d in 1794 was 1s 6d by 1812.[16]

Between 1793 and 1815, Britain was cut off from accustomed sources of continental grain. This not only forced up the price of the local product but also made it economic to produce, so that grain growing replaced animal husbandry in many rural districts. This situation was not alleviated by the ending of the war with Napoleon. Instead, it was artificially continued by the passage of the notorious Corn Laws which imposed duties on continental grain, raising its price to that which delivered profitability to landowners. This both hastened enclosure and changed the pattern of rural employment, for grain farming is characterised by seasonal fluctuations in the demand for labour.

A centuries-old pattern in which labourers lived and ate with the farmer and were typically hired by the year was replaced by one in which labourers were hired by the day and found their own dwelling. This meant that for significant periods of the year large numbers of agricultural labourers were out of work with no means of support. The Poor Law of 1600 and the Act of Settlement of 1662 envisaged the relief of occasional distress by taxing the property owners of the parish as the basic administrative unit, but this was something new. In 1795 the parish authorities in Speenhamland, Berkshire, developed a solution which became the universal model. They set a minimum standard of living based on the cost of bread, and taxed the parish to make up the difference between this and wages paid.

This system created what we would now call a poverty trap. Rural labourers could not leave their parish without losing access to relief. But local employers were able to keep wages down, secure in the knowledge that the whole parish, not they, would have to make up the difference. Large numbers of the rural poor were forced to live at starvation level. William Cobbett, who quartered the countryside on horseback in the 1820s, wrote:

> The labourers seem miserably poor. Their dwellings are little better than pigbeds and their looks indicate that their food is not nearly equal to that of a pig. Their wretched hovels are stuck upon little bits of ground on the roadside . . . In my whole life I never saw human wretchedness to equal this : no, not even amongst the free negroes in America.[17]

By the 1830s desperate and hungry people were finding extralegal means of eking out their existences.

The other significant social indicator of the dislocation brought about by rapid industrialisation of both industry and agriculture is the measurable rate of crime. Again, despite the lack of comprehensive statistics, the picture is clear enough:

> There was a slow increase in the crime rate throughout the eighteenth century. Crimes against property rose sharply between 1770 and 1800, reached alarming levels in the post war years (1815-17), and remained a matter of great alarm until the mid-nineteenth century. From the 1860s crimes against property and the person declined gradually. Can it be mere accident that in the worst years of industrial and urban growth up to the mid-century, crime was on the rise . . . the governing and propertied

orders felt that they were living through times of major crisis, one manifestation of which was a rise in crimes against them and their possessions.[18]

One historical study has collated the rural crime rates by county for the period between 1800 and 1830, and assessed the relationship between wages, good harvests and the crime rates.[19] The closeness of this relationship is uncanny. Until 1810 (a period of relative prosperity because of war spending), crime tended to fall. For the next two decades it increased significantly, and always in step with bad harvests. A more detailed study of the particular crimes of arson and poaching confirms the general conclusions.

This was the age during which the British government, under Sir Robert Peel, felt it necessary in 1829 to invent the police force. It is also the period during which transportation for criminal offences was greatly extended and the level of its use reached its peak. It is interesting to note that in 1835 the highest English county rate for committal to criminal trial (1 in 481) was in the manufacturing districts of Lancashire.[20] In a very real sense Australia was the child of the industrial and agricultural revolutions. Between 1793 and 1810 an average of only 392 persons annually were transported to New South Wales. By 1815 the average had reached 1,000; between 1816 and 1825 it was 2,600; and by 1830 it was 4,160. By 1831, 34% of those convicted at assizes were being sentenced to transportation, although only about 70% of these were actually sent to Botany Bay. Some

Many of the rural poor lived in miserable or insanitary circumstances. The interior of a cottage in Dorset 1846. (Illustrated London News)

For many people their working lives were as miserable as their domestic circumstances. This young woman is gathering fuel. (ATL)

of those transported had had their sentences commuted, often from the death penalty.[21]

Studies of the nature of the offences for which people were sent to New South Wales make it clear that typically their only crime was poverty occasioned by social dislocation. Almost all of these were crimes against property. In towns and in metropolitan London theft, fraud and picking pockets were favourites; in the countryside, it was more likely to be poaching. [22] The bitter ditty, 'The law locks up the man or woman/who steals the goose from off the common/but lets the greater villain loose/who steals the common from the goose', sums up contemporary sentiment precisely. Although as many as 1,000 individuals were transported between 1800 and 1840 for overtly political crimes – rick burning, issuing threats as social protests, forming 'illegal combinations' (trades unions, and the like) – almost all of those transported were making a political protest in the broader sense.

THE WORKERS PROTEST

Those most directly affected – working people – did not accept the social effects of change passively. Their protests took two forms. The first of these was a vigorous literature of dissent, much of which has been the subject of recent exploration as the ideological dimension of a contemporary culture of resistance.[23] That such a literature flourished should come as no surprise: literacy among workers in this period was more widespread than is sometimes imagined. It has been calculated that in 1816 about half of the 1.5 million children in England would have attended some form of schooling, albeit much of it cursory, and they would have been taught very simple reading skills.[24] At a slightly later date, 1839, two-thirds of men and half of women were signing marriage registers with their own names, suggesting at least a functional level of literacy. That workers were using this skill to read radical tracts is also suggested by the harsh sedition laws and the punitive use of taxation on periodicals which the rulers of Britain found it necessary to enact.

The market for political pamphlets and books among the working class was considerable. In 1791 Thomas Paine's *Rights of Man* sold 50,000 copies in a few weeks, and at an expensive 3s a copy. In 1821 William Cobbett's *Address to the Journeymen and Labourers* sold 200,000 in two months. William Pitt, who declined to ban William Godwin's libertarian classic *Political Justice* on the grounds that a six-guinea book could do no harm, was confounded when groups of working men clubbed together to buy copies between them. By 1821, too, the number of newspapers sold

Workers protested and organised against their circumstances. Chartists near Halifax stone troops called out to suppress them, on this occasion in 1842. (Illustrated London News)

annually had risen to 24 million, a fourfold increase over six decades. About half of these were Sunday papers of a radical complexion.

Many middle-class intellectuals were sympathetic to the plight of working people and produced works accordingly. But more than any paper protests, the workers themselves turned to various forms of mass mobilisation to express outrage at their predicament. Largely disenfranchised until the 1880s in the case of men, and for a further half century in the case of women, working people nevertheless had traditional forms of social protest available to them.[25] These usually took the form of an appearance on the hustings during elections, visiting the authorities in a body (until the end of the eighteenth century magistrates had the right to amend wage rates by court order) or mobbing unpopular employers and their premises. There was also the institution known in France as *taxation populaire*, also in use in Britain, in which in times of famine mobs broke open grain and flour warehouses and distributed the contents at a 'fair price' which was then conveyed to the owner.

The period from 1810 to 1820 was characterised by the growing use of these forms of popular protest as the effects of industrial and agricultural

Hungry workers sometimes took matters into their own hands and distributed food. An attack on the Stockport poorhouse also in 1842.
(Illustrated London News)

change became more apparent and oppressive. One of these has come down to us in popular folklore as 'the Luddite riots'. In 1812 the followers of 'Ned Ludd' (an apocryphal name used to avoid victimisation of the real leaders) began breaking up steam looms in Yorkshire and Lancashire districts previously the heartland of hand-loom weaving.[26] They have since been depicted as irrational and violent people who foolishly stood in the way of progress: the word 'Luddite' carries this connotation. In fact they turned to this course only after more traditional methods of protest had failed. All other avenues of redress were closed to them and the authorities almost entirely unsympathetic to their plight.

Few members of the British political establishment were prepared to speak on behalf of the Luddites. One exception was George Gordon, Lord Byron, who in his maiden speech in the House of Lords on 12 February 1812 referred to 'these rejected workmen [who] in the blindness of their ignorance, instead of rejoicing at these improvements in arts so beneficial to mankind, conceived themselves sacrificed to improvements in mechanism. In the foolishness of their hearts, they imagined that the maintenance and well-being of the industrial poor were objects of greater consequence than the enrichment of a few individuals.' Byron's savage irony could stand as the epigraph for the age. For the Luddites were by no means alone. Theirs was only one among dozens of protests.[27] These were mostly unsuccessful, but a decade of quiescence was followed by further disturbances in the 1830s. Known as the 'Swing riots' from their similarly eponymous leader 'Captain Swing', these were largely agricultural riots following the failed harvest of 1829.

The harvest of 1830 was almost as meagre, and the three months of autumn of that year saw spontaneous and widespread rural protests. Hardly an agricultural county of England was unaffected. Crowds of rural labourers roamed the countryside threatening landowners, demanding better wages and wrecking threshing machines. There is ample evidence that they were encouraged in some instances by tenant farmers who sympathised with them. Rick burning and the delivery of anonymous threatening letters to local magistrates and to landowners particularly perceived to be unsympathetic to the poor became endemic.[28] These disturbances, like those prior to 1820, failed, but both were significant in the creation of a culture which is now associated with the English working class. Indeed, in a very real sense, it has been argued that the working class as a self-conscious entity was created by these experiences:

> The making of the working class is a fact of political and cultural, as much as of economic history. It was not the spontaneous generation of

the factory system. Nor should we think of an external force — the 'industrial revolution' — working upon some undifferentiated raw material of humanity and turning it out at the other end as a 'fresh race of being'. The changing productive relations and conditions of the industrial revolution were imposed not upon raw material, but upon the free-born Englishman, and the free-born Englishman as Paine had left him, or as Methodists had moulded him. The factoryhand or stockinger was also the inheritor of Bunyan, of remembered village rights, of equality before the law, of craft traditions. He was the object of massive religious indoctrination and the creator of political traditions. The working class made itself as much as it was made.[29]

One of the most important dimensions of this act of self-creation was the developing knowledge that, if all else failed, it was possible to find one's way to a new land and begin on a new footing. The mass migrations which took place from Britain in the next five decades are ample evidence of that possibility and its realisation in myriad individual instances. Many working people, despairing of an improvement in their wretched conditions, took whatever opportunity they could to decamp. In the light of the ruling-class response to their distress, this reaction is hardly surprising.

THE RULERS RESPOND

The immediate response of successive Tory governments to the various manifestations of popular protest between 1810 and 1830 can only be described as one of exemplary savagery in each instance. Fourteen of the Luddite 'ringleaders' were hanged and some 12,000 troops drafted to York and its surrounding environs to keep the peace — that is, prevent any further public demonstrations of discontent. This did nothing to still popular outrage at the distress caused by the combination of social change, economic depression and official policy which was so dislocating the communities of the north of England. It culminated in a mass demonstration at St Peter's Field in Manchester in 1819 which was charged first by the Yeomanry (a militia cavalry made up largely of the local middle class and their retainers) and then by a detachment of the 15th Hussars who, in the space of minutes, killed eleven people and wounded hundreds with their sabres.

Percy Shelley, moved to fury by this brutal attack, wrote his *Masque of Anarchy* which, beginning 'I met murder on the way/He had a mask like Castlereagh', depicted the members of the government riding by in grisly apocalypse. Other critics of the government dubbed the affray 'Peterloo', a name it has since retained.

The government was not deterred. It passed six new statutes which variously prohibited drilling, restricted the right to bear arms and to assemble by way of public meeting, invented the offence of criminal libel and imposed a harsh punitive tax on newspapers. This last in particular bore hard on those papers which advanced radical political views by forcing up their price beyond the reach of working people.

The response to the disturbances of 1830 was similar. Reactionaries such as the Duke of Wellington rejoiced in the firm manner in which he and other large landowners had got together the local gentry and their servants and scoured the countryside for bands of protesting labourers whom they harried as if pursuing game.[30] The London poor, unimpressed, smashed the windows of Wellington's Apsley House. In the repression which followed, the government set up a special commission to deal with those arrested for protesting or destroying property. In all, 1,976 were indicted and tried in 34 counties. Of these, 19 were executed, 481 transported to Australia, 644 imprisoned, 7 fined and one whipped.[31] The extent of these punishments is a mark of the authorities' fright. But it also taught at least some of the labouring poor the dangers of organised and open confrontation. Henceforward their response to distress took a more individual form. Either they voted with their feet by emigrating to more congenial environments, or they turned to the purely personal solace of evangelical Methodism and its offshoots in various social movements.

By 1830 perceptive members of the middle class had developed a very strong sense that something was wrong with the fabric of English society, and that this endemic unrest could not simply be attributed to the inherent licence of an unchecked labouring class, nor to the presence of agitators who preyed upon them. Among these was William Cobbett who, responding to those who blamed outside instigators, cried: 'What! can these men look at the facts before their eyes; can they see the millions of labourers everywhere rising up, and hear them saying they will no longer starve on potatoes; can they see them breaking threshing machines; can they see them gathering together and demanding an increase in wages; can they see all this and believe . . . that these are the works of some invisible agency.'[32] He was seconded by an unlikely ally in Edward Gibbon Wakefield who, in his pamphlet *Swing Unmask'd*, invited readers to look more closely at the actions of rural incendiaries and in particular at whose property their actions were directed. Here was no outbreak of undifferentiated violence, but a carefully considered response to social distress.

But as the nostrums preached by both Cobbett and Wakefield make clear, it was one thing to agree on the existence of a problem, and quite another to agree on a solution. Nevertheless, on one matter they were clear. The prelude to any solution was political reform. The uprisings of 1830 were conducted against the backdrop of an election which, for the first time in almost five decades, broke the grip of the Tories on Westminster and returned a Whig government to power. Lord Grey, one of the Whig leaders, expressed scant sympathy with the actions of the labourers but was equally determined to get to the root of their distress and have done with it.

A first step in that direction was the Reform Act of 1832. While it enfranchised very few more than the 5% of the population already entitled to vote by virtue of property ownership, it revised and reorganised electoral arrangements so as to ensure that the new rich in the newly developed manufacturing centres were included among those who ruled England.[33] But beyond this the government would not go. On this point it parted company from the working class which had been its enthusiastic ally until now. These latter struck out on their own in what has become known as the Chartist movement, an agitation for the much wider extension of the franchise, along with a host of other reforms.[34] Although at its peak it numbered a mass membership of over a million, this movement had by 1850 clearly failed in its immediate object, and the British working class had to wait until 1887 to achieve universal male suffrage. Women were obliged to wait until after the First World War. Here was an additional reason for the working class to turn to emigration.

The authorities were determined to give them plenty of others. The Whig governments from 1830 to 1841, instead of instituting such crucial reforms as the repeal of the Corn Laws (which lay at the root of much economic distress, but which were not finally abolished until 1846, ironically by a returned Tory government), turned instead to a comprehensive series of social reforms.[35] In particular they concentrated on the effects of the Poor Laws which were forcing ratepayers to subsidise employers in providing a subsistence level of existence for labourers. One of their sternest contemporary critics summed up much widespread feeling when he remarked: 'The poor laws were intended to prevent mendicants; they have made mendicacy a legal profession; they were established in the spirit of a noble and sublime provision which contained all the theory of virtue; they have produced all the consequences of vice . . . the poor laws, formed to relieve the distressed, have been the arch-creator of distress.'[36]

Unfortunately for the poor, the distress that governments now had in mind to alleviate was that of ratepayers'. Under the Poor Law Amendment Act of 1834 no more 'outdoor relief' — subsidies on wages — were to be offered by the parish authorities. Instead, those seeking relief were obliged to apply to the parish authorities and, having satisfied them that they were genuinely destitute, were admitted to workhouses. Here, separated from spouse and children, they were set to work for their keep under a regime designed to make conditions within less pleasant than those without on the presumption that the lazy would otherwise be encouraged to rely upon charity for their daily bread. 'To this end,' remarks a recent critic, 'the new arrangements were meant to deter the poor from resorting to public assistance and to stigmatise those who did by imprisoning them in workhouses, compelling them to wear special garb, separating them from their families, cutting them off from communication with the poor outside and, when they died, permitting their bodies to be disposed of for dissection.'[37] Given that those responsible for paying the bills were also those in charge of the administration of the institutions, it is hardly surprising that subsequent studies of the dietary regimes of most workhouses have established that the inmates would have suffered from chronic malnutrition and lived in a state bordering starvation.[38] Understandably, the poor quickly came to regard the workhouses as distinguishable from prison only because they were worse, and stayed as far away from them as possible — even if that entailed going to another country.

By 1840 it was clear to most perceptive critics that the Whig programme of social reform was foundering, and that it was not alleviating distress. In some ways, as the experience of the new Poor Law revealed, it was making it worse. Among those critics were to be found some of the leading writers of the day. Charles Dickens's *Oliver Twist*, a damning indictment of workhouse regimes, still retains its power to sear. But it was Dickens's friend and mentor Thomas Carlyle who, in his seminal essay *Chartism*, dramatised the solution to the 'state of England question' towards which all had been groping: 'Overpopulation is the grand anomaly which is bringing all other anomalies to a crisis . . . And yet, if this small western rim of Europe is overpeopled, does not everywhere else a whole vacant earth, as it were, call to us, come and till me, come and reap me.'[39] This cry was to hasten two generations on their travels.

CHAPTER THREE

EMIGRATION AND NEW ZEALAND

There was nothing new or original in Carlyle's championing of emigration as the solution to Britain's woes. Rather, he was crystallising a mood which had been concentrating for two decades. By the 1830s it was widely accepted that the problem of excess population could not otherwise be resolved. The intellectual basis of this view was supplied by the economist clergyman Thomas Malthus, who had expounded it in his famous work, *An Essay on the Principle of Population* (1798).

Population, said Malthus, tended to reproduce itself up to the available limits of subsistence. This was because people bred geometrically, but food and other resources increased only arithmetically. Thus, unless moral restraint was exercised, the population had nothing to look forward to but hunger, pestilence and starvation. It was useless, said Malthus, to try to better the position of the masses by misplaced charity or state assistance. It only encouraged a further spurt in uninhibited procreation and returned the masses to the same miserable state as before. This very squarely defined the poor as the authors of their own misfortune — a comforting doctrine for the rich. Malthus himself, although a clergyman, placed little faith in moral restraint, and painted a gloomy prospect for humankind.[1]

He was seconded by his contemporary and fellow disciple of classical economics, David Ricardo, who propounded what he perceived as an iron law of wages, or what would now be called the equilibrium price of labour. This extended the theory of Malthus beyond charitable assistance to earnings themselves. A benevolent employer or the intervention of an outside force such as a trade union, said Ricardo, would have the same effect as charity. It would either encourage the labouring masses to breed up to the subsistence level again or, by increasing wages beyond their natural level, disrupt the forces of the market and thus throw thousands out of work.

This was a message even more welcome to the wealthy, especially employers, than that of Malthus. The official encouragement of such views and their consequent widespread currency is understandable.

Naturally there were critics, William Hazlitt and William Cobbett to name two.[2] Cobbett was particularly scathing. In his essay *Getting Rid of the Poor* (1826), he denounced 'the monster Malthus who has furnished the unfeeling oligarchs with the pretence that man has a natural propensity to breed faster than food can be raised for the increase' and went on to demonstrate with reference to a single parish that the poor produced more than ample for themselves. It was those who produced nothing and battened on them who were responsible for the miserable state of the labouring masses. The former and not the latter should be subject to enforced removal. An unfettered free market was nothing more, he considered, than liberty to starve quietly.

But even most of those who rejected out of hand the classical economics of Adam Smith (including Carlyle who had no time for the reduction of

Propagandists frequently contrasted the condition of those in England with those who emigrated. The needlewoman, at home and abroad. (ATL)

'Emigration a remedy', one of the most famous of all the emigration poster images. (Hocken Library)

humankind to statistical categories) saw no hope for an overpopulated nation unless the authorities turned to the expedient of emigration. The period 1820 to 1840 is replete with schemes and commissions directed to coping with the problem of paupers and what might be done to get them out of the country.

'SHOVELLING OUT PAUPERS'

In the forefront of much of this debate was the now forgotten figure of Robert Wilmot Horton. Although Horton, a liberal Tory, agreed with most of his contemporaries in politics that England's problem was too many people, he was no Malthusian. On the contrary, he believed that population pressure could be permanently alleviated by emigration. And although he followed Ricardo in his economics, he saw quite clearly that effective emigration could not simply be left to the vagaries of the labour market. Excess labour would have to be encouraged by subsidy and other devices to go where it was needed. The question was: who was to pay?

Horton's approach was novel, although not entirely original. Parishes, he suggested, should borrow against their future expectation of the poor rate, and ship their surplus labourers and artisans to where they were most needed in the British colonies. As under-secretary to the colonies from 1823, he presided over a range of schemes and commissions directed to this object.[3]

Over the four years to 1828, Horton sent groups of first Irish, then English and Scottish subsidised emigrants to Canada, the Cape Colony and New South Wales. Most of his schemes were only a qualified success, nearly foundering on a combination of landlord opposition, the indolence and incompetence of colonial administrators, the unwillingness of parish authorities to commit their Poor Law revenues in advance, and the cupidity of contractors who were more interested in their profit margins than Horton's schemes. But even limited success showed that Horton was right. He continued to have his critics, one of whom described his efforts as 'shovelling out paupers',[4] but he had shown that immigration could supply some sort of answer, if incomplete, to Britain's social distress, provided not too much attention was paid to the feelings and comfort of those sent to the colonies. And his efforts also created a climate favourable to

(ATL)

administrative measures which aided the process of emigration. The incoming Whig administration of 1830 contained many who saw it as the main hope in resolving distress. In June 1831 a commission was appointed 'for the purpose of collecting and diffusing information on the subject of emigration to the British possessions abroad and also for the purpose of rendering any such assistance as may be in [its] power to afford to persons desirous so to emigrate'.

In the commission's view, the parishes should find the means to assist labourers to emigrate, as in Horton's schemes, and the 1834 Poor Law Act incorporated a provision empowering boards of guardians accordingly. But well before this, in 1831, a sum of £10,000 had been set aside to supply assisted passages to would-be emigrants, and regulations governing who was to be assisted and how were gazetted. This was a crucial shift in policy and one which was to determine the nature of emigration from Britain for the next 50 years, although those who were responsible for it had little inkling of that at the time.

The 1831 commission was subsequently transmogrified into the London Emigration Committee (1832–1836), an agent-general for emigration (1837–1839) and, in 1840, the Colonial Land and Emigration Commission, which was to remain in being for the next several decades (although after 1848 its role in the encouragement of emigration to New Zealand was negligible).[5] These bodies effected two crucial administrative reforms. First, beginning with Plymouth in 1834, eleven emigration agents were appointed at the principal points of embarkation in England, Scotland and Ireland. Their tasks were to inspect emigrant vessels for seaworthiness and their compliance with requirements as to provisioning, water supply and accommodation; to ensure that prospective emigrants had not fallen into the hands of unscrupulous fraudsters who sold them tickets on non-existent vessels; and to ensure that the fullest possible information was available to parish officers, clergy and gentry who wished to assist labourers and others to emigrate.

Secondly, commencing in 1838, and arising from a controversy over the ship *Asia*, the agent-general, Thomas Elliot, arranged for the drawing up and implementation of a strict code of regulations governing the basis upon which emigration ships might put to sea and the conduct of the vessels during their passage. These regulations, although amended in the light of experience from time to time, remained in force during the whole of the nineteenth century, and in the majority of cases put an end to or limited the scandalous abuses and conditions of passage which had pertained up until then. They undoubtedly saved the lives of many prospective settlers.

That these regulatory activities should have been conducted during a period in which it was generally believed that the less intervention by government in the marketplace the better is a tribute to the central importance that emigration had assumed in the social policy of successive governments up to 1840. That it had done so is in its turn a tribute to the propaganda genius and political acumen of a significant group of reformers and, above all, their publicist, Edward Gibbon Wakefield.

EDWARD GIBBON WAKEFIELD AND 'SCIENTIFIC' COLONISATION

Robert Horton and Edward Gibbon Wakefield, notwithstanding their shared belief that the only lasting solution to the problems of England was emigration, differed crucially in their perception of the phenomenon with which they were dealing. To Horton it was a question of how to alleviate the pressures created in England by an excess, pauperised population whose personal situation nevertheless needed to be improved in the new country. Once they were got aboard a ship and landed at a new destination, he was concerned that they should be settled on land of their own as quickly as possible.

Wakefield also believed that what happened to people once they came to their new destination, and how they behaved there, were central to the success of any emigration scheme. But although he too considered that the key factor in the development of a new colony was land, and to whom it should be available, he was entirely against it being offered too quickly to the working men and women who went from Britain as colonists. In this difference lies the key to the acceptability of Wakefield's schemes and why he ultimately succeeded where Horton did not.

Edward Wakefield, who was born in England in 1796 and died in New Zealand in 1862, was one of the most seminal influences in British politics in the two decades from 1830. Denied the opportunity of a more orthodox political career as a member of parliament because of his conviction in 1826 for the abduction of an heiress (a felony which automatically disqualified him), and long regarded by many of his contemporaries as a scoundrel because of it, he instead devoted his considerable energies to the theory and cause of emigration.[6] Indeed, it was his three-year sojourn in gaol which brought him face to face with social distress and convinced him that the only solution to it was the creation of colonies and the shipping of the excess population of Britain to them. But he also thought that this should be done only on the basis of careful planning and execution.

While in prison he composed his *Letters From Sydney* (a place he had never visited), purporting to be an account of what was wrong with the settlement of New South Wales and published anonymously in 1829. All of his subsequent writings on colonisation are extensions and expansions of this first work. What was wrong with colonies, said Wakefield, was that too much was left to chance. To succeed and flourish they needed to balance the requirements of investment and labour. There was no use at all in simply dumping colonists down in a new place and leaving them to survive as best they might. The first, developmental stage of colonisation required significant investment. But those with capital would not invest it unless they could be assured of a return. This could be assured in its turn only by the application of labour.

Consequently, for a colony to flourish two conditions had to be met. The first was the need for a balanced mix of investors and labourers. Secondly, and even more important, labourers who were sent out to the new colony had to remain labourers for a sufficient period to ensure that the virgin properties in which investors had sunk their capital were sufficiently developed to return a dividend. If they did not, there was no

Edward Gibbon Wakefield in 1823. His lodgement in prison for abduction and the social distress he saw there turned his mind to emigration as the remedy for England's social ills. (ATL)

incentive to invest. There was the rub. Labourers in new colonies did not remain labourers. They had emigrated to escape the consequences of that status and as soon as practicable they went off and set up as small farmers on their own account. Unless this problem could be resolved, colonies would not succeed and attempts to relieve population pressure in Britain would fail.

Wakefield thought he had found the answer to this apparent conundrum in what he called the 'fair price'. This was a very simple concept. Land in colonies should be available only at a price which was beyond the immediate means of labouring immigrants. They might, after a period, diligently scrape together the wherewithal to purchase a smallholding, but this should take them two or three years. In the meantime they should work for the investors. When they did eventually find their way to own land, their place should be taken by other immigrant labourers on the same terms.

The elegance of this equation was particularly calculated to appeal to investors of capital, and explains why Wakefield was feted and Horton ignored. The latter offered nothing of advantage to the rich and powerful, whereas Wakefield appealed directly to their pocketbooks. This probably also explains why despite his notoriety, Wakefield found himself with many influential supporters, including members of parliament and those interested in investing in colonisation. In 1830 this group set up the National Colonisation Society, which was to have a significant influence on the pattern of British emigration for the next two decades.

The times were particularly propitious for this society. Not only was there a new administration in office which was looking for solutions to . social distress and the population problem which was considered to underlie it, but many of the politicians prominent in the society were friends of this administration. In addition, there was before the public the dreadful case of the Swan River Colony in Western Australia which in 1831 failed miserably, primarily because its founders were unable to retain the services of their labouring immigrants, who decamped to New South Wales and its generous land grants. The government in London was left to pick up the cost. This, said the society, was what happened when colonisation was conducted on an unsystematic basis.

Its message found ready ears in the Whig administration and particularly in Lord Goderich, the colonial secretary. It was the influence of the society which ensured the allocation of the £10,000 already noted for assisted passages to Australia. The important feature of this allocation was, however, that it was to be offset by the proceeds of the sale of land to prospective settlers in New South Wales. From this point on, land was not to be freely available but, in accordance with the doctrine of the sufficient price, to be beyond the immediate reach of labourers. The 5s an acre at which this price was set was, the society estimated, too low. But it was a start, and in August 1831 the society considered itself ready to proceed with its first planned colony in South Australia.

The Colonisation Society was interested in colonisation everywhere, and at first glance there seems no obvious reason why it should have selected the antipodes as the site of its initial sponsorship in this field. The traditional destinations for British immigrants were Canada and the United States. A thriving timber trade with Canada, in particular, had developed and by 1840 over 2,000 vessels each year were plying the trade, which was made economic by the shipment of emigrants, especially from Ireland and Scotland, on the voyage out.[7] But there were two very compelling reasons for looking south rather than west.

The first was simply that many of those interested in the affairs of the society had commercial interests in this part of the world. The Enderby Brothers and Joseph Somes, for instance, were principal figures in the south seas whaling industry. It was to their advantage to see the development of new markets in their area of operations. The second, more important reason, at least from the point of view of theoreticians such as Wakefield, was that for their settlements to succeed there had to be tight control of the price of land. This implied rule by the British government, which was committed to experimenting with this new form of colonisation. This ruled out the United States. It also implied a new colony in which a private market in land had not yet developed and in which, at least in the crucial first few years, the sufficient price could be strictly enforced. This ruled out Canada and South Africa. But Australia met both requirements.

From the point of view of the Colonisation Society, the experiment in South Australia was an unqualified success. In 1833 a South Australian Association was formed, and in 1834 an Act was passed establishing the new province. A commission was set up to establish the price of land in the new colony. This fixed, eventually, upon 12s an acre, a price quite self-consciously based upon the costs of transporting labourers to Australia and the expected period it would take them to save enough to purchase land of their own, but balanced against the price investors were prepared to pay.[8] A South Australian Land company was set up in 1835 under the chairmanship of George Angas to purchase land as an investment for settlement, and by July 1836 the first settlers were on the water.

By 1836 the society had also cemented its position as the arbiter of emigration policy through the Select Committee on the Disposal of Land in British Colonies.[9] This committee, convened in early June, reported on 1 August with a series of resolutions. They had given careful consideration, said their report, to previous practice in respect of lands, and had concluded that until 1831 this practice, which had taken the form of land grants and reserves, had been injurious to the public good. It was only with Lord Goderich's introduction that year of land sales for a minimum price for cash that this situation had been rectified. The committee therefore recommended that not only should Goderich's system be erected into law as basic policy but that its oversight should also be vested in a board in London 'with the care of so directing the stream of Emigration, which may be expected to flow into the Colonies from the Mother Country, as to proportion, in each, the supply of labour to the demand'. Each colony should, furthermore, receive emigrant labour to the extent that it had financed this by its own land sales. The welfare of the colonies and that of Britain were inseparable, the committee concluded, 'the one thing wanting in the colonies being precisely that free, or hired, labour, a superabundant supply of which is occasioning great local suffering in other parts of the Empire; while the transfer of this labour to the Colonies, by enabling them to turn to the best account the advantages they possess cannot fail to open new channels of industry and commerce.'

This ringing endorsement of its policies must have been a great encouragement to the Colonisation Society. It was not fortuitous. Indeed, it had been carefully stagemanaged. In all, the committee took over 200 pages of evidence. Of this, nearly 60 were contributed by E. G. Wakefield. Much of the balance was the work of prominent members of the society. Two of the latter — Torrens and Whitmore — were closely associated with the South Australian venture, as were three members of the committee itself — Hutt, Ward and Baring. And the following year they had evidence that the policies they were pressing were a success. There were to be subsequent difficulties in South Australia and the administration of the colony had in 1840 to be rescued by Captain George Grey. But by 1837, with their work in South Australia well under way, the Colonisation Society and its friends were casting about in search of new fields of endeavour. It was almost inevitable that their eye should fall on New Zealand.

NEW ZEALAND AS IMMIGRANT DESTINATION

The National Colonisation Society was not the first group to be interested in New Zealand as an immigrant destination. If we ignore the unsuccessful attempts of Sydney merchants in 1810 to obtain a monopoly charter to exploit flax, that honour belongs to a William Savage who had petitioned Earl Bathurst, the colonial secretary, for permission to 'form an agricultural settlement' in New Zealand in 1820. Sadly, he was obliged to write again later that year and confess that 'circumstances have arisen which make it doubtful that it will be in the power of the individuals to carry their plans into effect'.[10] There were others more than willing to fill his place.

In 1821 a Robert Sugden also wrote to Earl Bathurst on the subject of New Zealand,

> convinced an English colony would soon become flourishing and happy, the space being so ample for their industry, the soil so fertile, the climate salubrious, its capacious harbours and fine rivers — in fact they would have every natural advantage in their favour, added to which the cause of humanity would be served in a twofold manner, provision would be made to a class of enlightened person (now unoccupied from different causes), and the civilisation of a fine race who are now sunk in utter ignorance would by such an event be rapidly accelerated, and eventually England would benefit by it in an eminent degree.[11]

Bathurst was not impressed by this vista of splendours. 'I am in reply to acquaint you,' replied his secretary, Henry Goulburn, 'that he does not feel he has the power of approving any particular encouragement to the establishment of a colony there.'[12]

The fact was that successive British governments were interested neither in colonising lands over which they held no sovereignty nor in obtaining sovereignty over them. In 1817 they went as far as to pass an Act denying any such sovereignty over New Zealand. This signal lack of interest proved no discouragement. In 1823 a Colonel Nicholls proposed a military colony (to no avail), and 1825 saw the formation of the first New Zealand Company under the chairmanship of John Lambton, later Lord Durham. This got as far as sending out a party of 60 settlers who made landfall first at Stewart Island in March, and subsequently at the Bay of Islands and Hokianga. But they found the prospects so dismal that they sailed on to Sydney, abandoning all hope of a settlement in New Zealand.

The reasons for these failures and discouragements were plain enough. Asked what he thought of Nicholls' proposal in 1824, the missionary Samuel Marsden replied: 'If an effective government can be established in New Zealand to punish crime, a colony may be established, and benefit the natives, but if an effective government cannot be established, neither can a colony, in my judgement, without much danger.'[13] Marsden was

echoing the views of John Bigge, who had been sent out to New South
Wales by Bathurst in 1822 to look into the question of whether the colony
should continue in its present form, or might be reformed so that convicts
were excluded from the outset.[14] As a supplement to these instructions
Bigge was to look into the trade situation in New Zealand and its
relationship to New South Wales.

Although Bigge found New Zealand to be a place in many respects
more fertile and promising than Australia, there was a serious impediment
to European settlement — 'the savage and revengeful disposition of the
inhabitants'. Any settlement would, at the very least, require the stationing
of a substantial body of troops in the country to keep order between settlers
and the Maori inhabitants.[15] In Marsden's view, the savage and revengeful
disposition of the Maori was an understandable response to their treatment
by Europeans trading around the coast, but even the outrage of the brig
Elizabeth in 1832[16] occasioned no more than the stationing of a Resident,
James Busby, in the Bay of Islands to keep an eye on matters and report
any serious depredations. This was as far as successive London
administrations were prepared to go.

THE NEW ZEALAND ASSOCIATION AND
LAND COMPANY

It is against this particularly unpropitious background that the formation
of the New Zealand Association in 1837 by Wakefield and his friends,
fresh from their South Australian triumph, must be seen. It was an interesting body, not least because of the number of members of parliament
among its directors, including Lord Durham from the abortive 1825 venture and now a figure of considerable political significance. Its avowed
intention was the colonisation of New Zealand. In March 1839 it reconstituted itself as the New Zealand Land Company, absorbing both an in-
terim Colonisation Company and what remained of the company of 1825.
Interestingly, the group associated with it included the members and witnesses mentioned in relation to the 1836 committee.[17]

The New Zealand Company is sometimes presented as if it was a
philanthropic venture. No doubt concern for the good of humankind figured
somewhere in the breasts of its founders and directors. But they were, for
the most part, hard-headed businessmen and politicians. If doing good
motivated them to a degree, doing well motivated them more. The activities
of the company prior to the despatch of its first immigrant ship tell us a
good deal about its main aim.

The New Zealand Land Company was a venture in land speculation, and a very successful one.[18] Long before it owned any land in New Zealand, the company was selling New Zealand land orders on the London market for just over £100 each. They entitled the owner to 100 acres of farmland and a town section of one acre in the new settlement proposed. Anyone who bought one of these orders received a 75% discount on a first-class passage to the colony when it was established. Even on this basis it is astonishing that prospective settlers could be induced to purchase land which did not yet belong to the company at more than four times the price of land in Canada or even New South Wales.

In fact, what people were buying was a very cheap section in the prospective new town around which the colony would be based and some quite expensive land in the countryside as a condition of doing so. The expectation of those who bought the orders was that the town sections would rapidly appreciate in value once the new settlement of Wellington was established. This probably explains why the 1,000 orders floated in 1839 were snapped up in a month, and why they were changing hands shortly thereafter at an attested 10 times their nominal value and, according to some reports, significantly more.[19] The value of the orders was enhanced

---

FREE PASSAGE.

EMIGRATION to NEW ZEALAND.

The Directors of the New Zealand Land Company hereby give notice that they are ready to receive applications for a Free Passage to their FIRST and PRINCIPAL SETTLEMENT, from Mechanics, Gardeners, and Agricultural Labourers, being married, and not exceeding 30 years of age. Strict inquiry will be made as to qualifications and character. The Company's Emigrant Ships will sail from England early in September next.

Further particulars and printed forms of application may be obtained at the Company's Offices.

By order of the Directors,

JOHN WARD, Secretary.

No. 1 Adam street, Adelphi,
June 15, 1839.

(Auckland Public Library)

by every purchaser being entitled to take part in a lottery which would allow all an equal chance to choose the prime sites at Wellington in exchange for their order.

No one was under any illusions about the speculative nature of the proposed colonisation of New Zealand. Inducing investment by playing upon the incentive of greed was central to the Wakefield theory of colonisation. This was inherent in all the schemes from the earliest point. Robert Horton, whose influence was sufficiently significant for the National Colonisation Society to ask him to chair their initial meetings, parted company with Wakefield and his friends within a few months on specifically this point.[20] Colonisation based on selfish and speculative considerations was, in his estimation, bound to fail, because the interests of the investors would take precedence over those of the emigrant labourers who were the ostensible justification for the whole exercise. Wakefield and his friends pressed on without him. It was, said *The Times,* a very 'smuggish thing'.[21] Notwithstanding, with 150 years of hindsight, it still seems a remarkably risky venture to invest money in a land speculation on the other side of the world. That people were prepared to do so speaks volumes not only for the persuasive powers of Wakefield but also for the careful political groundwork undertaken by his friends.

REMOVING THE IMPEDIMENTS

A major obstacle to the colonisation of New Zealand was the complete lack of interest by successive British governments in establishing the sovereignty over the country which was the precondition for its success. There were three other impediments, two of which were specific to New Zealand. Firstly, there were already people living there. While the Maori inhabitants could hardly speak for themselves in the course of the political machinations which preceded New Zealand colonisation, they had powerful friends in the shape of both the Church Missionary Society and Aborigines Protection Society willing to do so on their behalf. Secondly, there was also a small European community living in New Zealand. These people too were of little account for themselves, but they had valuable connections in the New South Wales business community they largely served. If the Sydney merchants and investors claimed prior rights of purchase of New Zealand land, one of the preconditions of the establishment of a successful Wakefield settlement could not be met.

Related to this factor was the third and more general consideration. New South Wales was still regarded primarily as a dumping ground for British malefactors. Bigge's inquiry had made little or no difference to that.

Wakefield had, from the outset, opposed the introduction and use of convict labour in planned colonies as inimical to the whole venture. 'You may obtain, though not without trouble, one, two, or perhaps three, convicts, for the term of a few years,' he wrote in *Letters From Sydney*, 'but that they will rob you is almost certain; that they will murder you is by no means improbable; and that their labour will not be very profitable is beyond a doubt.'[22] Nor, he thought, would the supply of convicts be up to furnishing the number of labourers required once a colony began to expand and develop. It would certainly not produce the gender balance required and would, by the same token, deliver a population comprising the dregs of the metropolitan society. Drunken, foul, corrupt and brutified were some of the epithets Wakefield regularly applied to the involuntary settlers of New South Wales.

Many prominent citizens believed that emigration was the solution to the overcrowding of Britain and the terrible social conditions of industrial change. (ATL)

His colonising friends took a similar but more practically oriented line. They were well aware that as long as Australia remained a penal settlement insufficient free settlers would come to the south Pacific region to make their investments profitable. As a precondition of successful colonisation, it would be necessary to curtail transportation. Exerting their considerable political influence to this end, they arranged for the setting up in 1837 of a Select Committee on Transportation, and handed the task of managing it to one of their number, Sir William Molesworth, the member for Cornwall.

There is something faintly ironic about Molesworth having bequeathed his name to the street upon which New Zealand's parliament now stands. For, if anything, William Molesworth was as flamboyant and disreputable a character as Wakefield. Some of his contemporaries thought more so. Sent down from Cambridge for challenging his tutor to a duel, and a publicly declared atheist, his engagements to marry had twice been broken by furious fathers because of it. Twenty-six years old, a thoroughgoing disciple of Wakefield, and one of the inner circle of the New Zealand Association, Molesworth belonged to that small group of Radicals in the House of Commons whose espousal of such dangerous causes as the abolition of flogging in the armed services or the introduction of the secret ballot for elections usually united the Whigs and Tories against them.[23]

In this instance he had the support of the Whigs. Both Lord John Russell and Lord Howick (later Earl Grey), two of the most influential Whig parliamentarians, had already decided to severely curtail convict transportation, if not to abolish it. The setting up of the 1837 committee suited them very well. From the point of view of the Wakefield group it also did its work superbly, taking evidence from Australia-based clergymen such as the Presbyterian J. D. Lang and the Roman Catholic Bishop Ullathorne (who were in London at the time), and of 21 other bitter opponents of transportation such as James Mudie. The outcome of the committee's deliberations, given such self-conscious bias, was a foregone conclusion.[24]

If Wakefield himself had scripted the committee's report it could not have come to more convenient conclusions. Transportation was ineffective in discouraging crime; convict labour was inefficient and insufficient to meet the needs of the growing colony; and the only effect it had on the convicts themselves was to corrupt their morals in every degree. No respectable person would emigrate to Sydney while it remained a sink of iniquity. 'To dwell in Sydney,' Molesworth noted privately, 'would be much the same as inhabiting the purlieus of St Giles, where drunkenness and profligacy are not more apparent than in the capital of Australia.' No free settlers, he thought, would be prepared to subject themselves to an ordeal by which their feelings were 'constantly outraged by the perpetual spectacle of punishment and misery . . . till the heart of the immigrant is gradually deadened to the sufferings of others, and becomes at last as cruel as the other gaolers of these vast prisons'.[25] Transportation must go. And, of course, an end to transportation would also mean that the reason for maintaining the price of land in New South Wales at 5s when it was to be set at 12s to £1 in other settlements nearby would no longer pertain.

The inhabitants of New South Wales were infuriated by this caricature of their community when they became aware of it, but impressing them was not Molesworth's purpose. He had another agenda. There is a curiosity about this. It seems to the casual reader that during this decade a committee of the legislature was simply incapable of addressing any topic concerning matters outside Britain without somehow or other coming around to the subject of immigration. This becomes explicable only once the busy political work of the Wakefield reformers is understood.

Russell and Howick were not inclined to accept the recommendations of the committee all at once. Opponents of transportation they might be, but such a change of policy would cost a great deal of money. Nevertheless, sending convicts to Australia as a penological device was doomed. Although transportation to Western Australia continued until 1867, the last convict transport to drop anchor at Sydney had done so within four years of the committee's report. At the same time the Colonial Office began to pay a bounty of £30 for each young family, and lesser payments for the single and for children, who were willing to go out to Australia. By 1840 New South Wales was fast losing its stigma. Within a few years 18,000 settlers had entered the colony under the bounty system and a further 40,000 on their own initiative. There they found the price of land beyond their means until they had laboured for a time at earning its price. It had all worked out rather nicely for the Colonisation Society and, by implication, the New Zealand Association. But the latter had still to deal with, among other impediments, the powerful Church Missionary Society (CMS).

It is customary now to pour scorn on the pretensions of nineteenth-century missionaries. But there is no doubt that the philanthropy of the many missionaries who went out to bring the gospel to the heathen was genuine, as was their belief in their evangelising and civilising mission. The precise nature of this mission is conveniently summarised in the report of the Select Committee on Aborigines which painstakingly gathered evidence (not all of it from missionaries) over two years to 1837.[26] Its brief was nothing if not comprehensive. It was to inquire into the relations between incomers and aboriginal inhabitants both in British colonies and in those areas in which British subjects had made an impact on the indigenous inhabitants, and to make recommendations as to how these relations might be improved. The committee's conclusions were blunt:

> It is not too much to say that the intercourse of Europeans in general, without any exception in favour of the subjects of Great Britain, has been, unless when attended by missionary exertions, a source of many calamities to uncivilised nations. Too often, their territory has been usurped; their property seized; their numbers diminished; their character debased; the spread of civilisation impeded. European vices and diseases have been introduced amongst them, and they have been familiarised with the use of our most potent instruments for the subtle or the violent destruction of human life viz., brandy and gunpowder.

In arriving at these conclusions the committee drew on evidence from New Zealand and elsewhere, and quoted approvingly from a Mr Ellis who had said that he had scarcely ever 'inquired into a quarrel between the natives and the Europeans in which it had not been found to have originated either in violence towards the females or in injustice in traffic or barter on the part of the Europeans'.

But, said the committee, there was one bright spot on this desolate horizon — 'the effect of fair dealing and of Christian instruction upon heathens'. They had had abundant proof of how beneficent these two influences had been, and expressed their conviction that 'there is but one effectual means of staying the evils we have occasioned, and of imparting the blessings of civilisation, and that is the propagation of Christianity, together with the preservation for the time to come of the civil rights of the natives.' The ex-missionary William Yate had told the committee that he and his colleagues had laboured for 15 years in the New Zealand vineyard without any civilising impact on the Maori until, at the end of that time, they began to make converts and 'from that moment civilisation commenced'.

The committee had recommendations for advancing the cause of civilisation specific to all territories. In New Zealand this amounted to the establishment of consular agents who, unlike Busby, had the effective power to detain malefactors and impose punishments upon them. Within the framework of order thus created the missionaries could continue their civilising work. But the committee also sounded a note of caution:

> Various schemes for colonising New Zealand and other parts of Polynesia have at different times been suggested, and one such project is understood to be on foot. On these schemes your Committee think it

enough for the present to state, that regarding them with great jealousy, they conceive that the Executive Government should not countenance, still less engage in any of them, until an opportunity shall have been offered to both Houses of Parliament of laying before Her Majesty their humble advice as to the policy of such an enlargement of Her Majesty's dominions, or of such an extension of British settlements abroad, even though unaccompanied by any distinct and immediate assertion of sovereignty.

This was a clear shot across the bows of the would-be New Zealand colonisers. The CMS and the New Zealand Association could agree on one thing only, and that was the need for some sort of overall authority in New Zealand. Writing to the CMS in 1824, Marsden had remarked that 'the New Zealanders themselves are very sensible of the want of a protecting government, and would rejoice if anything could be done to prevent the strong from crushing the weak'.[27] Thirteen years later he was of the same opinion. In his final report on New Zealand to the society in 1837 he again remarked: 'You are aware there are no laws in New Zealand; they have no king.' But there the two divided. The society saw law as a necessary instrument to protect Maori from Pakeha, and the New Zealand Association as necessary to protect colonists from Maori and to impose the sufficient price. In their struggles to obtain their way, the association and subsequently the New Zealand Company initially got the worst of it.[28]

The CMS had powerful friends, not least of whom was Lord Glenelg, the colonial secretary, who had been an office holder in the Aborigines Protection Society, and both he and his permanent under-secretary, James Stephen, maintained close links with Dandeson Coates, secretary of the CMS. They were not opposed to some form of sovereignty being established over New Zealand, but they would not permit this to happen on terms favourable to the would-be colonists at the expense of Maori.

The New Zealand Association, having failed to negotiate an agreed basis for colonisation with the government of Lord Melbourne, in 1838 attempted to carry legislation in parliament to effect their object. They were unsuccessful. But the tide was turning in their favour. By the end of 1838 it was apparent to the policy-makers that the settlement of New Zealand was proceeding in any event and this made some form of intervention inevitable.

In August the first of the parliamentary committees on New Zealand recommended by the Committee on Aborigines was ready to report.[29] The evidence heard by this, the House of Lords committee, did not bear out the contentions of the earlier committee, which may explain why they made no recommendation. Typical of this evidence was that given by the trader Joel Polack who, in remarking the missionaries' opposition to European settlement, opined that this view was not universally shared by the Maori themselves. Indeed, he suggested, many thought that an influx of Europeans might well be beneficial.

Pressed further on why he thought so, he said that in encouraging Maori participation in farming activities, as was likely with an increased European presence, their minds would be diverted from their previous concentration on war; it would furthermore ensure that the lands presently lying empty would be profitably utilised. He even went as far as to suggest that the missionary opposition to European colonisation might not be wholly motivated by philanthropic considerations, but rather by the advantage they enjoyed both as residents and in their knowledge of the Maori language in purchasing land for themselves.

Polack was seconded on a more abstract plane by Francis Baring, a member of the government as well as of the New Zealand Association. Colonisation, he thought, would be 'indispensable' to the present European inhabitants of New Zealand by imposing order on chaos. It would be equally beneficial to the Maori inhabitants both for this reason and because it would quickly enhance the value of their lands.

Clearly, political forces were moving in the direction of what was shortly to become the New Zealand Company. Its business backers produced a petition signed by over 40 large merchant houses in the City of London urging intervention. Melbourne was impressed by this, particularly as his increasingly shaky hold on government meant he could not afford to upset important financial figures. Even more, in those days before tight party discipline he depended for his governing majority on the eleven members of parliament controlled by Lord Durham.

When, in February 1839, Glenelg was forced to resign from office as a result of events unconnected with New Zealand, he was replaced by Lord Normanby. The new colonial secretary, in office until the succeeding September, had not the same connections with the CMS and was thus not nearly as sympathetic to their views. On the contrary, he was a political associate of Durham. He had before him the report of Captain William Hobson who had been off the New Zealand coast the previous year, engaged in an attempt to impose law and order in what was an increasingly anarchic situation.

Hobson recommended the imposition of some form of sovereignty in some limited coastal areas at least, so that order for trading purposes could be maintained. His proposal led to a decision to appoint him consul in

New Zealand, and in August 1839 Normanby issued him with a fateful instruction.[30] The context of Hobson's mission, he was instructed, was to be found in three distinct groups of persons. There were those of Her Majesty's subjects who were already in residence in New Zealand; there were those who wished to establish colonies there; and there were the Maori people whose interests stood in need of protection. To ensure that those already in New Zealand were subject to some restraint and to create a situation suitable to receive those who had already sailed to the territory as colonists, he was to negotiate with the Maori inhabitants to establish some kind of British sovereignty. He was to do so, furthermore, in a manner which ensured the genuine consent of the native inhabitants, and in terms which protected their interests. But this was not his sole responsibility. The instructions continued:

> It is further necessary that the chiefs should be induced, if possible, to contract with you, as representing Her Majesty, that henceforward no lands should be ceded, either gratuitously or otherwise, except to the Crown of Great Britain. Contemplating the future growth of a British colony in New Zealand, it is an object of the first importance that the alienation of the unsettled lands within its limits should be conducted from its commencement upon that system of sale of which experience has proved the wisdom, and the disregard of which has been so fatal to the prosperity of other British settlements.

This was a reference to the 'sufficient price' and was Normanby's compromise between the demands of the missionaries and those of the systematic colonisers. How this was to be effected he left to Hobson.

Hobson carried out his instructions to the letter. In February 1840 at Waitangi, and subsequently at many other places, he and his officers induced some 512 chiefs to affix their signatures to a treaty which, in return for the cession of sovereignty, on the one hand protected their rights both to their traditional rangatiratanga and as British subjects, but on the other required them, by way of a pre-emption clause, to sell their lands in future only to the British Crown, thus establishing the conditions for the imposition of the sufficient price.

But Hobson's instructions had gone on ominously to remark: 'Extensive acquisitions of such lands have undoubtedly already been obtained; and it is probable before your arrival a great addition will have been made to them. The embarrassments occasioned by such claims will demand your earliest and most careful attention.' Around this instruction revolves the whole matter of the success or failure of the Wakefield colonising ventures in New Zealand.

CHAPTER FOUR

THE
WAKEFIELD SETTLEMENTS
IN NEW ZEALAND

One of the more beguiling myths of New Zealand historiography has been the assumption that serious colonisation began only with the arrival of the first Wakefield settlers at Port Nicholson in 1840, and that this had a crucial influence on the nature both of subsequent colonisation and the resultant society. Thus schoolchildren were taught until recently:

> No colony was ever so carefully and wisely colonised as New Zealand. To begin with, only men and women of unusual courage and enterprise were willing to cross the world in sailing ships and seek their fortune in so distant a land. For settlements such as those of Canterbury and Otago, colonists were specially selected, and those pioneers, many of whom were well-educated men of unusual ability, left a deep and lasting influence on the history of a young nation.[1]

Setting to one side the questions of the extent to which New Zealand was unique in attracting the courageous and enterprising, and the degree of volition involved, this ignores the existence of a vigorous community of some standing prior to 1840, and the continuing development and extension of this community subsequently. It was this community which formed the core of nineteenth-century immigration to New Zealand.

The number of pre-Wakefield settlers was not large — 2,000 to 3,000 in most estimates — but it was of considerably more significance than these raw figures suggest. This is because the settlers did not stand alone but were the New Zealand end of an economic relationship with New South Wales and the South Pacific trading economy. It was a relationship, furthermore, of some long standing. As already noted, it extended back at least four decades, and had been established to exploit the timber, flax and other raw materials New Zealand had to offer. The numbers involved in this relationship were also much larger than those who lived in New Zealand itself, and included, for instance, the crews of the visiting whaling fleets who together numbered many thousands of men (although obviously not all visited New Zealand at once) and those involved in processing or selling New Zealand products in New South Wales.

Most accounts of the pre-1840 New Zealand non-Maori community have, for various reasons, concentrated on the picaresque. Missionaries and would-be colonisers alike, each with their own agenda and upon whose accounts historians have tended to rely, stressed the lawlessness and violence which are endemic to all frontier societies. And there is no doubt that these were features of life in New Zealand between John Savage's sojourn in 1805 and the first imposition of settled colonial government. This was not a place for the nervous or faint of heart. But to perceive it as a lawless sink of iniquity is to caricature it out of all recognition. To the extent that New Zealand prior to 1840 was a lawless place, this was largely confined to areas inhabited by non-Maori. Maori society, although violent, was highly structured and controlled. To the extent that the latter was breaking down, this was in part a result of European incursions. And to the extent that violence was endemic in the European settlements, this too was largely a consequence of the circumstances in which those living and working in New Zealand found themselves. Those obliged to suffer those circumstances did not take kindly to them.

Early sealing gangs were often marooned in New Zealand or on offshore islands for extended periods to fend for themselves as best they might. Songs dating from this period express the bitter feelings of those so treated.[2] One of the best known of these, 'David Lowston', records the marooning of ten sealers, probably near Open Bay off the south-west coast, where they remained for four years after their ship was lost. By the time they were picked up in December 1813 they were eking out a miserable existence eating fern root and seal meat. One party taken off the Snares in 1817 had been there for seven years. They got little for their pains. Mostly they were paid in kind, offset against supplies at exorbitant cost, and ended their season of sealing in debt.

The life was a brutal and repressive one. John Grono, one of the main Sydney entrepreneurs in the field, was not above exercising his powers as a magistrate to do down his competitors. In 1823 he arrested a whole sealing crew at Chalky Inlet, using as his excuse the presence of runaway convicts in the gang. The Sydney bench was not impressed. Noting that the arrested sealers had been replaced with a gang of Grono's own, and that he had purloined the seal skins they had gathered, it ordered their return to New Zealand and the restoration of their property. In such anarchic and unpleasant circumstances, the trade attracted largely those who had no alternative employment available to them. These were not, generally speaking, the most civilised of men. This was a circumstance which prevailed into the whaling era after the seals had been hunted to near extinction.

The number of men engaged in the whaling trade was considerable. By 1839, one of the Sydney captains, Johnny Jones, was employing nearly 300 men in seven shore-whaling establishments south of the Waitaki, and there were dozens more dotted about Banks Peninsula and the coves and inlets between. Most of these stations were underwritten by Joseph Weller in Sydney, or the London firm of Enderby Brothers. For the merchants it was a lucrative business which brought them £120,000 annually by 1840 according to one estimate.[3] Little of this found its way into the pockets of the men involved in the hard, dangerous work it entailed.

Colonel William Wakefield, later principal agent for the New Zealand Company, has left an account of how the stations were managed:

> The Sydney merchants supply casks and freight for the oil and bone, and nominally pay the fishermen ten pounds per ton for the former, and six pounds per ton for the latter. The wages of the working men are paid in slops, [kind] provisions, and spirits, which are valued at an exorbitant rate. . . . A good hand in a whaleboat can earn thirty five pounds during a fair season; but his profits depend on the success of his party who have shares in all the whales caught by them.[4]

He thought the whalemen 'badly compensated for their labours'. In such a situation it is hardly surprising that violent disputes over ownership of shore positions and individual whales were commonplace. What the whalemen themselves thought is harder to document, but it is clear that they knew they were being cheated, and resented it. One of the longer established shore whalers in Cook Strait, Worser Heberley, was blunt:

> We could not get any money for our work, instead of money we had to take spirits, soap, sugar, clothing etc. Sometimes we earned two hundred and twenty pounds per year. The agent would give an order on the merchant in Sydney. The merchants sent down their order for the produce of the place and gave orders to the captain not to give anyone a passage to Sydney without charging an enormous price for their passage, their charge was sixty pounds. That was done so they could keep us there. We paid high prices for everything that we got, about eight hundred per cent, soap five shillings a bar, sugar one shilling a pound, and moleskin trousers one pound per pair, so the reader can see how we got robbed by the merchants and agents.[5]

Sydney employers maintained discipline over their crews through managers, known as headsmen, whose brutality was notorious. One headsman at Te Awaiti, when asked how he maintained control, replied: 'I knocks 'em down, sir.' Edward Palmer, a Sydney associate of Jones, managed a station at Preservation Inlet. In 1837 he was indicted for the manslaughter of an employee, 18-year-old Charles Denham, who had, from inexperience, allowed a whaleboat to be driven ashore and wrecked. According to the depositions of eye witnesses, Palmer responded by beating Denham to death with a knotted rope. He was acquitted.[6] This was doubtless an extreme case, but the incidental detail of the depositions, which give a rare insight into working conditions in pre-Treaty New Zealand, make it clear that the viciousness of employers and the drunkenness they encouraged were features of life on the New Zealand coast. By 1838, such flamboyant but reliable eye witnesses as F. E. Maning (later a judge of the Land Court) could characterise sites like Kororareka as

a sort of nest of runaways from whalers with whom were congregated certain other individuals of the pakeha race whose manner of arrival in the country was not clearly accounted for, to enquire into which was, as I found afterwards, considered extremely impolite . . . They lived in a half savage state, or to speak correctly in a savage and a half state, being greater savages by far than the natives themselves.[7]

The missionaries were appalled by all of this. Samuel Marsden described Kororareka in 1837 as a place where 'Satan maintains his dominion without molestation'. But churchmen had their own agenda — a fact well appreciated at the time. James Stephen, permanent secretary at the Colonial Office, minuted in 1843: 'One and all the missionaries seem to me too solicitous to produce a striking effect; and to have too large an infusion of dramatic nature for persons of their high calling.' Such a comment from one of their most sympathetic observers is revealing.

In fact there was a reverse side to this unrelievedly black portrait of New Zealand before 1840. While the population undoubtedly included 'many persons of bad and doubtful character', as Normanby described them to Hobson in his instructions, others had found in New Zealand a comfortable niche for themselves. This is attested by a number of unlikely witnesses, including Edward Jerningham Wakefield, son of Edward Gibbon. In his *Adventure in New Zealand*, young Wakefield painted a picture of the life of the whalers and others which, although characterised by sustained periods of hard work followed by bouts of hard drinking, was very far from the debauched bacchanal of the missionaries' accounts.

A whaler's house is generally built by the natives. It is either entirely composed of reeds and rushes woven over a wooden frame — or else the walls consist of wattled hurdle made of supplejack (kareao) covered inside and out with clay, and the roof thatched. A huge chimney nearly fills one end of the house — and generally swarms with natives, iron pots and kettles, favourite dogs, and joints of the whale's backbone which serve as stools. A view of some fine hams, bacon and fish repays the exertion of peering through the woodsmoke up the chimney. Bunks with neat curtains line the greater part of the sides of the house. A large deal table and two long benches stand in the middle of the hard earthen floor. The rafters support spare coils of rope, oars, masts, sails, lances, spades, and harpoons, and a tin oil lamp, carefully burnished. The square holes in the walls serve as windows, with wooden shutters for the night. The harness cask (for salt meat), flow key and water butt stand on one side, and a neat dresser, shining with bright tin dishes, and a few glasses and articles of crockery on the other side of the door.[8]

This account is similar to contemporary descriptions of the dwellings of the artisans in the community which had grown up around the timber industry in the Bay of Islands and Hokianga from the mid 1830s. In comparison with the living conditions of workers in Britain, this was an idyllic existence. Wakefield pays tribute to the hospitality of these settlements towards casual visitors, and notes that most of those living in them had stable relationships of many years' standing with Maori women.

Some historians have recently reconsidered the evidence concerning the nature of life for most Pakeha in New Zealand in pre-treaty times, and have revised the traditional view propagated by missionaries and others:

> Whaling settlements were . . . 'at once the embodiment of order and disorder' since 'excessive work' under rigid control was followed by periods of 'excessive idleness' during which boredom was drowned in massive consumption of alcohol sold by the companies. This service was provided partly in the interests of further profits but also because endemic drunkenness was a form of discipline, keeping employees dulled and 'captive' during their off duty hours.[9]

Whatever the truth of the matter, given the conditions under which many of the men were employed, it is hardly surprising that they established their independence from their employers as quickly as they could, and negotiated with local Maori for a plot of land which they farmed for subsistence. By the end of the 1830s the number of men living thus had grown significantly. When, in the wake of the establishment of British authority, those with land claims were asked to identify themselves, several hundred did so. In the north, in particular, a burgeoning society of over 500 people had developed.

Behind them loomed the investment and interest of the Sydney business community.[10] The latter were unenthusiastic about the prospect of Crown pre-emption of land purchase, for cross-Tasman exports from New Zealand were, by conservative estimates, bringing in well over £70,000 by 1840.[11] This may explain the attempts of W. C. Wentworth, leader of that community, to induce chiefs visiting Sydney to sign a version of the treaty without the pre-emption clause, and later to unsuccessfully claim land rights over vast areas of New Zealand by prior right of purchase. For the fact was that these prior settlers posed a particular threat to the Wakefield ventures. If these ventures were to be effective, they required a landscape free of settlement, as well as the absence of an existing market in land. The presence in parts of New Zealand of settlers who had the backing of a nearby powerful business community cut across those schemes. These were 'the embarrassments' which Normanby had noted in his instructions to Hobson and which he had instructed should 'claim Hobson's earliest and most careful attention'. As it happened, the New Zealand Company had already anticipated this difficulty.

'EXTENSIVE ACQUISITIONS OF LANDS HAVE ALREADY BEEN OBTAINED'

The existence of the prior settlements in New Zealand, and the despatch of Hobson's mission to establish sovereignty, placed the directors of the New Zealand Company in a quandary. On the one hand, the imposition of British rule so necessary to their schemes was now imminent. On the other, they would have to be quick to establish their rights to purchase land for settlement or they might be excluded from doing so by the very pre-emption clause which lay at the root of their chance of success. It is from this dilemma that the myths surrounding the despatch of the company vessel *Tory* to New Zealand in 1839 to purchase land have grown.

Throughout his life Edward Gibbon Wakefield liked to tell the romantic tale of how he had ridden post haste to Plymouth, galvanised the directors of the company into despatching the *Tory*, and thereby forced the hand of the government in the annexation of New Zealand. But this was mere self-aggrandisement. His motives seem, on examination, rather less exalted. If the *Tory* did not anticipate the arrival of Hobson, the New Zealand Company, hoist by its own petard, might be obliged to buy land at its own, loudly trumpeted sufficient price. This would have been a severe blow to the windfall profits expected by the directors.[12]

As it happened, by May 1840 the company was reporting to its shareholders that the *Tory* party had purchased in excess of a million acres of land for the use of prospective settlers.[13] Ultimately it was to claim the purchase of an astonishing 20 million acres. It had already, the previous August, despatched the first emigrant vessel with '216 settlers of the superior sort, and 909 labouring immigrants' aboard. What it did not tell its shareholders about this land was that much of it had been carelessly and hurriedly purchased from its putative Maori owners in an attempt to establish claims before Hobson could declare sovereignty. Many of these purchases were subsequently disallowed, and endless trouble arose from them over the next decade and a half. The purchases led to immediate difficulties in Wellington (where the owners had not participated in the sale but were driven off their lands nevertheless and obliged to accept inadequate compensation later), and were the root cause of the affray at the Wairau, and ultimately of the land disputes in Taranaki which led to the later wars with the Maori.[14] Perhaps even more to the point, the need

---

SHIPS FOR NEW ZEALAND,
for the Conveyance of Passengers and
Stores to the Settlement of Otago.

New Zealand House,
22nd September, 1847.

The Court of Directors of the *New Zealand Company* do hereby give notice that they will be ready on Thursday, the 30th day of September instant, at One o'clock precisely, to receive Tenders at *New Zealand House*, for the hire of two Ships, of not less than 450, nor above 650 Tons each, old measurement, to be ready to sail on the 30th day of October, 1847, the one from Port or Ports in the Clyde, and the other from the Port of London, to Otago, in New Zealand.

The Tenders to be made according to a Form, which may be had on application at New Zealand House, 9, Broad Street Buildings, London, and at 3, West Nile Street, Glasgow.

The Directors do not pledge themselves to accept the lowest, or any tender.

By Order of the Court,

(ATL)

to purchase land and establish sites at a distance from existing settlements meant that many of the locations chosen — New Plymouth and Wanganui, in particular — were isolated and not very suitable. Others, such as Wellington and Nelson, had good harbours but inaccessible or unavailable hinterlands.

Between 1840 and the end of 1850, the New Zealand Company, or companies which developed from it, established settlements in these four places, and at Dunedin and Christchurch. Overall, they sent out to New Zealand about 12,000 settlers.[15] But by the end of the same decade the Pakeha population was 21,912.[16] More than half of these people were settled in non-company centres, principally Auckland. Obviously the Wakefield settlements had accounted for a significant proportion of immigration to the new colony, but they were by no means responsible for it all. Planned colonisation to New Zealand had not been the success that Wakefield had hoped.

This was not for want of careful political manouvering in London. In October 1840 the company, obliged to admit that it was in financial difficulties and to throw itself on the mercy of the government, had made an arrangement with the colonial secretary, Lord John Russell. This arrangement was brokered by Sir Charles Buller, a close friend of both parties. An independent arbitrator would establish how much money the company had invested in land in New Zealand, and the Crown would subsequently grant four times the value of this in acres at Wellington and New Plymouth at £1 an acre (but amounting to no more than 160,000 acres in all). A further 50,000 acres might be purchased at a discount, and the monies paid over by the company would be used by the government to undertake emigration to New Zealand.[17]

This was a very favourable arrangement by any measure and it certainly saved the company's bacon financially, at least in the meantime. However, it rapidly began to unravel. Less than a year later the Whigs fell from power and were replaced by a Tory government, the colonial secretary in which was Lord Stanley. This new government was sympathetic neither to the notion of 'systematic colonisation' nor to those it perceived as the political friends of the outgoing administration. By 1842 Crown and company were in dispute over the matter of compensation to the previous Maori owners of the land the company claimed to have purchased. The notion that the Maori owned all of New Zealand, said Joseph Somes for the company, was preposterous and the Treaty of Waitangi 'a praiseworthy device for amusing and pacifying savages for the moment'.

Lord Stanley was not impressed. If the company wanted the agreement of 1840 honoured, he coldly informed them, then they must compensate those from whom they claimed to have purchased land. He had already, to the consternation of the company, appointed Robert FitzRoy as governor to replace the prematurely deceased Hobson. FitzRoy, also no friend of Whigs or Wakefield colonisers, had no scruples, when short of revenues, about abandoning the principle of Crown pre-emption upon which the schemes depended, and allowing free purchase in return for a transaction tax. Land speculators, mostly from New South Wales, rushed to buy up land, and nearly 100,000 acres passed out of Maori hands, mostly in the vicinity of Auckland.[18]

Nor was the adjudication on the validity of company purchases by land commissioner William Spain very helpful to their cause. The 20 million acres became 300,000 and then 240,000 after FitzRoy further reduced claims at New Plymouth.[19] In 1844 and 1845 the company could barely manage to arrange for the passage of any immigrants. Meantime, in New Zealand the company continued to experience considerable difficulties, particularly at Nelson and New Plymouth. At the former, attempts to survey land inadequately purchased from Ngati Toa led to the affray at the Wairau. Working men at both settlements, brought to New Zealand on the basis of a promise of work, demonstrated in protest when the capitalist investors who were to provide it failed to materialise and the company was unable to supply either the work or the rations it had promised in such a case.[20]

When the usual company devices of a parliamentary commission in 1844 (chaired by the sympathetic Whig, Lord Howick) and a full dress debate in the Commons (initiated by Buller) failed to budge the government, the company seemed headed for ruin. Fortuitously for them, however, the government fell in December 1845, and the Whigs appointed first William Gladstone, then Lord Howick (now Earl Grey) as colonial secretary. In opposition the Whigs had renewed their commitment to emigration as the basis of the solution to England's social problems.[21] Now with Grey, Buller and Benjamin Hawes, a director of the company, in the Cabinet, the government, while unwilling to give uncritical support to the more eccentric of the New Zealand Company proposals (including the suggestion that Auckland should be abandoned 'to native and hostile tribes'), was open to ideas on how this policy might best be implemented in New Zealand.

Suggestions were not long in coming. In response, the government agreed that the company had suffered as a result of the actions of the Stanley administration and proposed in May 1847 that it make a compensatory advance of £236,000, interest free and for three years, to carry on its activities. If, at the end of that time, the company could not continue, this advance would be written off and the company's remaining land purchased at 5s an acre. Otherwise it should be repaid.[22] The only concession to accountability required was a government appointee to the court of directors. The alacrity with which these terms were accepted is understandable.

The renewed lease of life this gave to the company enabled the settlements at both Otago and Canterbury to be set in train. This latter was effected in time for the company to uplift the government guarantee in 1851. In doing so the directors entreated Earl Grey 'to consider the relative position of New Zealand, regarded as a fair and flourishing possession of the empire, as compared with that of the New Zealand Company. New Zealand has, by its means been rescued from becoming a colony, and we believe a penal colony, of France.' This was meretricious nonsense, and the company, which had recently bought out the entirely private Nanto-Bordelaise Company for £6,000, knew it. Nevertheless it continued:

> But the company through whose means she has been called into existence, nursed, and advanced, lies prostrate; and the shareholders (by no fault or mismanagement of their own) must, in many instances it is to be feared, be absolutely ruined. My Lord, we cannot imagine, we will not believe, that the Government over one department of which your Lordship presides, or the nation over whose sentiments the British Parliament is the exponent, will permit the infliction of so grievous an injustice. [23]

The directors were justified in their faith. Earl Grey responded to this heartfelt plea and the shareholders ultimately received debentures worth £200,000 plus interest for in effect disposing of their colonising ventures in New Zealand to the British government. The London government, in its turn, passed on this liability in 1854 to the newly fledged government in New Zealand. In accepting the debt by way of a London loan, it began its career as it was to continue to the present.

In the meantime, FitzRoy, discredited by his unorthodox financial expedients and by his failure to prevent a war breaking out in the north of the country, had been replaced by George Grey. Grey, more politically acceptable to the new government and fresh from his triumph in rescuing the South Australian venture from collapse, was confidently expected to achieve the same in New Zealand. Armed with a land fund, he resolved the problems with Maori claimants for the time being by his judicious purchases, although ultimately these were insufficient to keep pace with rising immigration.

SUCCESS OR FAILURE?

By the time the company went out of existence in 1858, the non-Maori population of New Zealand stood at 59,277. This was a remarkable increase in less than two decades, but in fact the company could claim credit for only one in five arrivals. From both a business and a colonising point of view, the New Zealand Company had failed. Without significant and generous government support on at least two occasions, the company would have gone bankrupt — a circumstance which consorts oddly with the professed free-trade doctrines of many Whigs and of the promoters of the company itself. And it also failed to realise the creation of a new antipodean Britannia of investors and arable farmers served by hard-working labourers. What brought it to grief on that score was the nature of the New Zealand economy as it developed.

Wakefield's propositions concerning colonisation were simply unworkable in the New Zealand context. In the first place the proportion of employers to workers was out of balance. This had been the case from the outset.[24] On the four ships which came to Nelson in 1842, for instance, there were only 60 cabin passengers to more than 800 who might be prospective employees of these family groups. The company had neither the resources nor the inclination to fulfil its promises to these immigrants that they would be given work and subsistence until the new settlements

Auckland in 1851 was a small but developing settlement which owed little to the New Zealand Company. (Cuthbert Clark – Auckland Institute and Museum and British Museum).

were able to take care of themselves.

But beyond this, and of even greater importance, the heavy bush in the immediate hinterland of most company settlements inhibited the development of arable farming. Those with the wit to see this and the capital to act on it quickly abandoned any attempt at setting up as small employers close to the settlements and turned to the much more lucrative pastoralism offered by the Wairarapa, the Wairau and, eventually, the Canterbury and North Otago plains. This development was assisted by Grey who, through a judicious policy of land purchase, had by 1853 acquired 32 million acres of land from its Maori owners. In 1851 he had regularised the position of those who had hitherto squatted illegally on Maori leases. Two years later he reduced the cost of land to 5s an acre from its previous 30s. By the time self-government became a reality in 1854, New Zealand had become a flourishing pastoral economy.[25]

But this served merely to enable those who had the capital to expand their holdings rather than to encourage the supplementary small farming for which Grey had hoped.[26] Pastoral farming engages many sheep but few people. By 1843 the working men of Nelson were petitioning the company for their removal to some other country. By 1848 the population of Wellington was significantly less than it had been in 1842. The exception to this otherwise gloomy outlook was Auckland, not a company settlement but one which continued to flourish as both the political and business capital of the colony.

Part of the reason for Auckland's prosperity was the availability of arable land in its immediate vicinity, a fact to which attention had been drawn in the evidence to the parliamentary commission of 1844.[27] Auckland settlers, far from wanting to leave, wanted their families and friends to join them and were, in some instances, prepared to pay some or all of the passage money.[28] Earl Grey was not very sympathetic to requests for assistance, although earlier small gestures had been made, including the settlement of some military veterans in 1846. By 1848 most of the immigrants entering Auckland were coming from New South Wales, according to the regular returns furnished by Grey.[29]

THE CRITICS: MARX ON WAKEFIELD;
WAKEFIELD ON WAKEFIELD

The Wakefield schemes had had their critics from the outset. They included Lord Stanley and other Tory politicians, who saw no need to enrich large investors by underwriting their investment; Robert Horton, who saw the dangers in losing sight of the real problem — the need to relieve surplus population; and William Cobbett, who suggested that the rich rather than the poor were the basic problem.

One of the most interesting critics was Karl Marx, who devoted a whole section of his massive work *Capital* to a critique of Wakefield's theories.[30] Wakefield's great merit, said Marx, was not that he discovered anything new about colonies but instead 'the truth as to the conditions of capitalist production in the mother-country'. The sufficient price was nothing more than 'a euphemistic circumlocution for the ransom which the labourer pays the capitalist for leave to retire from the wage-labour market to the land'. It was from this, of course, that the investor/rentier derived the desired dividend. One may argue with Marx's analysis of capitalism but not with his final observation on the Wakefield system. Confronted with a choice of colonies, no labourer would go to one which forced him to labour long before acquiring land. Thus, said Marx, the net effect was to divert the stream of immigration from the English colonies to the United States. In this assertion at least he was borne out by the facts. Labourers would not

Edward Gibbon Wakefield in 1861. Older and perhaps wiser, he was critical of the outcomes of his own theories when he saw them in practice. (ATL)

come to New Zealand if by doing so they only exchanged one exploitative master for another. Besides, the passage to America was cheaper and shorter.

If Marx was trenchant in his critique he was, ironically, surpassed by another even more so. This critic was Wakefield himself. In 1853 Wakefield came out to New Zealand, where he was eventually to die in 1862.[31] To his considerable chagrin he was not feted in Christchurch as the colonial leader and hero he had hoped to be. The Canterbury settlers had their own leaders, who were not prepared to stand aside for any newcomer, no matter how celebrated. Wakefield quickly wore out his welcome and transferred his attention to Wellington. It was here that he became the improbable but politically successful champion of the labourers who were the harshest critics of the company he had fathered.

This is not to say that he had abandoned his belief in the sufficient price. In a series of speeches to prospective constituents in the Hutt Valley, he attacked those who argued for free land as the friends not of colonisation but of land speculators. But while it might be necessary for labourers who came to the new country to work for a while to gain experience, this period should be as short as possible and should lead to the acquisition of freehold land. Only in this way could the industry so crucial to the development of colonies be encouraged. According to Wakefield's biographer, the labouring men who had come to listen to Wakefield 'pricked up their ears' at this.[32] For Wakefield, with his references to 'the malice of thwarted speculators and monopolists', was dramatising the failures inherent in the outcome of his own efforts. Whatever he may have thought his efforts were about over the years, the gentlemen investors who had backed him so vigorously, and who had directed their considerable political clout accordingly, had not shared his illusions.

To them this had always and invariably been a question of profitability first and immigration second. That the bulk of the prospective emigrants were seeking a new life was nothing to them. It was of particularly little interest to those of their number who had felt constrained for whatever reason to come out to the new settlements themselves as employers and investors, and who now constituted the self-appointed political leaders of these settlements (always excepting Auckland). It meant a great deal, however, to the furious inhabitants of the Hutt Valley (and other places) who now felt that they had been cheated in their desire to have that new life in a new place.

That Wakefield was so naive as to have only discovered these truths in New Zealand after 1853 is unlikely. He had experience of other colonies and was no fool. The illness which forced him back into private life shortly after his election to the new Colonial Assembly prevents us from assessing his sincerity against a subsequent career. But that he had touched upon a real grievance is clear enough from the response of his constituents to his proposal that their path to freehold land ownership as small farmers should be eased. This was to be the agenda of the abiding political debate in New Zealand for the next five decades, and the backdrop against which immigration proceeded.

That aside, the Wakefield colonisation schemes in New Zealand were not entirely the failure they sometimes appear to be. There is no doubt that they were responsible for the creation of New Zealand as an immigrant destination at a particular moment in its history, and were similarly responsible, within that context, for ensuring that New Zealand became a Crown colony in 1840. By the end of the first decade and a half of comprehensive settlement, two winners and two losers had emerged from this process.

The first of these winners were the directors of the New Zealand Company who had made significant dividends and protected their investment in the venture. From 1855 they disappeared in that guise from the New Zealand scene, although they remained present in another — as general investors in the City of London. The other winners were the financial and business community of New South Wales who, as original exploiters of the resources of New Zealand, had feared that those opportunities would be lost to them in 1840. By 1855 they had reasserted their earlier role, and for the next two decades they supplied most of the immigrants and much of the business underpinning of the developing colony.

The first of the losers were the Maori inhabitants, who saw their land begin to slip away at an accelerating pace. The second were the labouring immigrants and their families who, having dared the voyage, found New Zealand was not quite what they had anticipated. To immigration as experienced by this last group, both as individuals and as families, it is now appropriate to turn.

CHAPTER FIVE

POOPDECK AND STEERAGE
1840–1855

Adieu! Adieu! my native shore
Fades o'er the waters blue;
The night winds sigh, the breakers roar,
And shrieks the wild sea mew.
For pleasures past I do not grieve
Nor perils gath'ring near;
My greatest grief is that I leave
The friends I hold so dear.[1]

It is nearly impossible for us to conceive what the experience of emigration to a new land might have meant to an immigrant New Zealander in the nineteenth century. In an age when security, both individual and social, came from one's surrounding family and other immediate relationships, and when few people moved far from the environs of their birthplace, undertaking a journey of 12,000 miles to an unknown land where they knew, at best, a handful of other people and from where they were unlikely to return, must have been a wrenching leap into the unknown. Adding to that the known hazards of travel by sea, and taking account of the length of the voyage, it is, however, possible to begin to understand the courage and the determination required to make the decision to go. It is also an indication of how people felt about the unacceptability of the conditions they were leaving behind that large numbers of them took this step.

Two things help us to get to grips with what the experience of emigration must have meant. The first is the known objective circumstances of the voyage as described in reports, letters and diaries. The other is the thoughts and feelings expressed in those same diaries and letters as people assessed the experience and tried to come to terms with it. Such source material itself poses problems. Although literacy was more widespread in the early nineteenth century than is sometimes believed, the habit of keeping diaries and writing letters was largely confined to a narrow social group. Mostly these were people who occupied the cabins on board the emigrant ships, and these are a very small and unrepresentative sample of the emigrants. We are obliged, therefore, to rely on the relatively rare records from the steerage or the comments of the cabin passengers concerning their less propertied fellow passengers to establish how the great majority of emigrants responded both to the voyage itself and to the experience of arrival in the new land.[2]

To those who arrived to take up their passage on the eve of their departure, the sight of a ship preparing to sail cannot have been very comforting. Many of those who recorded their impressions of the voyage began by saying so.

> An emigrant ship on the eve of her departure presents an extraordinary spectacle to the inexperienced eye. The noise, confusion and bustle on board — the busy hammering of the carpenters finishing the different cabins, — the gangs of 'lumpers' hoisting in the huge casks and packing-cases and stowing them in the ample hold — the constant arrival of the different classes of passengers, anxiously watching the descent of their little property down the gaping hatchway, or turning to console some weeping wife or mother, quitting, perhaps for ever, her much-loved home, or gazing with eyes of wonder upon the busy scene — bewilder the

A time for leaving. Embarkation day was often a confused and confusing experience. (Auckland Public Library)

novice as he first sets foot upon the deck. The state of the "tween decks' also, as it is termed, is little different. The chief cabins are crowded with confused heaps of furniture, which the owners are endeavouring to arrange and reduce to order — servants are running hither and thither, and in their embarrassment, hindering rather than assisting their masters — outfitters are looking for their customers, with articles forgotten or not ordered until the last moment; whilst the half-distracted passengers are almost ludicrously endeavouring in the midst of the unaccustomed tumult, to get their furniture and luggage securely stowed in their little cabins, as though in anticipation of the immediate presence of the dreaded sea sickness.[3]

In fact this apparent chaos both of luggage and passengers was ordered and regulated much more comprehensively than it appeared. The New Zealand Company in particular issued very clear and detailed instructions as to who might expect an assisted passage and how they should prepare themselves for the voyage.[4] Labourers had to belong to specified occupations which were calculated to be of value in the new colony. The list of 26 preferred occupations included agricultural workers, smiths, those who worked with horses and agricultural machinery, and those engaged in the various building trades. If they were also engaged to work for an emigrant capitalist, so much the better. Men were obliged to supply testimonials as to their qualifications, character and health; to be not less than 15, nor more than 30; and married (with a certificate to prove it). Only if they had a large family might the age limits be lifted. Oddly, children had to be under one year or more than seven to qualify for a free passage, otherwise they would be charged at £3. Single women might also emigrate if they had another person with whom to travel and with whom they had some family or employment relationship, and provided they too had a suitable occupation upon which they might fall back on arrival.

If they met other requirements but did not qualify for a free passage, intending emigrants could pay at the rate of £18 15s. But like everyone else they had to be vaccinated against smallpox, find their own way to the port of embarkation and bring with them their own tools of trade, 'clothing, bedding and other necessaries for the voyage'. Few in the steerage can have reached the maximum adult allowance of half a ton of baggage or 20 cubic feet of hold space.

The minimum outfit requirements were extensive, including not only the clothing which might be expected but 4 lb of marine soap per person (i.e. soap that was supposed to lather in salt water but often did not), blankets, sheets, a mattress and bolster, eating utensils and, for the women, 2 lb of starch, a pair of stays and a comprehensive sewing kit. Basic rations were supplied to a strict schedule. Three days a week, for instance, an ounce of suet or a third of a pint of peas was issued to the steerage. This diet was not very varied, comprising mostly biscuit, salt meat, flour, rice and potatoes. Passengers were advised to carry supplementary rations, and most did. Food was prepared by the steerage passengers themselves, who were divided into messes for the purpose.

The steerage passengers were accommodated below decks: single men, if there were any, in bunks six and a half feet long by two feet; married couples in bunks an extra foot and a half in width. This space had to accommodate not only the people concerned but everything they needed about them for the whole voyage. What privacy they sought, or the little others felt they required, was supplied by a curtain. Down the centre of the steerage space ran a large table at which people had to eat and do anything else public which required a flat surface. Washing and laundry arrangements were by way of buckets of water drawn up as needed. Periods on deck for this and other purposes were sometimes limited. There was usually also a hospital served by a surgeon who was supposed to inspect all passengers at intervals but sometimes did not. He would normally be assisted by four 'constables' appointed from among the passengers or crew,

This idealised 1849 view of the interior of the steerage leaves out the crowding and, unavoidably, the stench, while accurately depicting the gloom of the between decks. (Illustrated London News)

and a matron appointed to oversee any single women on board, although these minor officials were as much to act as beadles to keep order as to see to the welfare of the steerage passengers. The emigrant William Nichols noted in May 1849 that 'the whole of the single females owing to the misconduct of a few are sent below at eight o'clock and their lamp taken away and locked in the dark until seven the next morning. The doctor keeps them very strict, the doctor's assistant counts them every night after they are in bed like a flock of sheep.'[5]

Cabin passengers, of whom there might be as many as 40 including children (as on the *Bengal Merchant* in 1839) or as few as eight (on the *Coromandel* in the same year), fared rather better. They had much more space and privacy, and were significantly better fed. Mostly the live animals carried were sacrificed to their wants, and stewards cooked and served their meals for them. Interestingly, there was provision for some cabin passengers to travel free, particularly clergy of all denominations and sometimes other professionals such as the surgeons, who were effectively working their passage and who accordingly sometimes showed little interest in the welfare of their ostensible charges. Captains generally received an additional 40 guineas for each cabin passenger to provide the extras they needed by way of food and drink for the voyage. Some could not, of course, resist the temptation to profiteer on this, and there were often regular disputes.[6]

One of the immigrants, Alfred Fell, subsequently published some advice for intending cabin passengers.[7] They should choose the poop cabins, which would be more light and airy, and the larboard in preference to the starboard, because the former was the weather side and allowed fresh air to blow through — a great boon in the tropics. Bunks were to be preferred to hammocks, and all furniture and boxes should be firmly lashed or bolted to the floor. Passengers should also, he thought, bring their own supply of bottled water or at least some filtering device because the ship's supply quickly became brackish. A straw hat was indispensable in the tropics and 'you cannot have too much linen. A candlestick with a glass shade is requisite to suspend, with a lot of sperm candles.* A metal footbath is useful for many things, as well as a water-can or two. By attending to a few little comforts like these, and living in harmony with each other, the voyage to New Zealand, although a long one, nevertheless to a young person may be rendered a very agreeable period of existence.' This and other evidence

---

*Clear- and clean-burning candles made from the spermaceti wax found in the head cavity of some species of whales, and much prized by whalers.

suggests that older people with families did not find the three-month journey quite so agreeable.

Fell also remarked upon the good messing arrangements he enjoyed. On one Sunday in the tropics 'we had an excellent dinner: a salmon preserved and as fine as ever I tasted, soup (and sailors make capital soups), a roast goose, a saddle of mutton, a couple of fowls, with curry and a Westphalia ham, plum pudding and apple tarts, cheese and bottled porter, champagne and sherry, with dessert consisting of apples, nuts, almonds, raisins &c.' This was among 22, including the officers.

The contracting arrangements between immigration entrepreneurs and the shipowners could be complex. In the 1840s, for instance, the New

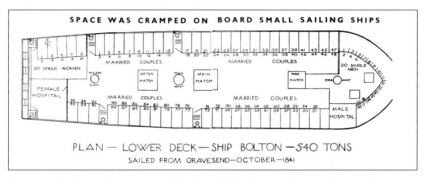

This 1841 plan gives some indication of the discomfort and lack of privacy of the crowded steerage compartments on a typical emigrant ship, in this case the Bolton *(ATL)*

What most plans do not show is the use of the central space as an eating and living area. In stormy weather steerage passengers could be battened down here for days on end. (ATL)

Zealand Company contracted with its shippers at the rate of 1s 6d per day for each steerage passenger carried. The shipowner on a well-conducted ship in which rationing and other requirements were fully met might expect to profit at the rate of about a penny a day per person from this.[8] Presumably this was worthwhile or the owners would not have entered into the arrangement. But as with the victualling of the cabin passengers, there was always the temptation to skimp. There was not much the immigrants could do about this except complain when the voyage was over. Such complaints were usually ineffective, and many were undoubtedly forgotten or abandoned as the prospective complainants scrambled to establish themselves in a new country.

Most of these details were known in advance to those who chose to emigrate either through the publications of the company and other contractors or, as the period progressed, through the accounts of those who had experienced the voyage. So why did they choose to emigrate in the first place? At a public and official level, most emigrants may have shared the motivations advanced by those who had the authority to act as spokespeople on the occasion of their taking their leave, an event often marked by a formal gathering at which speeches were made by prominent citizens. Thus, speaking at a Glasgow banquet to farewell the first New Zealand Company ships in 1839, the sheriff, a Mr Allison, responding to the toast of the lord provost, envisaged a time when 'the British race' would people western and southern hemispheres with 200 millions 'speaking our language, reading our authors, glorying in our descent'. And he went on to ask:

> Are we oppressed with a numerous and redundant population? Are we justly apprehensive that a mass of human beings, already consisting of five and twenty millions, and multiplying at the rate of a thousand souls a day, will ere long be unable to find subsistence within the narrow space of these islands? Let us turn to the colonies, and there we shall find boundless regions capable of maintaining ten times our present population in contentment and affluence, which require only the surplus arms and mouths of the parent state, to be converted in gigantic empires.[9]

Sir William Molesworth was even more expansive. Speaking to a dinner at Plymouth to farewell settlers leaving for the newly acquired lands in Taranaki on 20 October 1840, he announced: 'We are by nature a colonising people. God has assigned to us the uninhabited portions of the globe, and it is our duty to take possession of them . . . to found an Empire which might in future ages become the Britain of the Southern Seas.'[10]

No doubt most of his listeners were more interested in contentment than empires. A subsequent meeting in Dublin, attended by the lord mayor and some dignitaries of church and law (although others were conspicuous by their absence from what they divined, probably correctly, to be a Whig gathering), passed a resolution noting the need to promote emigration from Ireland for the relief of the destitution of labouring people, to improve the condition of all classes of society and to encourage settlement in countries 'where they will be likely not only to thrive in fortune, but to lead good lives, and to bring up their children in virtuous habits'. New Zealand, the resolution noted, appeared to offer all these advantages.

More personal thoughts and feelings upon departure are harder to catch, although it is clear that while hope of self-improvement was usually the motive to emigrate, the experience of leaving was a bitter-sweet one. Susan Meade, travelling to the southern hemisphere with her sister and brother-in-law in 1842, confided to her diary:

> The white cliffs of my native isle have faded from my sight — where the happy years of childhood have glided swiftly away in the society of my affectionate parents, sisters and brothers of my happier hours — but for these dear ones I have left I do not regret leaving England — I am fond of travel, and hope seems to shed a halo round my pathway whispering scenes of happiness yet to come in the terrestrial land of promise to which I am bound.[11]

Jane Bannerman, departing for Otago on the *Philip Laing* in 1847, and then just 12 years old, later recounted that: 'Never while I have power of memory will I forget that sad dreary day. I cannot describe the discomfort around us. The poor passengers looked so dispirited and weary; women weeping and little children looking so homesick, there seemed no room for them on the deck. I turned down into our cabin in the stern of the ship to be out of the way of so much sadness and discomfort.'[12]

Many of the letters and diaries of emigrants made specific reference to Bunyan's *Pilgrim's Progress* in trying to explicate their feelings and motives. In 1852 Henry Whittingham, himself an emigrant, wrote grimly to his brother, who intended to follow him: 'Remember that your voyage is for your own benefit, taken voluntarily by you. To lament this is to lament your own act, and to lament what cannot be undone.'[13] Others were more cheerful and forward-looking, if equally portentous. Alexander Marjoribanks noted, as his ship cleared Scotland: 'We were all full of hope and anxiety to see what had been represented to us as a sort of earthly paradise — a smiling land, the very sight of which was at once to have banished away all our cares and all our sorrows.'[14] Many, including George Angas, tried to express their feelings in verse:

Away, away — let visioned scenes
Of other lands elate thee,
Nor vainly cling to those behind
While brighter ones await thee.
Though many a thousand weary miles
Of ocean are before thee
The beacon star of hope shall shed
Her cheery influence o'er thee.[15]

Angas was bound to be optimistic. In the wake of the Wairau affray which had disposed many would-be settlers against choosing New Zealand as their destination, he had been engaged by the New Zealand Company (of which his father was a leading luminary) to prepare an illustrated work of propaganda with heavy emphasis on the cheerful good humour of the Maori. But even he was caught up in the ambivalence of departure.

LIFE ON THE OCEAN

Once on board, the emigrants had more pressing and immediate concerns to deal with. Some of the steerage passengers, having established themselves in their new situation, were outraged to discover that they were expected to play their full part in the running of the ship, not only in respect of the preparation of meals but also in keeping their quarters clean and aired, and in standing watches. Dr Alfred Barker, on board the *Charlotte Jane* heading for Canterbury in 1850 with his wife Emma, and with 100 steerage

In the tropics most passengers spent the day on deck, protected by an awning. This rather idealised depiction purports to be on the Randolph *in 1850. (ATL)*

passengers under his control, began each day with a roll call, the airing of mattresses on deck, and a roster of eight men to scrub the steerage compartment floors and sprinkle chloride of lime. But first he had to quell an incipient mutiny: 'Several stoutly refused, and said they hadn't been accustomed to scrub etc etc., and one mutineer held out stoutly against a compulsory task, and we were ultimately obliged to put him to sleep by himself in one of the boats hanging over the ship's side on a wholesome diet of biscuit and water, after which he thought it advisable to knock under, and has worked well ever since.' Barker went on unwittingly to reveal what conditions must have been like in the steerage: 'The filthiness of some of these folks should be seen to be appreciated, and as long as the sea sickness lasted the work of getting them in order was really no trifle, in addition to the fact that going below made me invariably seasick.'[16]

Most of the passengers, however, and especially the single men, took to their new roles as cook or laundry hand with zest, and some discovered skills and a resourcefulness in themselves they had previously not suspected. Francis Taylor commented ironically in 1850 that in rising at 4 a.m. to take his turn at doing his laundry it was 'laughable to see so many men in the washing buckets up to their elbows, lots of fun, more fun than dirty clothes. I find I can do it smartish. Think something about taking a laundry maid's place [on arrival].'[17] This boded well for their progress in their new country.

From the extant accounts it is clear that the voyage was mostly boring. 'Nothing worth mentioning except sky and water, water and sky,' remarked Henry Widdowson on his way to Australia in 1825. Nearly 30 years later Byron Ronald likewise confided to his diary: 'As every day is little different from the one preceding, I thought it not worth while to write every day.'[18] This monotony was interrupted by storms, of which there are many compelling descriptions in letters and diaries ('confusion and awful noise; the waves tossing themselves almost mountains high, and every now and then one sea larger than another would sweep the decks, poop, and everything. I could neither sit nor stand, and it was with great difficulty that I could keep myself in bed'[19]). There were also deaths, commonly of children, recorded in a manner we would now find callous or even shocking: 'the children throve every day. Three or four deaths of little children from natural causes took place, but no serious sickness', or, 'Two children died on the passage one of whom was not expected to live when it came aboard — this is a very small mortality considering that we had forty cases of measles, some of them followed by whooping cough'.[20] Seasickness was ubiquitous, along with illnesses, some of them startling to say the least:

'One of the cabin passengers, Mr Rankine, who during the voyage has been drinking heavily, was this day attacked with the Blue Devils and conducted himself in a very riotous manner like a lunatic.'[21]

But the journey was also enlivened by events such as the sighting of unusual fish, the hailing of other vessels, the apparently obligatory ceremony associated with crossing the line, and a range of entertainments got up by the passengers among themselves. Thus Mary McKain on board the *Olympus* in 1841 remarked: 'One of the immigrants has a violin and plays on it most evenings, and many of the people dance on deck. We have singing and jokes of all kinds.' She then rather spoiled the effect by continuing, 'and as a contrast a man was put in irons one day for striking his wife. The assistant superintendent is not liked, and has this week been suspended for striking one of the emigrants. So you see, we have sport of all sorts.'[22] But incidents of this kind notwithstanding, passengers of all classes often went to extraordinary lengths to pass the time pleasantly, setting up choirs and debating societies, and even an occasional newspaper. Beneath these high jinks, however, a curious tension runs like a theme through many of the accounts kept by the cabin passengers.

Alfred Barker was not alone in his patronising attitude towards the steerage. Others made comments which are equally revealing. Martha Adams, travelling to Nelson as a cabin passenger in 1850 aboard the *Eden* with her two children and husband William, after commenting on the unbearable heat in the tropics and bemoaning how she had been obliged to dress her children less formally than usual, drew a distinction between them and 'the common children, going without shoes and stockings'. She also stayed well clear of the steerage passengers: 'I have never been myself into the steerage, as William says it is not fit for me to go, and besides it is now so filthily dirty, that it can only be wondered at, that there is not more disease on board.'[23] This was not simply an isolated snobbishness. Alfred Fell spoke disapprovingly of

> one or two of our fellow passengers who will go amongst the emigrants and make themselves familiar with them. The captain is very much annoyed at it, as it tends to lower our dignity by familiarity, and, of course, lower the dignity of the ship. One of them absented himself from our meeting on last evening, and was found amongst them. The captain felt himself insulted at his preferring their society to ours, particularly at our weekly festival. We passed a vote of censure upon him immediately, and this morning he apologised. But if such a thing is repeated he will certainly be sent to Coventry by all of us. It is very foolish of them, as we have no business to come in contact with them at

all, living in different parts of the ship. I have never spoken to one of them yet.[24]

This same captain surprised even Fell by forbidding the steerage passengers to come on deck to sing hymns as a group on a Sunday because they had impertinently done so without his leave.

A number of writers on southern emigration have commented on this phenomenon.[25] No doubt the ships were a microcosm of the social structure of Victorian Britain, with its firmly delineated class distinctions. On some larger vessels the distinctions were even more minutely maintained by the existence of an intermediate class between cabin and steerage in which the passengers had their own companionway and cabins but ate their meals in messes. What particularly concerned those such as Fell and Adams was not so much the failure on the part of the ship's authorities to maintain distinctions, but the disinclination of non-cabin passengers to do so. 'Some of the second class (i.e. intermediate) passengers are very troublesome,' recorded Rachel Hemming indignantly in her diary in 1854. 'The first day one of them, with his wife, took their seats at the captain's table, and refused to show their tickets, alleging that they were first class passengers.

Emigrants on deck, 1849. There is no sense here of the overcrowding which bedevilled steerage passengers taking the air. (Illustrated London News)

Cabin passengers considered the poop deck their exclusive preserve and vigorously resisted any attempts to open it to the steerage. (ATL)

However, the purser enforced the appearance of the ticket, and the steward expelled them.'[26]

What especially raised the ire of the cabin passengers was the sight of steerage passengers trespassing on the poop deck. This was the stern area below which lay the first-class cabins and other amenities. The officer of the watch commanded from the poop, and as a recreational space it was regarded as the prerogative of the cabin dwellers. Steerage passengers who trespassed on it were usually unceremoniously chased off. Some captains allowed access to the poop from time to time, particularly when the 'tween decks and maindeck were being cleaned, but the regular occurrence of this caused many cabin passengers deep offence. John Whiting for one complained of his captain's doing so in 1854, and added: 'if he understood his business and looked after them and saw them all turned up on deck while their place was cleaned and they were all washed and properly clean in their person there would be no fear of disease. It is certainly very unjust towards the cabin passengers — I would strongly advise any persons of respectability if emigrating to Australia to do so in a merchant ship and not in an immigrant one.'[27]

John Fenwick, writing his diary also in 1854, could see the inequity of the poop, 90 feet long and 35 wide, being reserved for about 50 people while the much smaller available space on the main deck had to take the remaining 500 aboard — 'a dense crowd of men, women, and children — ropes, luggage and confusion of all sorts — some read, one knits, others smoke, and most are idle.'[28] But such sympathy was rare. Martha Adams' attitude was much more typical: 'We are sorry to find that the regulations of the ship are not adhered to as much as we expected; the intermediate and even the steerage passengers walking on the poop with the greatest impunity; so there is very little advantage in paying extra for this privilege which now is open to all.'[29]

It is nevertheless hard to escape the impression from many of the extant diaries that the farther from England the voyage progressed, the harder it became to keep up the social distinctions so important at 'home'. Martha Adams fulminated against attitudes whereby

> everybody on this ship think [sic] a great deal of themselves, and even the poorest imagine that they will be grand folk in New Zealand, it can easily be pictured what disturbances are constantly taking place among them owing to this cause. There is not I believe a single young woman on board but scouts the idea of being a servant when they land: nothing less than a piano forte and crochet seem compatible with their ideas of their own dignity; on which account, it is so difficult to get any little service performed for you, presuming you have no servant of your own. For instance, should you require an article of children's clothing washed: you *may* find someone who on Friday, which is a washing day, will attend to it for you: but if you offer payment you will be told 'they could not think of such a thing, as they only did it to oblige you, and that their papa means to buy them a *piansy* when they get to New Zealand.'

There was sometimes even collective action against privilege and the pretensions of the cabin. Towards the end of some voyages water was inclined to become extremely foul and even to run low. On the *Eden* there was a concerted, albeit unsuccessful, attempt to force the captain to make for port at the Cape of Good Hope when it became clear that the water was running out but that rationing would be confined to the steerage. In the event rain resolved the crisis, but not before the captain had been obliged to cancel his rationing order. Nor had Alfred Barker quelled his last mutiny. As his ship neared New Zealand he recorded: 'A few days ago we had a quarrel with some emigrants who struck work and gave us a good deal of trouble, but the assurance that the galley fire would be put out and no food cooked for them, together with the sight of the arms chest which was brought on deck, made them listen . . . and [they] knocked under in time to get their dinners.'[30]

One of the most interesting of these incidents occurred on the *Timandra*, bound for New Plymouth in 1841, over the sprinkling of chloride of lime in the steerage. This was a common enough measure to ensure hygiene, but there had already been some stormy scenes over the extraordinary insistence of the ship's surgeon that he should carry out a post mortem on those steerage passengers who died en route, and of whom there had been a number. These had caused such an uproar that the ship's captain, Skinner, had had to intervene and tell the surgeon that his safety could not be guaranteed if he persisted. When the first mate tried to sprinkle the lime, the passengers protested that it burned their clothes, and in the ensuing altercation the mate was assaulted and the captain was obliged to threaten the steerage by drawing up his crew and reading the ship's rules. The mate's assailant was put in irons until he apologised, which he initially refused to do. No doubt Captain Skinner was relieved to see Mount Taranaki come into view eleven days later.

But if the occupants of the cabin imagined that landfall would put an end to the impudence of the steerage, they were mistaken. Many cabin passengers discovered, once ashore in the new land, that social niceties were not of an order to which they were accustomed, and that many of the distinctions they took for granted in Britain were not, and indeed could not be, observed in the new land. Not only that, but attempts to affirm them often ran into strong opposition.

UPON ARRIVAL

After the long voyage the emigrants, now become immigrants, looked forward with longing to the sight of their new home, and waxed lyrical at the prospect. Alfred Barker, whose first glimpse of New Zealand was the southern point of Stewart Island, took a hasty sketch of it as the sun set, and wrote: 'tonight we had to welcome us to our new land the most beautiful sunset we had ever beheld, indeed neither tongue nor pencil would give the slightest idea of its splendour.'[31] But closer inspection often dashed high hopes. 'With very long faces we saw what a fearfully rough country we had come to, and the gloom was not abated by the sight of three small vessels lying wrecked on the rocks,' wrote one early arrival in Wellington. ' "What a country to come to," said Mr Cullen, a Somerset farmer. "But see what a fine harbour we have got," said the boatman. "Dang the vine harbour," said farmer Cullen, "What's the good ov a vine harbour whar you can't graw nothen?" '[32] Lieutenant John Wood, on board an early New Zealand Company vessel, was blunter: 'The passengers were all on deck straining their eyes to catch a glimpse of civilisation. Little was said, though disappointment was visible on the countenance of everyone.'[33]

New Zealand Company secretary John Ward might dilate at length in 1840 upon the preparations the company had made to assist the new settlers with 'machinery, mills, steam engines, agricultural implements, the frames of houses, and goods of various other descriptions now on their voyage'.[34] The company might very well have sent out buildings for first shelter and 'a considerable stock of provisions to supply the first wants of the settlers, and prevent the possibility of a scarcity'. But the arriving immigrants had to turn to at an initial level of plain subsistence.

'To our utter astonishment,' William Bannister was to write of his arrival in 1840, 'there was not a house or place to receive either steerage or cabin passengers, so that we were obliged to remain on the ship fourteen days — I mean the women and the children. The men and all the boys that were able went on shore every morning for the purpose of making houses for their future abode.'[35] Of her arrival in 1847 Jane Bannerman recalled:

> We had to take up our life, and very rough it was at first. Our boxes were piled one above the other in front of the house and it was six months before we could get at them unpacked. There was no room in the house and we had a fire outside to cook at. . . There was abundant food. How sweet we thought were the potatoes, beef and mutton good, and plenty of fish and pork could be had from the Maoris. We had come to a land without scarceness. We had no luxuries but abundance of wholesome food.[36]

Some of the colonists had come with unreal expectations.'They expected,'

Immigrants were often surprised and indignant at the conditions they were expected to live in on arrival. These huts at Petone were sketched by William Swainson in 1841. (ATL)

'Our kitchen' by William Bambridge (1819-1879). By 1845 many of the immigrants were reasonably well established although the conditions for ex-cabin passengers were still often well below what they had known in England. (ATL)

said the company surveyor Ernest Dieffenbach, 'with the help of the labour which was provided for them in return for their purchase of land . . . to produce those articles which the country was said to offer available for export . . . and having thus made a rapid fortune, to return to their native country.'[37] Quickly disabused of this illusion, these people either dissipated their little capital idling in the coffee rooms and public houses of the new settlements (where, according to George Angas, 'billiards are played without interruption, and liquors and champagne circulate rather too freely for a new colony'[38]) or, as Warren Adams reported from Christchurch, they were 'reduced to work on the roads, or employed at daily wages by those they had brought out as servants'. Their wisest course, Adams thought, was to leave their money in the bank and go up country for a few years to learn the business of runholding from an experienced farmer. He was particularly contemptuous of those who had fitted themselves out with well-furnished guns, kid gloves and evening dress. 'If they expected to continue the habits of the old country in the new colony, these adjuncts would be appropriate; but it is difficult with such views to comprehend the object for which they quitted England.'[39] The social distinctions so important in England did not apply in the new colony and expectations were quickly overturned, as

Martha Adams discovered:

> All labourers, mechanics, and those who can work with their hands,
> succeed excellently, soon purchase a cow which increases to a herd, and
> are fed on the hills at a very small expense — build their house, which
> however rude and ugly is soon covered with vines and creepers; and
> keep geese etc on the common land. Thus far once, and they soon grow
> rich; but those who require people to work for them have to pay such a
> high ratio of wages, that the profit is small, and they are slower in
> gathering around them the comforts of life than the industrious
> labourers. Cabinet and furniture makers are at a high premium: there
> are plenty of unmarried young girls here too proud to go to service and
> too idle to get husbands, who only marry active, useful wives, they get
> about ten pounds the first year, and rise afterwards according to their
> acquirements: one who can cook, wash and iron well, or can take the
> charge of a dairy would have twelve to fourteen pounds *at once*.

Snobbish to the last, she added, 'There is a good day school here for the
poop children, and the clergyman who attends to it has also a salary from
funds for the grammar school, but as this is at present held in the same
room as the daily school, of course people do not like to send their children
there unless they have no objection to their mixing with the lowest.'[40]

If Martha Adams could get servants at whatever price, she was one of
the fortunate. In 1842 Jessie Campbell, her husband and children were

*As experience of emigration developed, so did the recognition of the need
for buildings of substance to house newcomers at the point of arrival. The
scene at Lyttelton in 1851 must nevertheless have been daunting. (ATL)*

removed from their original destination, Wellington, to Wanganui, and on 4 December she wrote to her family in England for only the second time since her arrival. This was a short letter, and 'when I tell you the reason you will not complain, for the last fortnight I have had no servants; the damsel I've had since coming here chose to get a beau and left me at ten minutes notice to prepare for her marriage. I cannot get her place supplied here, the only help I have is from a smart little girl about twelve years old who comes in every evening.'[41] In Christchurch a few years later Emma Barker encountered a similar problem. She and some other ladies rose from a communal breakfast 'and afterwards dispersed; the ladies making no secret of their household occupations, as they are occasionally without any servant. The want of domestics is much felt in this colony.' And she added feelingly, 'the independence of those who go to service is often very annoying.'[42]

It was not just the servant problem which agitated the immigrant middle classes. Wages everywhere were an outrage. Writing about the same time from her new home in Canterbury to her sister Letitia, Georgiana Bowen alluded twice to the cost of labour, which she described as 'enormous'.[43] Two months later, in March 1851, she was still exercised by it: 'Labour is enormous, for example a man and his wife require fifty pounds per year with their maintenance and that of their children — which must be good and abundant, and many of them are so independent as it is termed and they often leave their employers for to do their own work. Our man Simpson and his wife, like many others left us after landing having refused to take forty pounds per annum.' Others made similar comments. Mary McKain at Port Nicholson referred to the outrageous wages for carpenters at 12s and sawyers at 15s a day. Even labourers might make £1 a week and generous rations from cutting horse trails through the bush.[44]

No doubt it all came as rather a shock to those used to the low wages paid to British workers. But there was worse. To its original settlements at Wellington (1840), New Plymouth (1841) and Nelson (1842), the New Zealand Company, in the guise of the Otago Association, had added Dunedin in 1848 and then, as the Canterbury Association, Christchurch in 1850. Those promoting emigration and a new start in the Canterbury settlement had particularly directed themselves to the 'uneasy classes', by which they meant downwardly mobile gentlemen and their families whose 'hearts are failing with fear' at the political and social upheaval of Europe. They should make their way to Canterbury, urged the publicist author of the *Canterbury Papers*. There they might not make their fortunes but 'they would have comfort and plenty'; from there they might listen with interest but no anxiety to the din of war and 'to the tumult of revolutions, to the clamour of pauperism, the struggle of the classes, which wear out body and soul in our crowded and feverish Europe'.[45]

Unfortunately for the peace of mind of these gentlemen, such tumults had come with them in the steerage. Ominously for the quiet and happy life they had been promised, the regulations of the New Zealand Company had made it clear that emigrants would 'be at perfect liberty to engage themselves to any one willing to employ them, and will make their own bargain for wages.'[46] Given that the social composition of the new settlements ensured a shortage of skilled labour, this freedom of contract was bound to cause difficulties. Combined with the failure of the company to provide the employment which their posters and propaganda had promised, and a determination on the part of many labouring immigrants not to put up with the conditions they had fled, it is hardly surprising that these difficulties appeared sooner rather than later.

'A RIGHT AND LEGAL THING'

That the social tensions liable to surface on the immigrant ships remained to simmer on arrival is clear from most accounts. These tensions took interesting forms. In Wellington, for example, there was an almost immediate dispute over whether the celebration of the anniversary of the arrival of the first ships should be a popular or an exclusive affair.[47] That these tensions were long lasting is also clear from the political support already noted as being given by working men to Wakefield himself when he came to New Zealand over a decade later to pursue his political ambitions and spoke up for better availability of land to the populace at large, and against the landowners and speculators many of the cabin immigrants had become. But the tensions were most likely to break out into open disputes over employment and wages. These became so widespread and apparently endemic that at least one historian has characterised this as the period of 'the labourers' revolt'.[48]

The New Zealand Company had promised employment to intending worker emigrants, and in default of this wages of £1 a week and rations. Once they had arrived in New Zealand, however, this and other promises that they would be decently housed were quickly forgotten. Even some of the cabin passengers were moved to protest. Alexander Marjoribanks was one who subsequently expressed his outrage at seeing his fellow passengers 'driven out of the ship like oxen upon a Saturday night in the midst of a storm of wind and rain, of which you can hardly form any conception, many of them having no place to which they could fly for shelter until the fury of the storm was overpast'.[49]

By 1842 it was clear in most settlements that there was not enough work to meet the needs of the large number of labourers the company had brought to New Zealand and which it continued to send without regard for the consequences. Instead it published propaganda accounts denying reports that there was a problem. 'The happy effect of the Wakefield system,' Charles Heaphy, company draftsman, wrote in 1842, 'has been to cause the supply of labour and demand to be at all times equal, and neither have the rate of wages been high, or labouring classes in want of employment.'[50] He was seconded by another company employee, William Petre, who was, if anything, even more emphatic: 'It has been frequently stated in some of the newspapers of New South Wales and of this country, that the first settlers at Port Nicholson suffered great privations, and even sometimes were in want of food. There never was the slightest foundation for such statements.'[51] Both men were well aware that what they were saying was untrue.

The fact was that the company was in financial difficulties and in no position to make good its promises, and by January 1843 it was instructing its agents 'not to employ any labourer whatever on any account at any of the settlements except those who are indispensable for the Company's purposes'.[52] Those hitherto on relief work, mostly cutting tracks and lines, and on a subsistence wage far less than the promised £1, were either dispensed with or had their wages further reduced.

In England, any protests at such treatment would have been swiftly suppressed. But this was not England and the labourers had come to the new country to escape both the treatment and the suppression. A protest meeting at Thorndon, after Colonel Wakefield had tried to force the unemployed out to subsistence plots in bush country, resolved 'that the alarming condition of the labouring classes of this settlement requires on [the part of the Company] the most strenuous exertions . . . to prevent the well disposed and industrious workman from becoming a pauper or felon in this distant land'.[53] This protest fell on deaf ears.

In Nelson and New Plymouth the protests were more vigorous. At Nelson the working immigrants politely petitioned yet another Wakefield brother, Captain Arthur, drawing attention to the company's commitment to provide work and noting that they and their families would starve if there was none, that they had been seduced to the other side of the world with false promises and that they only wanted 'a right and legal thing'.[54] The company did not respond favourably to this petition, and instead sent

its agent Frederick Tuckett to impose some discipline on the recalcitrants.*
The labourers responded by invading his office armed with sticks and guns,
and faced him down. The company then sent a Mr Valle, who confronted
the disgruntled labourers at their work site and accused them of slacking.
They threw him into a drain and pelted him with stones. Valle, badly shaken,
enlisted the support of the authorities, and the police magistrate, White,
subsequently tried to arrest and handcuff the men's leader. There followed
what White described as a 'scene of the wildest disorder and impertinence'
when the other workers came to the rescue and White was forced to beat
a retreat.[55] Tuckett then sent for the military and had five of the men
arrested, although the magistrate prudently released them with a lecture
on civil obedience to help them on their way. Notwithstanding the sneers
of Alfred Domett, editor of the *Nelson Examiner* and a future prime
minister, who took to referring to the roadmakers as 'a privileged class',
the company was forced to rescind its decision and continue to employ the
men.

Similar scenes were enacted at New Plymouth where the labourers had
retained the handbills issued in England which promised them work. These
they thrust under the noses of the outraged company officials. No doubt
they had not forgotten the *Timandra* and the chloride of lime either. When
a polite petition succeeded only in having the petitioners characterised as
'a mob' by the company agent, the attitude of the labourers became so
threatening that attempts to end relief work and the issue of supplies had
to be abandoned.[56] Eventually the situation was relieved by a growth in
employment as the new settlements began to develop and expand. Nor
was the problem confined to the company settlements. In 1844 Governor
FitzRoy spoke in a despatch of 'a relative over supply of labourers, with
consequent distress' in Auckland. The government had taken this in hand
by offering relief work at 2s a day, and in deserving cases a licence to
occupy small sections of land for subsistence purposes. FitzRoy went on to
complain that many of those who arrived as immigrants were used to
living and earning their wages in industrial towns, and that they were of
little use in a colony which could not yet be sure it could feed and house
itself adequately.[57]

But it was not simply a matter of protest against the activities of the
authorities. Many of those who came to New Zealand as steerage passengers
in this period would have had contact with the Chartist movement in Britain

---

* Captain Arthur Wakefield had meantime been killed in the clash with Te Rauparaha at
Wairau in June 1843.

and been well aware that one of its key demands was for a limitation on the daily hours of work. Those who found their skills in high demand were not slow to capitalise on this, most famously the carpenter Samuel Parnell who, shortly following his arrival in Wellington on the *Duke of Roxburgh* in 1840, told the scandalised shopkeeper George Hunter that he would work no more than eight hours a day for him, commencing not at the customary 6 a.m. but at 8. When Hunter protested, Parnell bade him good day and Hunter, suddenly aware of what a free market in scarce labour might mean, was obliged to agree to his terms.[58]

The practice became widespread, and in Wellington it became customary for delegations of tradesmen to meet arriving ships to explain the new arrangement to those on board. In Auckland from 1851 the painter and Chartist William Griffin led a campaign for limitations on Saturday hours and ultimately an eight-hour day. He was also active in successfully promoting the candidature of working men for the Auckland Provincial Council. And in Dunedin, from the outset of settlement in 1848, a strict eight-hour day was observed by the public ringing of a bell. This outraged William Cargill, the company agent, who castigated the labourers for having come out to New Zealand with 'an exaggerated belief that they are to have large wages and shorter hours of work, making them in reality mere drones'. When he attempted to reassert the 'good old Scotch rule' of a ten-hour, five-shilling day, the 'drones', ably led by Samuel Shaw, faced him down and the eight-hour day remained in force.[59]

By the early 1850s the steerage immigrants in New Zealand had made two important discoveries. The first was that in a new land there was significantly less social constraint on what they might achieve by way of a comfortable living than there had been in Britain, particularly if they had a skill which was in short supply. But they had also been made aware that success in attaining such a level, or even striving to do so, was not necessarily welcome to those who might have been expected to enjoy a considerable social distance over them if they had remained at home and who resented the disappearance of such distinctions. As the new colony began to find its way to a reasonable level of prosperity, this latent tension remained unresolved. In the meantime, the immigrant ships continued to call. In the decade from 1861 alone 195,000 immigrants entered New Zealand — something over 50 people a day, day in, day out, for ten years.[60] And beyond New Zealand the world economy was changing in ways which were bound, as always since, to bring changes to New Zealand.

CHAPTER SIX

THE STATE OF BRITAIN
1850–1870

An observer who, with the advantage of present statistical techniques, looked back down the long vista from the death of Queen Victoria in 1901 to her accession in 1837, would have seen what appeared to be a period of unparalleled economic growth. Many Edwardians did so and congratulated themselves accordingly. Superficially they were entitled to their pride.

Since that time there have been various attempts to assess the achievement of the Victorian economy. These have varied in their detail, but their conclusions have been of a piece.[1] Between 1801 and 1901, according to a 1967 estimate based on incomplete but adequate runs of data, the British economy grew fourteenfold in terms of gross national product (GNP) at constant prices. This represents an annual average growth rate of 2.7%. Subsequent and more conservative estimates have reduced this to about 2% per annum, and have set the overall growth rate between 1830 and the First World War at between five and six times. Whichever of these estimates is chosen, and however modest the annual growth rate may look, there is no doubt that compounded over six decades it presents a remarkable picture of growth and development over time.

Key factors in this development were the growth of both labour productivity and capital accumulation. Again, because of the lack of robust and long-term data there is debate over the extent of this growth, but the conclusions generally drawn by analysts are congruent. From around 3% per annum at the end of the seventeenth century, capital formation rose sharply to 6% in the last decades of the eighteenth, and from the 1850s consistently reached 10% every year — a remarkable accumulation over the century.[2] Labour productivity is harder to assess, but seems to have reached an annual average rate of 1.1%.[3] Compared to its continental neighbours, Britain, on the statistics at least, was doing very well. Production of pig iron per head reached 29 kg in 1830, and 132 kg by 1860. Comparable levels for continental Europe were 4 kg and 10 kg. Statistics for the consumption of raw cotton show a similar picture: 4.7, 15.1, and a derisory 0.3 and 1.1 kg.[4]

But these figures are misleading. Firstly, they do not differentiate between sectors of the economy. While industry grew almost exponentially at an average 4.7% per annum from 1801 to 1841, and at the slightly less spectacular rate of 3% per annum to 1871, agriculture languished by comparison, with annual rates of 1.2% and 1.3%. Nor do these figures tell us anything about the distribution of income.

During the whole of the nineteenth century the United Kingdom enjoyed the highest per capita GNP in Europe, but the average income per capita was still quite low, probably about £38. If this had been evenly distributed, it might have assured a modestly adequate standard of living at contemporary prices. It was not. In 1867, for example, the upper 0.5% of families received 26% of the national income. The next 25% of families accounted for 35% of income, and the rest had to make do with the 39% that remained.[5] These proportions remained much the same until after the First World War. Real wages may have increased by fits and starts as the century progressed, but at the end of Victoria's reign probably between 25% and 30% of the population still lived in poverty — either unable to maintain themselves and their families in good health, or just able to survive but with no margin against a sudden fall into penury as a result of unemployment, illness or old age. The best that could be said was that this situation had been significantly worse earlier in the century.[6]

But the most significant drawback of averaged growth rates is that they are precisely that — averages. They take no account of cyclical activity within an economy. Most economists in fact distinguish at least four broad periods within the British economy from 1815 to 1915. These stretch variously from the end of the Napoleonic Wars to the end of the 1840s; from about 1848 to about 1873; from then to 1896; and finally the period to the beginning of the First World War. It is the second of these, and in particular the two decades from 1850, that we are concerned with here.

Within periods themselves there are usually significant cyclical fluctuations. Booms in 1826, 1835 and 1845 were promptly followed by slumps and depressions in which a combination of bad harvests and high food prices overlapped with industrial overproduction and increasingly severe unemployment to create the period of social distress known, with chilling accuracy, as 'the hungry forties' — a period which coincided with the Irish potato famines of grim memory.[7] The years from the end of the

Napoleonic Wars to 1850 can be characterised by a prolonged fall in prices (43% overall) and in interest rates. Although these offset one another to a degree, the first was by far the most significant, impacting on profit margins and thus on wages which, in the absence of any labour market regulation, fell significantly from 1830 to the mid century. At the same time, and after 1830, most industrial activity was by way of consolidation rather than innovation, so that opportunities for adjustment of employment by transfer to new or extending industries did not exist to the same degree as before. Between 1830 and 1850 there was very little change in the distribution of the labour force. About 40% continued to be engaged in industry and about 25% in agriculture, with the balance largely in trade and transport, and domestic and personal services.

But some things did change. This was also the period during which the urban population of Britain grew to exceed the rural population for the first time. The population overall grew from 16.3 million in 1831 to 21 million in 1851. In the crowded towns of industrial Britain it was the angry new industrial proletariat and those displaced from the land by enclosure who had largely supplied the immigrants brought to New Zealand by the New Zealand Company, as well as those who had come of their own volition. Among the latter were some driven out of Ireland by famine, or of Scotland by land enclosures, who found their way to New Zealand through Australia or Canada or the United States, as well as directly.[8]

From the mid 1850s this pattern changed as the British economy changed. For two decades Britain appeared to experience an unprecedented boom. In the five years to 1849 Britain had produced just over a million tons of iron and steel per annum. Twenty years later the comparable five-year figure stood at 4 million. Almost every set of statistics of industrial production illustrates a similar development. It was a period of enormous expansion which has been characterised by one of the leading analysts of the Victorian economy thus:

> Profits, prices and wages rose instead of falling. The economy showed a remarkable dynamism and achieved a striking expansion in production, investment, and exports. The growth of product, both national and per capita, gained speed and reached its highest levels for the nineteenth century. Although the growth of industrial production seems to have been slightly lower than in the preceding period (which has been denied), agriculture prospered again and the services sector developed rapidly. Inflation created a climate of optimism among businessmen, in clear contrast to the gloom which they had known during their long fight against deflation in the preceding decades, and which they would experience again after 1873. Above all, the mass of

the population began at last to enjoy the benefits of industrialisation. Real wages increased markedly, and wealth spread in a way never before known.[9]

This is not to say that social distress disappeared. It continued to be widespread. Bouts of inflation in 1853–55 and 1870–73 quickly ate up the real increases in wage rates of preceding years. There were also severe slumps in 1857, 1862 and 1868 which took their toll on employment. The diet of the poorest continued to comprise almost entirely bread, tea and potatoes.[10] A parliamentary committee of 1864 had recommended a prison diet of bread, gruel, suet pudding and potatoes on the grounds that this was the minimum sufficient to maintain a prisoner at hard labour. It was widely adopted.[11] That those not in prison fared little or no better is apparent from the remark of a magistrate in Reading that if the authorities 'wished imprisonment to deter crime, they must cease to supply an excessive diet as to afford temptation to a poor man to commit crime in order to get into prison'.[12]

But the most important change during these mid-century decades was the internationalisation of Britain's economy. Overseas investment expanded

Social conditions for the poor, particularly the British unskilled, continued to be miserable in the mid nineteenth century. It was largely not they but those who feared they might fall to share their fate who emigrated. (This from Henry Mayhew, London Labour and the London Poor *1861)*

very strongly both absolutely and as a percentage of GNP.[13] The value of exports increased rapidly, by 23% between 1851 and 1871 — twice as fast as national product. This development is often attributed to the comprehensive adoption of a policy of free trade as the 1840s progressed (the Corn Laws were abolished in 1846 and the Navigation Acts in 1849) and to the progressive liberalisation of tariff regimes beginning with a bilateral agreement with the French in 1860. As Europe's leading manufacturing nation, Britain was bound to benefit from a policy which not only opened new markets but also reduced the costs of many raw materials, while at the same time a fall in the costs of foodstuffs on the domestic market stimulated domestic demand.[14] The expansion of steam shipping and of railway systems also played its part in the development of international commerce and trade. But to attribute the prosperity of the British economy in mid century solely, or even largely, to free trade is to allow ideological perception to override reality.

No doubt free-trade policies played their part, but the growth of trade and of the domestic economy would not have been as spectacular had it not been for the immense expansion of available capital which flowed from the gold discoveries in California and Australia after 1848. Within seven years the world gold supply increased sixfold. For the next 20 years credit was cheap and almost endlessly available, enabling an expansion of industrial production by the application of capital to technology in ways which made the unit cost of each item progressively cheaper. The age of the mass consumer had arrived.

It was not the British economy alone which was internationalised by these developments. Between 1800 and 1840 world trade had not quite doubled; between 1850 and 1870 it increased by 260%.[15] By 1875 British investors had over £1 billion invested abroad in every sort of venture. For the first time in human history there existed a truly world economy.

> Capitalism now had the entire world at its disposal, and the expansion of both international trade and international investment measures the zest with which it moved to capture it . . . The remaining institutional barriers to the free movement of the factors of production, to free enterprise, and to anything which could conceivably hamper its free operation, fell before a world wide onslaught.[16]

During the great mid-Victorian boom two developments occurred which were to have significant consequences for New Zealand. The first was a fundamental change to the nature of English agriculture; the second was the parallel internationalisation of the labour market.

THE DEVELOPMENT OF 'HIGH FARMING'

'The nineteenth century,' remarks Eric Hobsbawm in *The Age of Capital*, 'was a gigantic machine for uprooting countrymen.' Attention has been drawn earlier to the effects of the agricultural enclosures of the late eighteenth and early nineteenth century on the rural population of England. What is often not well appreciated, however, is that the combination of enclosures and early industrial development produced in Britain a system of agriculture unique in Europe. Alone among its neighbours, Britain had large estates characterised by tenant farmers, most of whom enjoyed effective security of tenure. There were no peasant proprietors; those who actually worked on the land, supplying the muscle power upon which agriculture still largely depended, were mostly landless labourers.

The relationships this entailed were primarily contractual and economic, rather than social. Farming in nineteenth-century Britain was a business activity.[17] It was also an activity in which margins of profitability depended on relatively low wages being paid by farmers to labourers and relatively high rents being paid to landowners. For most of the century the association of land ownership with social and political leadership continued to be of major significance. Without possession of an estate, it was impossible for any person, no matter how wealthy, to be accepted by the traditional ruling elites. The maintenance of this system of privilege was a key objective of agricultural policy throughout the nineteenth century.

During the Napoleonic Wars, and thanks largely to the blockade of British trade, arable farming had been a lucrative occupation, with the price of grain reaching the unheard-of height of 124s a quarter in 1812.[18] This impacted very harshly on the mass of the population.[19] As with any other staple commodity, demand for bread was highly inelastic among the poor. Throughout the period 1793 to 1838 the proportion of agricultural labourers' household expenditure on bread was never less than 46%, and in 1812 rose to nearly 75%. The dire effects of this were exacerbated by the abolition of the assize of bread, a system which had for centuries regulated the price of flour and the local level of wages to ensure that the poor could always afford sufficient bread to survive in times of dearth.

With the end of the war the price of British wheat collapsed, and in doing so threatened the whole social fabric. A parliament of landowners hastened in 1815 to enact the notorious Corn Laws which protected British arable farming and its landowners by banning the import of wheat until the domestic price reached 80s a quarter. This caused widespread protest, particularly among those who were poor and had no margin to absorb food price increases, and who were prevented from increasing their wages by a repressive political system. But the protests were in vain. The law remained in force in one form or another until 1846, when bad harvests and the Irish famine forced an uncomfortable Tory government to repeal it.

Notwithstanding dire predictions that its repeal would destroy British farming, this did not happen — despite wheat imports growing from an average of 7% of total production for the period 1829–1846 to 40% in 1868. Nor did the price of bread fall significantly during the two decades following the repeal of the Corn Laws — by only about 4%, according to one estimate.

There were several reasons for this unexpected outcome. The first was that there were no large, cheap international surpluses to flood the British market as alternatives to domestic wheat. Those belong to a later era. In some years Britain was actually a net exporter of wheat and other grains. It was a singular bone of contention in Ireland that while the peasantry starved during the potato blights of the 1840s, fully laden grain ships regularly left Dublin and Cork for European ports where wheat fetched a higher price. At the same time, population growth and the development of a lower middle class and a prosperous layer of skilled workers meant increased demand both for bread and for a much more varied range of foodstuffs over the two decades from 1850. During this period Britain continued to produce 80% of its own foodstuffs.

British farming survived the repeal of the Corn Laws by adaptation. More farms became pastoral, or combined livestock farming with the growing of grain, and the new networks of railways allowed readier access to urban markets for the wider range of products they produced. But this adaptation entailed the development of what has become known as 'high farming' — the application of much higher levels of capital in the form of fertilisers, land and building improvements, and the development of new strains of crops and livestock to improve output. Farming was, from the 1850s, a risky business which yielded about a 4% return on investment. It was possible to conduct it profitably only because interest rates and wages were both low. In fact the farming sector was seriously overcapitalised. The danger signals, such as the continuous fall in the real value of rents throughout the mid century, are clear with hindsight, but to contemporary observers farming seemed to be in a stable and prosperous state.

This prosperity did not, however, extend to those who did the heavy manual work on the farms. Between 1851 and 1871 the rural labour force diminished by 300,000 people, or about one-seventh overall. During the same approximate period agricultural production increased by about 14%.

But this staggering improvement in labour productivity was not reflected in the wages and standard of living of rural labourers. The workforce itself was casualised, depressed and underemployed.

The phenomenon we are pleased to recollect as the 'traditional' English village dates largely from this period. The industrial revolution had destroyed most of the traditional rural industrial occupations which had transferred to the towns and factories, taking the workers with them. Villages were now mainly places where agricultural labourers lived. The cottages they inhabited mostly belonged to the farmers who employed them, and went with the job. Typically they were ramshackle hovels, damp, insanitary and partly derelict.

A procession of government inspectors wrote reports on the state of the rural labouring poor for parliamentary commissions during the mid 1800s. In the labourers' cottages they found leaking roofs, rotten floors and endemic overcrowding. In one study only 5% of cottages had more than two bedrooms, although the average number of occupants was 4.87.[20] Most had only one room in which the whole family congregated and another in which they all slept. Farmers were reluctant to improve this situation; they mostly could not afford to, and if they could they were likely to see their poor rate go up as a result. Francis Heath writing in 1874 was succinct: 'The cottages as a rule are not fit to house pigs in.'[21]

Workers who objected to these conditions usually lost their job for their pains, and their house with it. If they fell ill or became unemployed, they had little recourse but the charity of the wealthy or the dreaded workhouses. Agricultural work was dangerous and back-breaking, and accidents were common and could be severe, especially when children or the elderly (who stayed in work as long as possible for fear of losing their cottage) could not cope physically with the tasks expected and demanded of them.[22] Broken backs and the loss of limbs were not unusual consequences of workers falling from ricks or carts, or becoming trapped in machinery.

Farm workers who were disinclined to put up with the bad wages and conditions found that they could not break their contracts without committing a criminal offence. In 1854 there were 2,427 summary convictions leading to prison for breach of contract in neglecting work or leaving service during the course of that year. [23] As late as the Master and Servant Act of 1867, workers could be sent to prison for three months for refusing to carry out a task allocated to them by an employer, even though the task was patently dangerous.

Most agricultural workers earned about 10s a week, and this paltry sum might be subject to deductions for rent of a small garden plot or the miserable hovel in which the labourer lived. In 1863 a Dr Edward Smith was engaged by the Privy Council to conduct a survey of the diet of 'the poor labouring classes'. Among his sample were 370 rural labourers. His findings varied from region to region, but these men were reasonably well fed, even if at barely above subsistence. The wives and children of agricultural labourers, however, often starved so that the breadwinner could be sufficiently fed to stand the hard work expected of him. Staples were bread, potatoes, oatmeal and dried peas. Meat was a luxury, and was consumed mainly in the form of bacon or discarded offal — a pluck or a head. Even those who worked with cows ate almost no dairy produce. The cost of bread might account for half the weekly wage.[24] Those who felt tempted to supplement their meagre diet by trapping a rabbit or game bird were advised not to get caught. Savage game laws reserved the animals of the field for a small social elite. The penalty for poaching was transportation as late as 1857, and thereafter imprisonment or a heavy fine, with loss of job and cottage, and a family destitute into the bargain. After 1862 new laws provided that labourers carrying bundles after dark could be searched by the police without consent. These laws were no joke. Several women in Warwickshire were almost immediately reported as having been searched

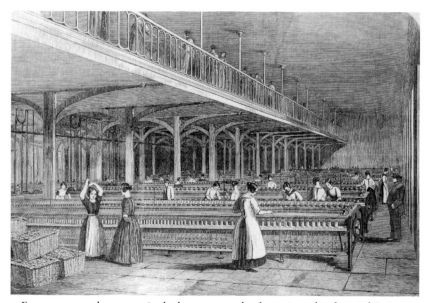

For many workers, particularly women, the factories of industrial Britain offered little by way of wages or a future. Emigration was the only way out.
(Illustrated London News)

and charged with stealing turnips.

Some, at the time, preferred to perceive in the condition of rural workers a form of bucolic idyll. This romantic notion rarely survived first-hand experience. The *Morning Chronicle*, which set out to report on the condition of the rural poor in mid century, described the outcome as 'a sentimental journey in search of the horrible'.[25] Even the regular festivals workers were said to enjoy existed largely in the imaginings of urban romantics. Some farmers might supply a dinner at the end of harvest, but in 1870 one careful observer of the state of life of Yorkshire farm labourers commented: 'The labourer's life was work and rest; of honest healthy whole-hearted play he had none . . . his only amusements were the drinking of a pint of beer at the village inn, and the enlivenments of the village feast which was celebrated once a year.'[26]

These agricultural workers in Yorkshire at least had the advantage of alternative work in the relatively accessible factories, although the better wages were little compensation for the degraded circumstances in which industrial workers often had to live and work. The response of many who suffered under these regimes was to leave altogether.

THE INTERNATIONALISATION OF LABOUR

Whereas prior to the 1850s there was much theorising about the desirability of emigration as the cure to Britain's ills, and companies had to be established with the specific purpose of effecting this remedy and convincing and subsidising workers to adopt it, from the fifties on the workers of Britain appear to have required no encouragement. With the hungry forties and the failure of Chartism as a political movement behind them; with no foreseeable improvement in their situation before them, and with the possibility for those in slightly improved circumstances of saving their passage money, they left in droves and without any encouragement from their social betters.

It has earlier been remarked that this was one of the great population movements in human history, and that no one will ever know its full extent. The statistics which were kept are spectacular enough. A total of 45,000 exited in 1835; by 1854, the number had grown to 323,000.[27] As those responsible for collecting these statistics counted only those who left on emigrant ships carrying 100 or more, and sometimes not even those, the figure of overall departures may be double the 4 million who left between 1853 and 1876.

Where did they go? In the main to British North America and the United

States, which meant a shorter and cheaper passage. It often cost more to get to Liverpool or London, the main ports of embarkation, than it did to cross the Atlantic. A steerage berth could be had for about £5 if one did not mind sharing an open space, six feet by six, with three others, sometimes of the same sex as oneself.[28] Even the cost of a relatively comfortable cabin passage nearly halved between 1850 and 1880, although at about £36 at its cheapest it was still far beyond the reach of working people.

Notwithstanding that it was relatively more expensive to emigrate to the South Pacific, between 1835 and 1860 alone a goodly number made the journey to Australia and New Zealand, probably in excess of half a million. That it happened should surprise no one. Hobsbawm comments:

> Population movements and industrialisation go together, for the modern economic development of the world both required substantial shifts of people, made it technically easier and cheaper by means of new and improved communications, and of course enabled the world to maintain a much larger population. The mass uprooting of [the] period was neither unexpected nor without modest precedents.[29]

He might well have added to these motivations the horrors of the life many emigrants left behind them. Mostly they were Irish, Scots and English, although Germany and Scandinavia contributed more than is usually appreciated, mainly to the United States. Some, like the men who engineered

Notwithstanding the development of trade unions in this period, most workers were unprotected and exploited. Tailoring as depicted here in 1863 was notoriously a sweated industry.

and built the world's railways, were highly skilled specialists not unlike those who work in the oil industry today. But most were simply ordinary industrial or agricultural workers or their offspring, depressed or outraged by conditions in their home country, and convinced that anything elsewhere had to be better.

The British government, despite being wedded to a policy of *laissez faire*, made some attempts to regulate this traffic, co-operating in some instances with colonial governments, particularly in Canada and Australia, to ensure that those who went were those who were wanted at one end and could be spared at the other. The Board of Emigration Commissioners, which could award free passages to Australia paid for from the sale of Australian land (from whence, no doubt, some came on to New Zealand), preferred, on Australian instructions, to send labourers, shepherds, miners and female domestic servants. Young couples with no children, or at best a maximum of two under seven, were the most sought after. The colonies emphatically did not want the residents of workhouses. Attempts were also made to balance the sexes. Young women travelling alone had to be 18 to qualify, although this was no doubt often breached.*

Successive British governments passed laws which attempted to establish at least minimum conditions of travel on immigrant ships. These included requirements as to victualling, the licensing of passenger agents, the carriage of sufficient water, the space available to each passenger, the carrying of surgeons and cooks, and facilities for the preparation of food. Ships carrying more than 50 passengers had to have a between-decks ventilator. According to an enactment of 1842, each passenger should be given a minimum weekly allowance of 7 lb of bread, biscuit, oatmeal, rice or potatoes. This was regarded as a supplement only, and steerage passengers might have to find their main provisioning themselves. This ration was increased in 1849 to include tea, sugar and molasses, and again in 1855 to include meat and peas. From that time on it was a requirement not only that the shippers should provide all the food needed by passengers but also that the passengers themselves were no longer required to cook it.

These attempts at regulation, particularly on the Atlantic passage, were mostly vain. The Emigration Commissioners did not consider they had much of a responsibility towards those going to the United States. Besides, with an annual budget of something like £17,000 to cover all their expenditure, and burdened by the continuous carping criticism of those

---

* One of my great-grandmothers and her sister, aged 14 and 15 respectively, came to New Zealand together and without any parents in this way, masquerading as older women.

who sat in parliament to represent shipping interests as much as their constituents, they were restricted in their effectiveness.

The burden of enforcing the legislation governing the conditions of emigrants fell largely on a maximum of 17 immigration officers, usually naval officers on half pay, distributed over the eight main emigrant embarkation ports. Liverpool, one of the busiest ports, had three of these. With an average of eight ships leaving daily, there was no way in which they could enforce the regulations, even as to the number of passengers carried. There were no musters to enable the counting to be done; vessels were sometimes in the process of casting off while passengers and their baggage were still being hurried aboard. Numerous reports of the period make it clear that victualling arrangements were often laughable, that the water on board was foul, and that sick passengers with evident signs of epidemic diseases were sometimes accepted for passage despite a compulsory medical examination. These medical examinations were often likewise a farce, with the passengers simply required to file past a doctor in a continuous stream. Unless the doctors were themselves cabin emigrants working their passage, the less said about the ships' surgeons and their qualifications to practise medicine the better, in many instances. Despite these shortcomings being common knowledge, prosecutions were rare — about seven a year on average — and convictions rarer.

From time to time a scandal might surface, as in the case of the *Blanche* out of Liverpool to New Orleans in March 1851, aboard which disease broke out, killing 25 passengers and incapacitating over 100 more. So many of the crew came down with the same illness that the captain had only four men to sail the ship; he said afterwards that providence alone had brought him safe to New Orleans.[30] It emerged from the subsequent inquiry that the ship had been overcrowded and the emigration officer had not checked passenger numbers before certifying the vessel could sail. It was not his fault. He was overworked and it was a physical impossibility for him to be present at all departures. Indeed, the inquiry revealed so many customary irregularities in the implementation of the passenger acts that the commissioners contented themselves with making a scapegoat of the unfortunate officer. With a shudder at the hopelessness of trying to enforce the regulations they had been set up to oversee, they closed the papers on the case.

Preyed upon by crimps, who cheated them by overcharging for accommodation and supplies, and runners who bullied them into the hands of their crimp employers while they waited for their ship to sail (and in the United States in particular by a similar fraternity at the other end), steerage immigrants travelled in conditions which almost beggar description. Their quarters were often wet and the air foul. The food was frequently unspeakable. A Dr William O'Doherty who, for reasons of his own, made eight or nine trips on emigrant ships, told a select committee in 1854 with masterly understatement that the food 'is not what you would give your servants'. [31] Potatoes were never distributed and the biscuit was not fit to be eaten. A mess of pulses more usually distributed was so hard that it had to be broken up with an axe prior to distribution.

Crews could also be brutal in their exploitation of passengers, with little or no prospect of redress when port was made; and burials at sea of those who had succumbed to the rigours of the voyage were sometimes perfunctory. Voluntary agencies issued advice to intending emigrants in an attempt to ameliorate conditions, but some of it was patently inadequate in the face of dysentery or worse. The Society for Promoting Useful Knowledge sagely opined that 'the smell of soap is a great enemy to all fevers'. In 1854 *The Times* published a graphic account based on first-hand knowledge of the experience of steerage passengers on emigration ships:

> The emigrant is shown a berth, a shelf of coarse pinewood in a noisome dungeon, airless and lightless, in which several hundred persons of both sexes and all ages are stowed away, on shelves two feet one inch above each other, three feet wide and six feet long, still reeking from the ineradicable stench left by the emigrants on the last voyage . . . After a few days have been spent in the pestilential atmosphere created by the festering mass of squalid humanity imprisoned between the damp and steaming decks, the scourge bursts out, and to the miseries of filth, foul air and darkness, is added the cholera. Amid hundreds of men, women and children, dressing and undressing, washing, quarrelling, fighting, cooking and drinking, one hears the groans and screams of a patient in the last agonies of this plague. [32]

Such hazards notwithstanding, hundreds of thousands of people were willing to subject themselves to such journeys.

Emigrants bound for New Zealand and Australia usually escaped the worst of these abuses, although the journey was no bed of roses for steerage passengers. There were a number of reasons for this, but the most considerable were distance, and government initiative and regulation. By conscious acts of policy, successive British governments had declined to 'interfere' in emigration matters. They might monitor and oversee certain aspects of the business, and even act to prosecute abuses from time to time, but this was usually only after scandals of such magnitude had been exposed that they had to do something or look ridiculous. Even then, they usually did the least possible and for the shortest time. They preferred to leave initiative to the market.

The Australian colonies, self-governing in many matters from an early date, declined to adopt this posture. From the outset they used the offices of the Board of Emigration established in 1840, and stationed officials in London to ensure that only the categories of immigrant they wanted, in the numbers they required, were sent to the antipodes. The New Zealand provincial governments, although they did not align themselves as closely with the board as the Australians, also established offices in London for the same purpose.

But it was distance which proved to be the greatest friend of the emigrants. The southern colonies were at a disadvantage in attracting immigration in what was becoming a competitive market for labour. It was cheaper and quicker to go to the Americas. Intending emigrants to Australia and New Zealand had to be encouraged. This meant that there was always an element of subsidy involved in the longer journey, and thus more prospect of ensuring accountability against abuses by unscrupulous shipowners and emigration agents. But it also meant that the journey was a good deal longer — three months at a minimum, instead of one. Until the end of the 1870s the voyage was invariably under sail. Ships from Britain sailed south to the Canaries or Cape Verde Islands, picked up the north-east trade winds across the Atlantic towards Brazil and, having crossed the equator, swung south-east to pick up the westerlies which would take them in a great arc towards the Antarctic and back up to Australia or New Zealand. Even after the opening of the Suez Canal in 1869 it was a long and tedious journey. These circumstances would not tolerate the bad rations and conditions of the Atlantic run without the certainty of serious disease. Consequently, the emigrants to New Zealand and Australia enjoyed relatively better conditions than almost any other group.

This is not to say that the journey could not be difficult, even horrendous, as has been noted for the period from 1840 to 1855. The layout of the ship remained in many ways as much a social as a physical space. The bulk of emigrants continued to travel by steerage, but now the accommodation was slightly more spacious, although not lavish, and those steerage passengers who paid their own fare (not an inconsiderable number as the century progressed) began to demand better conditions. Notwithstanding, the steerage area remained essentially a converted cargo space, with rows of bunks and a long table down the middle. These fittings were temporary because the space had then to be converted back for bulk cargo — usually wool — on the return. This was reflected in the roughness of the arrangements, and the cheapness of the materials used, so that they often deteriorated during the voyage. There was still a considerable lack of privacy.

But broadly speaking the steerage passengers did better than their counterparts bound for the Americas, and the cabin passengers could do very well indeed if luck was with them. This may explain why the number travelling in this way rose from 6% in 1854 to nearly 18% by the decade from 1876, despite the fare being three times more expensive more or less throughout the period.[33] Given that most agricultural labourers earned about 10s a week, and given that the fare even in steerage might be as high as £15 at some periods, the wonder is that any came at all. That so many did is a tribute to the strenuous initiatives of the New Zealand agents from 1855. What it was that stimulated these initiatives should now be explored.

CHAPTER SEVEN

THE PROVINCES AND IMMIGRATION 1855–1870

By the early 1850s New Zealand had become an economy. The country was no longer a miscellaneous collection of settlements, producing what they could for their own subsistence, importing what they could not manufacture (which was most things), and exporting small and irregular surpluses when they had them. Instead the foundations of the economic pattern which was to characterise New Zealand for the next century had been laid. This was to be a one-crop economy — grass — with some associated extractive activities, producing primarily for export to a few countries within the general ambit of British influence and control. This change was underscored by the establishment of self-government in 1854 under the Constitution Act of 1852, although for the first 20 years this was a government based on provinces rather than a single national centre, reflecting a pragmatic acceptance of the problems of communication and the continuing local focus of much activity.

The main economic characteristic of the 15 years to 1870 was growth. This might be patchy — Auckland and Taranaki, for example, were preoccupied for most of the period by land disputes with the Maori — but it was steady overall. Between 1853 and 1861, for instance, the total value of exports per annum rose from just over £300,000 to nearly £1.5 million.[1] By 1870 it had more than trebled again from its 1861 level.

In some areas the growth was spectacular. The most important of these were in respect of people and sheep. As to the former, a population of just over 26,000 in 1851 had become about 100,000 a decade later, and risen to over 250,000 by 1870.[2] Between 1861 and 1870 New Zealand records show that 194,975 people entered this country as immigrants.[3] Not all remained. In any year as many as the equivalent of a third of those arriving left for other immigrant destinations, but it was still a large influx of population.

As with most nineteenth-century colonies, the occupational mix of the workforce was a relatively simple one, with agricultural and pastoral workers, skilled trade workers and non-agricultural labourers each accounting for about a quarter of the workforce, and those engaged in the professions, trade and commerce, and domestic service the rest.[4] It was also a predominantly young population, in which about two-thirds were recorded as being the wives and children of those who were working. This too was typical of new colonies. Perhaps less to be expected, nearly seven out of 10 could read and write in 1861.

The workforce also seems, in rural occupations certainly, to have been chronically underemployed at certain times of the year, although the extent of this has been the source of controversy. Winter urban unemployment has been traditionally estimated at a low of 6%, but more recent estimates suggest that it may have been significantly higher.[5] Judging by the patterns of later periods, there was a summer peak and a winter trough. The labour market had both core and fringe occupations, the former comprising all-year-round employees, and the latter a more casual and seasonal group which might experience significant hardship in the off season. Quite minor economic downturns or a sudden influx of immigrants could extend the casual group significantly. That litmus test of social hardship, public drunkenness, was much in evidence in the developing colony, astonishingly accounting for more than half the total convictions in the courts between 1861 and 1867.

But when workers were in work they could do quite well, and were not slow to say so. In a letter to his family in Shetland about 1870, an immigrant wrote:

> I invite you all to come out here; we are getting fine wages. The country is fine and healthy. Wages are for labourers eight shillings a day, carpenters twelve shillings, blacksmiths ten to fifteen shillings, shoemakers three pounds a week, tailors three pounds a week. My girls are engaged at ten shillings a week and the other two at twelve shillings and thirteen shillings. Sailors are getting eight pounds a month. We are all getting eight shillings a day. Come away; and if your daughter is married let her husband come.[6]

Much work and such prosperity as there might be were based upon the even more spectacular growth in the number of sheep. Wakefield and his fellow promoters had had a vision of New Zealand as a land of small arable farmers, but this dream was stillborn. From the mid 1850s, more and more land was given over to pastoral farming and its associated activities. Some 220,000 acres under cultivation in 1861 had become nearly a million in 1870, and more than doubled again in just five more years.[7] Mostly this was land in sown grass. Nearly three and a half million acres of land was sold for cash between 1861 and 1866 alone, and a good deal more was taken into effective ownership by wealthy pastoralists. Much of this had passed out of Maori hands in highly questionable ways.[8] This was then sold to Pakeha landowners at effective knockdown prices. When the provinces took control of land sales and revenues in 1858, they accelerated this process by generous loans and lease-to-buy arrangements. To all intents Wakefield's 'sufficient price' was dead, although the main beneficiaries were those with capital. Working people still found the price of land beyond a small section well out of their reach.

Most of the land purchased was for large sheep runs. Some 233,000 sheep in 1851 had become 10 million by 1870. They were kept principally for their wool, which far outstripped any other export commodity in value, being surpassed only by gold for a few years in the 1860s. The next item after wool, timber, accounted for less than 4% of the value of the wool clip. Most of these exports found their way to Australia or Britain, and the latter took most of the wool. These two countries also accounted for the bulk of imports. These included not only expected items such as agricultural machinery, galvanised iron, coal, tea and sugar, but some which might well have been manufactured locally such as boots and shoes, a wide range of items of apparel, sacks and bags, and furniture. Obviously the tradition of sending away raw materials and buying back the added value later has a long history in New Zealand.

There was also a persistent deficit in the trading account and a growing burden of public debt throughout the sixties. By 1870 every European New Zealander owed an averaged £30 to a public creditor, another tradition which began early. Periodic attempts to get a grip on these problems were unavailing; the temptation to borrow for public works and the relief of unemployment was probably too great to resist. After 1870 it became central to much policy.

A visitor to New Zealand in this period would have seen few unemployed or distressed workers. Sheep might have been harder to avoid, but what struck local observers most was the settled and prosperous nature of the place. In 1856 one writer cited a letter from a Christchurch settler to his family in Britain in which he remarked upon his new environment as possessing 'all the refinement and civilisation already of a country town in England. Our dress, habits, manners and every thing are the same . . . Believe me, there is nothing wild or savage (hardly colonial) in our mode of life.'[9] When those who came to New Zealand as immigrants were asked to account for the success of the settlements, they usually stressed the personal qualities of the incomers, rather than any fortuitous or institutional factors. Thus, Charles Hursthouse, writing in 1861, attributed the development of a prosperous new community to 'a social variety, a vigour, boldness, and originality of character [of] these little antipodal communities, which we should find little trace of in the small town populations of the mother-country'.[10]

Visitors from elsewhere tended to notice rather different things. Anthony Trollope, in an observation befitting the author of the *Barchester Chronicles*, marvelled in 1872 at the lack of deference, especially to bishops, and went on to report, in an unconscious echo of Martha Adams: 'Even servant girls will refuse money offered to them. One poor girl whom I had injured, knocking down into the mud the line on which all her clothes were drying, although she was in tears at the nuisance of having to wash them again, refused the money that I offered her, saying that although she was only a poor Irish girl without a friend in the world, she was not so mean as that'.[11] Samuel Butler, who lived in Canterbury for four years from 1860 and invested his money in sheep farming so skilfully that he was able to retire to the life of a London gentleman, was a more searching observer. Christchurch he found estimable enough as a place, although he thought the inhabitants talked rather too much about sheep. But what fascinated him was the nature of the character most suited to thrive in the new colonial environment. Especially he advised young men of breeding with nothing but health and strength for their capital not to come to New Zealand unless they were prepared to work up country and to put their money by for later investment. He particularly noticed, and liked, the lack of deference of skilled workers who 'will be respectful and civil [but] there will be a slight but quite unobjectionable difference in their manner towards you'.[12] This he attributed to the readiness with which a skilled and steady rural worker might find alternative employment.

Encouraging such young men, who had the skills required and who could be relied upon not to drink away their wages, as well as the women who might become their wives, was a problem to which the provincial governments almost continuously turned their attention in the 1850s and sixties. The means of encouragement they found were often novel and creative. Mostly they revolved around passage money and land.

ENCOURAGING THE RIGHT IMMIGRANTS

The newly enfranchised leaders of the provinces were well aware that they could not sit back and wait for immigrants of the right calibre to arrive on their doorstep of their own accord. It was a long way to New Zealand, and many other colonies were competing for the same population. Worse, without their intervention, New Zealand might very well end up with the sorts of immigrants it most emphatically did not want.

Throughout the century the debate over what purpose was served by emigration continued in Britain. The many disciples of Malthus, Robert Horton and Edward Wakefield all contributed, and the views of Thomas Carlyle, who thought emigration a panacea not only for solving the population problem but also for ordering the universe through labour have been noted.[13] That their theories were taken seriously is demonstrated by the actions of the unions representing, in particular, engineers, iron moulders and compositors, which maintained funds with which to assist their members to emigrate whenever an economic downturn caused a labour surplus which threatened their wages and working conditions.[14]

But these theorists were also coming to appreciate that Britain's problems could not be resolved without co-operation and active assistance at the other end. This was the age of the Durham Report, which heralded a new beginning in relations between Britain and its colonies. In future the latter were to have more say in their governance; it was to this that New Zealand owed its constitution of 1852. But they would also have to accept greater responsibility for both conducting and, particularly, paying for their new freedom of manoeuvre. These new relationships, and especially the part about financial responsibility, took a little while to settle down. In New Zealand there continued to be some confusion in the minds of settler governments whether the role of British troops was to protect them from marauding savages or to dispossess the indigenous inhabitants of their land. The British government rather thought the latter, and first charged the local government £40 a year per soldier for their use and then withdrew them completely. But despite teething problems of this sort, the colonies accepted their new responsibilities readily enough.[15] Immigration was clearly one of them.

The provincial and central governments in New Zealand had to deal with two varieties of problem with regard to immigration. The first of these was the sheer difficulty of conducting relationships at such a distance and with such extended lines of communication. This went well beyond problems of governance.

It was not, of course, a problem unique to New Zealand. In 1833 the London government had created the Office of the Agents General for the Crown Colonies to handle the commercial and business requirements of the colonies in the imperial capital. From 1840 the activities of this office extended to New Zealand. But this relationship had still had to be conducted largely through the Governor, and the colonists' experiences at the hands of the autocratic George Grey had made them anxious to exert their own influence over these sorts of relationships. From 1854 this became more significant as the colony and its provinces took over responsibilities previously within the realm of the crown colony administration. From 1858, when the use of land revenues for a variety of purposes, including immigration, also became a provincial responsibility, the need became pressing.[16] From 1855 the provinces therefore began to send their own agents to London or to appoint companies there to act for them. Their primary function was quite explicit. Otago's ordinance, for example, specified that the purpose was to be 'for promoting immigration to this province, [and] for protecting and advancing in Great Britain the political and other interests of the said province'.[17] Others made similar provisions. Immigration may not have been the sum total of the interests involved, but it far outstripped others.

The second difficulty the agents had to confront was essentially one of information in a competitive emigration marketplace. From the outset the New Zealand Company had used its considerable propaganda skills, in particular arranging for the publication of the accounts of its own officials on the spot, to paint a favourable picture of New Zealand. But there were plenty of others engaged in the same business, and not necessarily with an axe to grind, and sometimes their accounts of New Zealand were more accurate and truthful than those which emanated from company sources. Typical of these was one published as early as 1842 which described New Zealand as 'an uncultivated waste either of mountains covered with dense forest, of plains and lowlands covered with high fern shrubs, or of swamps and marshes covered with rush and flax, without any open spots of grassland for pasturage'.[18] By the mid fifties this was no longer entirely the case, but even an enthusiast like William Swainson was advising would-be immigrants that only the industrious should bother to come, and was warning off those 'who have already failed at home — for decayed tradesmen, for clerks and shopmen, for young men who have neither capital nor skill and who are too proud or too weak to earn their bread by the sweat of their brow — New Zealand cannot be recommended as a field for emigration.' But he went on to say that industrious artisans, domestic servants and small farmers with a family would find that 'the country affords a congenial field on which an early independence may with certainty be earned'.[19]

With the company agents no longer active, it was useful to have agents in London able to speak up for New Zealand and to combat negative perceptions. Judging from their extant efforts, the New Zealand Company publicists had no monopoly on hyperbole. The *New Zealand Emigrants' Bradshaw* for 1858, for example, urged 'the toiling tenant farmer, the competition stricken tradesman, the drudging clerk, the embarrassed merchant, the struggling professional man in populous city pent' to hurry to New Zealand 'where they might enjoy rude health and plenty'.[20]

Between 1855 and 1870 the provinces pursued a range of initiatives to ensure that New Zealand got the preferred sorts of immigrants. Mostly these entailed the kinds of activities that Robert Horton had been recommending two decades previously, with the difference that this time they were successful, because a way of financing them from the colonial end had been found in the effective sequestering of Maori land and then selling it or turning it into income as rapidly as possible. Canterbury, for example, quite specifically broke with the doctrine of the 'sufficient price', leasing grazing runs for as little as two pence or even a penny an acre once a basic lease for a minimum acreage at a rather higher price had been granted. Otago sold smallholdings up to 10 acres for a flat price of 10s. In Auckland, blocks of up to 300 acres could be bought for as little as 15s an acre. All of this was calculated to make New Zealand a very attractive destination for the would-be emigrant.

But it was not enough to offer land. There had to be those ready to buy it, and those willing and able to work it. Canterbury offered assisted passages to labourers and domestic servants under the age of 50 years on the basis of a 50% subsidy, provided they were prepared to repay the passage money at the rate of £5 a year following their arrival. By 1861 initiatives of this sort had lifted the Canterbury population from 6,000 five years previously to 16,000. The original desire to create a slice of English society in the antipodes seems to have been abandoned in the rush to attract labour to the growing pastoral economy. Subsequent research has revealed that by the seventies it was impossible to distinguish the social mix of Canterbury immigrants from that of any other province.[21]

Otago was, if anything, even more vigorous in its endeavours. In 1856 the southern province voted the very large sum of £20,000 for immigration purposes; despatched an agent, James Adam, to London; and engaged the firm of J. Macandrew to bring out 2,000 suitable immigrants at £16 a head on vessels at six-weekly intervals. Assistance was offered on the rough calculation that each arriving immigrant ensured a subsequent average addition of £2 a year to the excise revenues. By 1861, when Otago raised a loan of £58,000 to assist further immigration, previous initiatives had already raised the population to 28,983. In combination with the gold rushes, it ensured that by 1870 the overall population of the province stood at 67,842.

The Otago landholders preferred to engage their workers directly from Britain rather than to take on former miners, who tended to be rather too independent for their taste. 'Farmers and runholders entertain a prejudice against engaging immigrants from other colonies as shepherds and farm servants, the preference being always given to those from the Mother-Country,' was how the local immigration agent Colin Allan delicately expressed it.[22] In 1869 Otago obtained central government approval to establish three new settlements at Martins Bay and Preservation Inlet, comprising in total 100,000 acres, with the first 10,000 offered free to those willing to take them up; but by now the limit had been reached, there were few takers, and the scheme petered out. Despite this, by 1876 Otago, now separated from Southland, was the largest of the provinces, with a population of well over 100,000.

By comparison the North Island languished. This was partly because of the preoccupation with wresting land from its Maori owners, an activity which ended in war — and the ramifications of which remain an abiding problem.[23] Taranaki and Wellington did encourage would-be settlers by offering assisted passages, but this was on a much less comprehensive basis than in the southern provinces. In Wellington any householder could nominate a person for assistance, provided they were prepared to put up a surety; if accepted, this entitled the prospective immigrant to a passage to the value of £20 for an adult or £10 for a child. This money had to be repaid by the immigrant; in the event of default it was the original guarantor who became responsible. Full payment did also entitle the immigrant to a small land grant, but the endeavour was distinctly small scale compared to the southern initiatives.

This less enthusiastic attitude may explain why the populations of the two provinces grew extremely slowly, in the case of Taranaki from 2,044 in 1861 to only 4,749 in 1870. Wellington, where the provincial council was dominated by large landowners and their wealthy town supporters, who were not as enthusiastic about encouraging small proprietors as elsewhere, did not do much better, with an increase of population of less than 10,000 from a base of 15,177 in the same decade.[24] The single variant was Hawke's Bay, established as a separate province in 1859. The same policy as Wellington was followed until 1863 when the election of Donald McLean as superintendent saw a change of policy towards wholesale assisted immigration and public works which prefigured the later national policies of Vogel.[25]

Auckland took a rather different tack. There, there was a distinct feeling that what was needed was not prospective settlers, who would almost certainly be drawn away to other areas by the availability to the south of land unbeset by problems with Maori owners. What was needed was immigrants who would stay in the Auckland area and enhance its business base. Fewer immigrants were thus required, and although various inducements were offered, particularly by way of land orders in return for passages taken, the population of Auckland grew from 18,177 in 1858 to only 24,420 in 1861, a much smaller percentage increase than in the south.[26] By 1864, however, the population had almost doubled to 42,484. This was largely because of central government initiatives in relation to war with the Maori.

While the provinces had been pursuing their immigration ventures with various degrees of enthusiasm, the central government had also been active. In 1858 the government had received a suggestion from a John Morrison that New Zealand should appoint its own London agent. This was not a disinterested proposition; when the government accepted the proposal the next year, Morrison was offered the job. He was the first of a series of such agents.

It was only in 1863, however, that immigration, as opposed to more mundane business matters, featured largely in the concerns of the central government. The refocusing of immigration concerns on the provinces in 1858 had left one significant responsibility in its hands. This was the creation of military settlements in Auckland, Taranaki and Wellington. From the late fifties it had been obvious that sooner or later there would be conflict with the Maori if the settler government persisted in its policy of obtaining Maori land despite the Maori's increasing unwillingness to sell. This particularly applied in the Taranaki and Waikato. Even if the contemporary uneasy peace persisted, there would be a frontier region which would require settlers able to farm with one hand on a plough and the other on a gun, trained to assemble rapidly in military detachments if there was trouble, and to overawe the Maori population generally.

By 1863 war had indeed broken out in both areas, and the government moved swiftly to ensure that by the time it was over its military settlements would be in place. The government, nominally headed by Alfred Domett, but in practice controlled by the Auckland bankers and land speculators Frederick Whitaker and Thomas Russell, borrowed £3 million in December 1863 for the purposes of 'suppressing rebellion'. Of this, one-tenth was to be spent bringing in and locating immigrants on military settlements, half of it in the Auckland area. Land seized from Maori without compensation under the New Zealand Settlements Act of 1863 would be available for this purpose, with the balance sold to repay the loans raised. That the expectations of the government were high is clear from the setting aside of £900,000 for land surveying purposes. It is also an indication of how much land the government anticipated seizing.

The intention was to bring in as many as 20,000 immigrants, not only from Britain but also from the Cape Colony, Australia, the southern provinces, and even from Germany. Labouring and artisan immigrants were to have free passage and a generous land grant which converted to freehold after three years' occupation by the settler. If they brought a wife and family, additional land was to be added to the basic grant. Small farmers and those with money to invest were encouraged on similar terms. During 1864 emigration agents put together parties of some 3,000 emigrants from both Britain and the Cape Colony, and these were dispatched. Then the scheme fell apart.

Evidently not everyone was as enthusiastic as the Auckland land speculators who had been responsible for concocting the scheme. The other provinces perceived it simply as a device for assisting Auckland, and in particular a clique of its leading citizens, to riches, while saddling the rest of the colony with a massive debt. Their opposition was significant, and was shared by the British military authorities in New Zealand who were sceptical of the claims often voiced by settler politicians such as William Fox, Domett and others that they were bringing civilisation to the Maori and saving them from the 'beastly communism' of their land-owning system.[27] This unease was conveyed to the War Office, the British government and the families of many officers in their letters home, some of which found their way into British newspapers. The disquiet spilled over into the London money market, and the loan float was a flop, even in a marketplace usually awash with available funds.[28]

When it became clear that the central government could not fulfil its promises, the Auckland provincial government, which had been sufficiently enthusiastic to offer its own small contribution, found that even its initial excitement had cooled. It became even cooler when it was suggested that the province might like to take over a significant portion of the funding of the scheme. Setting up a scheme to make money on the basis of a loan which others would have to meet the major share in repaying was one thing as far as the merchants and land sharks of Auckland were concerned; paying for it themselves was another entirely. When it became clear that the Maori did not intend tamely to give up their land at the first whiff of powder smoke but to fight tenaciously for it, and when arriving immigrants found that there was no land ready or even surveyed for them, and that they must cool their heels in Auckland until it was, the scheme went entirely to pieces, to the accompaniment of raucous and public acrimony over who was to blame. Nevertheless the population of Auckland had risen to 54,448 by 1870, an increase of about two-thirds over 1861.

What was really attracting immigrants to New Zealand during the 1860s was probably its developing reputation as a place where any intending immigrant might expect to better their condition: it was an emigrant destination as good as any other, and better than some because of the assisted passages and land grants on offer. And there was the prospect of making a lucky strike as well.

SERPENTS IN PARADISE: MINERS AND WOMEN

What had been, until the discovery of gold in Nelson, a grass-based economy was given a further fillip in June 1861 when Gabriel Read discovered gold in Otago. Canterbury and Westland joined the resulting rush in 1864, when large new discoveries were made, particularly in the latter.[29] This had the effect of changing the pattern of immigration into New Zealand for the next decade. Many miners who had already followed the gold to California and Victoria came on to New Zealand, a phenomenon so marked that Sir Julius Vogel was subsequently to describe the west coast of the South Island as 'an appanage of Melbourne'.[30]

The most significant immediate effect was a change in the balance of population between North and South Islands. In 1858, 43% were living in the latter; by 1864 it was 62%. Between 1861 and 1863 more than 64,000 mining immigrants entered Otago; and Dunedin, hitherto a small and exclusive Presbyterian settlement, found its relative tranquillity and isolation rudely interrupted by this distinctly unsaintly influx. Although this population ebbed and flowed, the net gain is unlikely to have been less than 40,000. Between 1865 and 1867 there were 17,000 arrivals in Westland, a net invasion calculated to be about 10,000.

The importance of this sudden population gain lies in the dimension it added to New Zealand's social mix. These men — they were mostly men — were not at all the sort of immigrant who had previously come to New Zealand, nor were they necessarily the sort the provincial authorities wished to attract. Whereas most immigrants had so far been working people displaced by change in Britain, or middle-class people with a little capital to invest and uneasy in their status at 'home', the miners were an important element in the new workforce created by the relative prosperity of the international economy of the mid-century and who followed work wherever it took them. A random sample of 50 miners taken by one historian shows them to have been a remarkably heterogeneous group, with all sorts of countries of origin, trades and even professions represented.[31] One thing was constant, however, if their detractors are to be believed. Their deference rating was as low as their noisy radicalism tended to be to the fore. Dunedin's 'old identity', the original settlers, were scandalised by them.

The miners also outraged the good burghers of Christchurch, whose province extended to the western coast of the South Island. By 1867 it was the most populous in the country, but Canterbury's ruling clique was little inclined to do anything to extend westwards facilities such as roads, ports and bridges, beyond the construction of the Arthur's Pass route to the goldfields to take this rowdy and unwelcome addition as far away from Christchurch as possible. In 1868, following protests about this failure, Westland was, by an illegal act subsequently validated by the imperial parliament, created New Zealand's first independent county. From now on the miners could take responsibility for building their own roads and bridges. The end of the gold consequently required no particular initiatives from Canterbury. The surplus miners mostly either returned to Australia or were absorbed by the continuing demand for rural labour on the eastern side of the Alps. Those who were not stayed on to work in the developing coal and timber industries, giving the region a distinctive cultural and political atmosphere it has since retained.

Nelson alone of the provinces seems to have found the gold discoveries of the sixties an unalloyed bonus. As a province it had languished until 1864, when the gold discoveries both there and in northern Westland began to attract the usual influx. By 1870 the population had increased to over 23,000. Unlike Canterbury and Otago, Nelson welcomed this increase whatever its social composition, and proposed to reinvest all of its goldfields revenues in roads and other infrastructures calculated to open up the area. It had, however, barely begun to do so when colonial political events took a more dramatic turn. These we shall shortly explore.

For the moment one final matter remains to be canvassed, and that is the problem which bedevilled all of those interested in ensuring the success of the nineteenth-century emigrations — the imbalance of women in the receiving colonies and territories.[32] New Zealand was no more a stranger to this problem than any other, and had tried to deal with it in the same way by encouraging family immigration. But it was particularly exacerbated in the 1860s by a significant intake of miners. It was part of the received wisdom of the age that if men were to be induced to settle and to make useful colonists of themselves by investing their labour in breaking in country, then they would do it best if they were anchored to the soil by the responsibilities of family.[33] This perspective sometimes even took the

NEEDLE MONEY.

Women were particularly vulnerable in the unregulated labour markets of mid-century Britain. Earning opportunities were often restricted to low-paid piecework. Emigration and the chance of a good marriage beckoned. (ATL)

extreme form of a demonisation of single men, particularly labourers in groups. Charlotte Godley, one of Canterbury's founding settlers, wrote to a friend from darkest Riccarton in 1852 to express such fears: 'I am a little afraid of being alone. There are a number of somewhat disreputable people among our neighbours in the bush, some thirty or forty men, I should think, living [in] it for the present, to cut timber, and whose songs and jollifications at their evening tea parties, we can hear till late at night.'[34]

Her anxieties were at least soundly based in the statistics. In 1851, when New Zealand conducted its first census, there were 776 non-Maori women to every 1,000 non-Maori men. By 1861 this had declined to 622, and although by the end of the decade it had climbed again to 705, this was still significantly below the figure for 20 years previously.[35] There is ample evidence that the authorities were as alarmed about this as Charlotte Godley, and steps were taken from the outset to do something about it.

At the British end, the encouragement of single young women emigrants by the New Zealand Company (provided they were suitably chaperoned) has already been noted. Two voluntary societies, the National Benevolent Emigration Fund for Widows and Orphan Daughters of Gentlemen, Professional Men, Officers, Bankers and Merchants, devoted to the genteel, and the Fund for Promoting Female Emigration, for the poor, illustrate not only the contemporary tendency to leave social amelioration to private initiative but the Victorian propensity for the rigorous division of every endeavour into cabin and steerage categories. These two societies sent some emigrants to New Zealand in the 1850s. Their efforts were seconded by the British Ladies' Female Emigrant Society which mainly devoted itself to improving shipboard conditions and to ensuring that proper provision was made for young women on arrival.

This effort, and the continuing activities of the provincial immigration agents to achieve the same into the sixties, was not entirely based on a disinterested wish to advance civilisation and assist distressed young women. It also integrated nicely with the demand for domestic servants which was deeply felt by the cabin passengers after their arrival in New Zealand. Otago in 1862 mounted a special effort and brought 1,350 young women to Dunedin in 14 vessels the following year.[36] Initiatives by other provinces brought similar but smaller groups to New Zealand throughout the decade. Two impediments stood in the way of these efforts and their prospects of greater success. The first, as shall be seen, was the conditions aboard the immigrant ships, although these were somewhat improved after Maria Rye, a philanthropist closely associated with the work of the London societies, came out to New Zealand on an immigrant ship in 1863. She was so shocked by what she was able to see both of the conditions on board and the state of the barracks on arrival that she agitated vigorously for improvements. The result was the more rigorous enforcement of the 1855 emigration regulations, although this tended to be on a less than comprehensive basis and there were continuing complaints throughout this period and into the 1870s and eighties.

The second impediment was the unrealistic expectations of the colonists as to who might be attracted to come to New Zealand. The Canterbury agent, John Marsham, was particularly criticised on one occasion for sending what was described as 'a collection of the prostitutes and thieves of London' and women unsuitable for rural life. He defended himself vigorously by drawing attention to the probable real source of the problem:

> If nothing short of first rate cooks will satisfy the ladies of Canterbury, they are not likely to get them at thirty pounds a year; such people can do better than that at home. The Canterbury people are getting particular. They must have an article exactly according to pattern, at a low price, and 'no Irish', or they won't take it at all . . . While men earn three times as much as they do here, it is sinful to pay a dairymaid only thirteen to fifteen pounds a year . . . It is totally impossible to send out young women who shall exactly please everybody, and only exactly as many of them as are asked for.[37]

During the 15 years from 1870 this remained an issue, but it became of secondary importance to the effect of important changes to Britain's economy and the eventual collapse of the international economy which seriously affected New Zealand's immigration patterns in the eighties.

Before turning to this, however, it is appropriate to try to summarise the experience of New Zealand in attracting immigrants in the 15 years from 1855 and what lessons the authorities had drawn from this:

> [T]he rapid increase of population and capital created by the goldfields did arouse the interest of the central body. Here was the capital to provide the revenue for that policy of expansion by which it was hoped to compel the Maori to desist in his struggle against encroachment of the white; and here, too, were the labourers being thrown on the market as their gold claims were worked out who could provide the hands to inaugurate the policy.[38]

But there was equally a realisation that this was too big a matter to be left to the provincial governments. This was a problem which concerned the relationship between the New Zealand economy overall and the international trade through which it earned its living, then and for the next century. More particularly, it was a problem of New Zealand's relationship with Britain through which it largely traded and from whence its immigrants mostly came. In 1868 parliament recommended that a prize of £100 should be offered for the best essay on turning the miners into settlers.[39] The prize was never offered, but if it had it would have been interesting both to read the winning entry and to know the identity of its author. Instead, by default, the prize goes to Julius Vogel, who in the next decade invented a way of resolving the immigrant conundrum —although not everyone thought so at the time.

Before entering this debate, however, we shall once more canvass what the experience of being an immigrant meant in the decade and a half from 1855.

CHAPTER EIGHT

ALTERED DAYS 1855–1870

But now it's altered days, I trow
I weel I wat, I weel I wat,
The beef is tumbling in the pat
And I'm both fat and fu' sirs
    John Barr, *New Zealand Comforts*[1]

John Barr of Craigielee, who emigrated to Otago in 1852, and who kept up the Scottish tradition of popular versifying and recitation in his new land, wrote in one of his verse sketches that it was a happy day for him when he first came to New Zealand 'poor and dirty'. Among other advantages such as eating adequately for a change, he would no longer have to tip his hat and bow to the laird. These seemed to him to be more than adequate justification of his decision to emigrate.

Alexander Bathgate, who emigrated with his family to Otago in 1863 at the age of 18, and who subsequently enjoyed a legal and business career of some prominence, similarly recorded his early colonial experiences, in prose, in 1874. In his book he asked the rhetorical question as to what induced people to emigrate. 'The answer which is most frequently given to this question is, "Because I hoped I should better myself".'[2] And although he did go on to remark that within that rubric there were as many personal circumstances and stories as there were immigrants, this desire to better oneself is attested by almost all contemporary accounts as the reason for emigration to this part of the world in the nineteenth century. During the middle decades it was complicated by the arrival of significant numbers of miners following the gold, but it nevertheless remains the single most compelling reason.

Thomas Coggan, who left England for New South Wales at the age of 25 in 1857, summed up the reasons for a generation of emigrants when he subsequently recalled that

> like many others I had worked constantly from the age of eleven for wages ranging from two shillings to twenty shillings per week, which seemed to be as much as I had a chance of getting by remaining at home; and, although my parents did rear a family on such wages, I did not mean to try to, so I thought I would devote ten years to money-making in Australia and go home a bloated capitalist.[3]

He never did go back to England; Australia became his home. His words were echoed by many others. 'If I could have obtained the commonst nessasarys (sic) of life at home I would never have emigrated,' Abijou Good confided to his journal on 4 March 1863.[4] That it was possible and desirable to emigrate to gain material advantage in life was a commonplace of the time, and was implicit in the many books of advice published for intending settlers in this part of the world:

> The man who will go out to the southern colonies, having no capital but his labour, with stout arms and a stout heart, with no old-world prejudices hanging about him, determined to work with a will and adapt himself to the new country and its ways — such a man will be sure to find what he seeks and cannot get here — certain and constant employment at more than ample wages.[5]

Not just men. In her pioneering and comprehensive study of nineteenth-century women immigrants,[6] Charlotte Macdonald canvasses the reasons, as far as these are available, which brought single women in particular to New Zealand at this period. The occupations of the majority prior to emigration are not known, but where they are the vast preponderance were either in domestic service or were farm workers, with a sprinkling of teachers, nurses and laundry workers. Some who were workhouse inmates were given little choice as to whether they wished to emigrate, although there are few cases of outright opposition recorded among those directed to go, and clearly others who embraced the prospect of a new start enthusiastically. Some went to New Zealand to join those with whom they had an arrangement to marry, or, conversely, to escape an unsatisfactory relationship. Most women travelled with their families, but those who did not, and who had nothing much to look forward to in England but a poorly paid life of service, went to improve their position in life. Many must have been aware that in the new colony the likelihood of improving their situation through marriage was much greater than it was in their country of birth.

Nevertheless, the emigrants generally continued to regard the prospect of a lengthy voyage and an unknown country with, at best, mixed feelings and at worst something approaching dread. They had good reason to do so. Passengers, many of whom were from rural areas or smaller towns and cities, found the uproar they encountered on the wharf prior to embarkation bewildering, even frightening. Alfred Withers, travelling in 1857 on the *James Baines*, remarked in his journal upon the immense piles of luggage, and thought that the metalware being loaded by way of pannikins, baths and water cans would be enough to open a tin ware shop: 'The squeezing, crowding, pushing and confusion is fearful.' Emma Hodder, sailing on the *Hydaspes* for Lyttelton in June 1869, felt 'thoroughly wretched': 'Goodbye how easily said, but oh what hearts are wrung . . . the future seems very dark.' She was not reassured by the sight of her berth where 'I am packed in like so many cattle . . . steerage passage is anything but comfortable . . . it seems like so many convicts.'[7] Elizabeth Ankatell, on board the *Queen of Australia* in 1865, 'felt very dreary and lonely and unhappy, could do nothing but cry and wish I had not ventured, everything seemed so confused, comfortless, and wretched.'[8] Fanny Davis, writing in her diary for 5 June 1858, felt much the same as the *Conway* left Liverpool but resisted the temptation: 'Nearly all the single women sit down and have a good cry the first thing, and I feel very much inclined to join them; but first ask myself what there is to cry about and as I cannot answer it to my own satisfaction, think it would be very foolish, so begin to put things in order in our berths.'[9]

The apprehensions of Marianne Manchester, who sailed for Auckland in April 1870 in the *Excelsior* at the age of 16, cannot have been improved when they were '[o]bliged to have a steam tug down the river when the Emigration Commissioners came on board and found all the sailors drunk'.[10] Although she did not know it, she was one of the luckier ones. The emigration authorities seem at least to have taken their task seriously. Archibald Moire aboard the *John Duncan* in 1862 confided sarcastically to his diary that the doctor and government inspector 'are either very clever men here, or else very careless for the Doctor only needed to look at the person as he was passing in order to ascertain whither (sic) they were all in good health or whither there was any infectious disease about them and the inspector or Emigration Officer as he was called to us, only needed a glance at our outward appearance in order to conclude that we had all a sufficient supply of clothing . . .'[11]

Often, as soon as the vessel was properly under way, those passengers keeping diaries or journals confided their thoughts and apprehensions to paper. These could sometimes be bitter. Abijou Good 'stood alone that night on the deck after most of the passengers had gone below i could not help reflecting it was a cruel destiny which had thus compeled us to leave our nativeland our freinds & homes to face we knew not what in a foreign land . . . if a man may be excursed for being down hearted & sad it is at a time like this.'[12] Now and again one encounters a rather more robust attitude. Joshua Hughes, writing in 1863, made no bones about his view of leaving: 'Many of the passengers regret they ever left Old England; I don't know why, there was not much to stop for.'[13] But feelings of loss and desolation could continue well into the voyage. Emma Hodder, after a month at sea, was still writing : 'I am very low spirited. I have taken my likenesses out and looked at all my family, and read their letters again which ended in me having a good cry. Oh, that I could feel more cheerful and have more trust in God, but it is indeed hard to bear.'[14]

A HAZARDOUS UNDERTAKING:
THE MID-CENTURY JOURNEY

There was indeed a great deal to bear with, and to adapt to. Some were still surprised to discover that they had to clean out their quarters by roster, arrange their own messing and oversee the cooking of their food, and even stand watch in some cases. 'We have to get up early,' wrote Anne Gratton in 1858, 'each one folding up their bedclothes & roll up the mattrass, sweep out her own Berth. Then we take it in turns for cleaning out the Cabin, Wednesdays & Saturdays it is scoured & the rest of the week swept & rubbed with a stone & with sand, all done before breakfast at eight o'clock.'[15] Long days at sea with little to do but sit or stroll on the maindeck left many of the emigrants listless or quarrelsome. Their quarters, very cramped, also quickly became noisome.

In general during the mid-century period the steerage was divided into three compartments: for married couples and children, for single men, and for single women and girls. The term 'single women' was an elastic one. According to the official New Zealand government regulations for emigrant ships, it was to be understood as including 'all those whether single or married who are berthed in the single women's compartment'.[16] Usually there were two tiers of bunks, with a curtain or sometimes a partition to allow families in particular some privacy. Emigrants brought their own mattresses. The bunk spaces were not large — six feet by 20 inches at most for single men. Married couples shared a berth at six feet by three feet. Smaller spaces were provided for children, but there was no provision for those under one year. Presumably they were expected to share with their parents.

There was a long table with forms down the middle. A series of hooks for storing clothing, food, eating utensils, water bottles and other items in bags completed the arrangements. Many passengers were surprised to be given these bags, which were quite small, on arrival on the vessel, and told to put in them everything they would need for the next month because their boxes containing all their other supplies would be stored in the hold and brought up at intervals for them to change clothing and so on. When the boxes were raised during the voyage the damp had often seeped in, and clothing and other items become spoiled, much to the dismay of their owners. Anything else the steerage passengers wished to keep by them, such as writing and reading materials or small personal items, they had to keep in their sleeping space. Theft, in these circumstances, could be a serious problem.

Even the best-appointed ships could not last a voyage of three months without these arrangements deteriorating and becoming oppressive. It was impossible to maintain even the most basic privacy. We catch a rare glimpse of a ship on the eve of its departure in 1864 in a report in the *Cork Herald* of the *Ganges* bound for Auckland with 393 emigrants aboard, 125 of whom were children.[17] The ship was only eight years old and had been previously used in the emigrant trade, so its owners must have been at least aware of what was involved.

> The 'tween decks space is airy, lofty, (nine and a half feet) and comparatively well lighted. The berths, too, are roomy and judiciously arranged. Two transverse bulkheads divide the passenger space into three compartments — that nearest the stem of the vessel being appropriated to single males, the intermediate to the married passengers, and the after compartment to single females. The utmost cleanliness and regularity pervades the ship in every part, sanitary precautious (sic) and provision against accident being well attended to. A portion of the deckhouse or saloon has been partitioned off as a hospital, and on account of its position on the upper deck, distinct from the passenger space, is far preferable to the similar institution we usually see between decks. The ship is supplied with a patent distilling apparatus capable of converting 500 gallons of salt water per day into a pure and wholesome liquid for consumption by the passengers; and in addition to this a large stock of fresh water has been laid in for the voyage.

Notwithstanding that this was probably as good as the conditions on any vessel attained and significantly better than most, disease broke out on the *Ganges* and there was 'great mortality . . . from bronchitis and whooping cough', according to a subsequent inquiry report. More than 20 passengers died, most of them children.

Children and infants seem to have been particularly vulnerable to epidemic diseases and fevers. In 1863, 46 people died on the *Brothers Pride* bound for Lyttelton; of these 31 were babies and children. Charlotte Macdonald has compiled a sample list of passengers known to have died on voyages between 1855 and 1870. Where the cause of death is known, the majority seem to have succumbed to infectious diseases.[18] Contemporary medical knowledge provided little succour once illness broke out, and immigrants were mostly obliged to rely on their innate resistance. Descriptions of burials at sea are a constant and poignant feature of shipboard journals.

It may well be imagined what privations were suffered by steerage passengers on vessels less salubrious then the *Ganges*. Rats and cockroaches abounded. Privies were often simply erections on the deck voiding directly into the sea. Finding one's way to these at night was not easy, especially in bad weather when it might be impossible, as a heavy sea could sweep passengers away. Alternative arrangements for such circumstances were often not made, and people had to shift as best they might. The imagination boggles at the outcome. The reticence of our Victorian forebears usually draws a veil over such matters but we catch the occasional glimpse. One passenger at a slightly earlier period complained that for want of anything else some were forced to use their eating utensils. Similar strictures applied to laundry arrangements in bad weather. Given that the passengers' small supply of linen had to be washed regularly to be kept clean, this obviously caused problems. Some steerage inhabitants were so unfastidious as to cause protests from their fellow passengers. At least one man, it is recorded, had his vermin-infested bedding thrown overboard by order of the captain after numerous complaints. Presumably he and his lice made themselves as comfortable as they might on bare boards for the remainder of the voyage.

It is small wonder that most historians dealing with emigration have shudderingly described the steerage as dark, unwholesome and, by the end of a voyage through the tropics, stinking. During the gold-rush period, with space at a premium, entirely unsuitable vessels were sometimes pressed into service to meet demand. Some steerage passengers were accommodated on the orlop deck, so close to the waterline that even in calm weather the scuttles could not be opened. Lights had to be kept burning continuously, and human ingenuity turned to the ventilation of such deep spaces. Interestingly, the device adopted, the windsail, had first been invented for the ventilation of mines. According to the report of a Victorian health officer in 1855, it comprised a two-part tube which penetrated the decks from above and allowed the stale air to exit and its replacement with fresh by the action of a wind-driven sail set to catch the breeze.[19] It cannot have been much help, and had to be sealed off in bad weather.

There was also the omnipresent danger of fire on a wooden vessel. Marianne Manchester remarked almost casually that 'the cook-house chimney has been on fire again, also a paraffin lamp was knocked down and all ignited in a sudden blaze.'[20] Obviously this was brought under control, but at a later period there was at least one serious fire on an emigrant ship, with great loss of life.

The hardships and the dangers which continued to be associated with long sea voyages in the nineteenth century should not be underplayed. Although most of the emigrant ships were thoroughly surveyed and were not in the shocking state of some of the cargo ships that put to sea,[21] the hazards associated with ocean voyaging were very real. By our standards nineteenth-century sailing ships were small and frail, and the voyage to New Zealand took them through particularly stormy seas. At least 30 ships making the passage to New Zealand and Australia in the nineteenth century are known to have foundered with serious loss of life. In 1855, for example, the *Guiding Star* out of Liverpool with 546 people on board vanished without a trace, probably, from the accounts of last sightings, as a result of a collision with an iceberg.

Passengers encountering a storm for the first time were understandably fearful, and few journals do not contain an account of such an experience. The steerage passengers tended to get the worst of it. In 1858 Fanny Davis recalled:

> Of all the nights we have had yet last night was the worst. The wind rose to a perfect hurricane; they fastened down the hatches but that did not prevent the water making its way down to us. . . All at once there arose a cry that we were sinking and, of course, that added to the general confusion and many were on their knees praying who had perhaps never thought on the name of God before . . .[22]

And a passenger named Mathieson, travelling on the *Jura* to Dunedin in 1858, recorded his impressions in his curiously misspelled but entirely literate journal:

> had a ver ruf day the sea running mountans high, the ship realing to and frow like a drunkin man, chists upsetting, watter cans pots & pans tumbling in all directions — and some of us a little seek to day again but for all that none of us seemed to be afraid of going down. Mr Adams [another passenger] said that he never saw as ruff a day. some of them that knew a little about sailing said the Captin acted very cautiously.[23]

MANNERS AND MORALS

Ships continued to be a microcosm of the class structures that many of those in the steerage hoped they had left behind. Even those in the first class were sometimes astonished to discover that if the ship foundered the available lifeboats would be reserved for the cuddy, that is, the cabin passengers. Safety arrangements for emigrants, it appears, were not included in the price of the ticket: they were expected to drown if the ship went down, or to cling to convenient wreckage. This remained the situation well into the next century, until the loss of the *Titanic* forced its reappraisal.

The casual and arbitrary tyranny of those set over the mainly working-class steerage passengers, and the callous indifference towards their welfare on the part of the middle-class cabin passengers, also shocks the twentieth-century reader. Emma Hodder drew much comfort from, and several times alluded to, the support of a dissenting clergyman on board who had arranged regular services and a weekly Bible class. Then, for no apparent reason, 'prayers and bible class forbidden by the doctor. I am very much disappointed and surprised that we cannot enjoy liberty if not in anything else in religious matters.' Hodder obviously found this curtailment by an official appointed to look after her well-being deeply hurtful. 'It could not be much worse if we were convicts,' she confided to her diary.[24]

Most cabin passengers continued to refuse to mix with the steerage even at the most casual level, although there were some who expressed a

The journey to New Zealand, although a long one, remained a fairly comfortable experience for most cabin passengers throughout the nineteenth century, as in this scene on the poopdeck in 1865. (ATL)

sympathetic concern without necessarily doing anything about it. 'I feel very sorry for the people on the main deck,' wrote Isabella Turner during a storm in 1868. 'They cannot come out in this weather owing to the water covering the deck, indeed sometimes they have to keep their door shut for fear of the water getting inside. It must be so uncomfortable for them.'[25] Rather rarer were those who actively engaged themselves with the steerage, a practice much frowned upon by the cabin. One of these was Samuel Butler who, on the voyage to Canterbury aboard the *Roman Emperor* in 1859, set up a steerage choir and afterwards remarked that he had been glad 'to form the acquaintance of many of the poorer passengers'.[26] Others went below decks for rather less altruistic reasons, although they would not have seen it that way. Edward Cornell went into the steerage in 1856 to distribute uplifting tracts, which 'were gratefully received by most'; but he seems to have been dimly aware that many steerage passengers resented this sort of patronage. After commenting favourably on the fact that so many were reading their Bibles, despite the poor light, he admits that 'by far the greater number were playing at cards or dominoes', and were oblivious to his presence.

And of course the significant matter of who should and should not be allowed on to the poop deck continued to exercise the indignation of the first-class passengers. This was compounded by the relative prosperity of the mid century which enabled some *nouveaux riches* passengers to purchase cabin tickets — an outrage which their fellow travellers thought should have been forbidden. 'Hogan ought to have been in steerage,' said Solomon Joseph of a fellow passenger in 1859. 'We tried to induce him to change but without success.'[27] Other features of the period also exacerbated the cabin passengers' problems. One of these was the growing use of the intermediate class between cabin and steerage. Some of these passengers, feeling that as they had paid their way they were entitled to some privileges, complained that they were excluded from the poop. Captains must have been exasperated by their responsibility to arbitrate such disputes. Robert Corkhill recorded in 1855 that following the use of the poop deck by the second-class passengers, and complaints by the first, the captain installed a spar dividing the poop in two. This simply served to incense the second-class passengers, and so failed to achieve its object. Steerage passengers also objected to this 'downright humbug', as George Randall described it in 1868;[28] he suggested that the steerage passengers put up a notice excluding the first- and second-class passengers from *their* part of the ship, although he seems not to have done so in the event.

But what caused a significant difficulty was the developing practice of sending parties of young single women emigrants. The problem was how to protect their morals during a lengthy voyage when they might be prey to the attentions of the men aboard, including the crew. The problem did not just exist in the fevered imaginings of our Victorian forebears. The women were very vulnerable and were sometimes exploited.[29] They were accordingly usually placed under the authority of a matron who had significant disciplinary powers, was required to keep a diary of the journey, record any breaches of requirements and furnish a report on arrival. Sometimes this was helpful and sometimes not. The matrons' effectiveness rather depended on their personality, although they did have some sanctions available to them. Usually they distributed needlework, and those who had 'behaved' were allowed to retain the product of their labour at the completion of the voyage.

The restrictions designed to protect the single women understandably sometimes irked them, and they responded in kind. In 1866 the captain of the *John Temperley* cabled his owners before he had even left port that he had had some trouble with the unacceptable use of language by some of the women, their insistence on consorting with the men, and their disruption of a church service by the singing of music-hall songs when they should have been singing hymns.[30] Ridicule was quite often used by the women as a defence against the arbitrary authority of male officials. When the surgeon on board the *Montmorency* in 1863 sent the women below after they complained of his refusal to allow them to dance with the men, 'they for revenge made a song up & sung it about him,' according to Joshua Hughes. 'He listened to it along with the others & got quite mad when the people cheered the song & sent down the purser to find who sang, but he was pulled about in every direction while the people on deck shouted "Doctor the purser is among the women."'[31] The doctor was not amused at being made a fool of, and had the women placed on bread and water. Such punishments were not uncommon. On the *John Duncan* in 1863 the captain actually put three women in irons when they repeatedly refused to leave the deck at a specified time. On the *Sirocco* two women were tied to the rigging and drenched with a hose for making too much noise after their lighting failed, although this led to a successful prosecution for assault against the second mate when the ship arrived in Lyttelton. Emma Hodder on the *Hydaspes* noted: 'A great stir this morning. Two girls very rude put in prison and fed on biscuits and water.'[32] They were still there the next day. Emma did not much sympathise with them, but found herself on the outer because of this. Other passengers tended to take the side of the unruly women against the authorities.

It is easy enough to appreciate why. Even attempts to protect the single women sometimes backfired. On one vessel they were confined to their between-decks area when there was a storm — a stipulation kindly meant, but described by another passenger as 'positive cruelty'. It was nevertheless a dilemma. Where were the women to exercise? They were already locked up at night. 'The Matron must see that every woman is in her berth before dark every night, and lock the door, and keep the key of the single women's compartment. The door is not to be unlocked except in the case of illness before 7 o'clock in the morning,' said the official instructions to matrons. But if the women could not exercise on the main deck, where they might fraternise with those who put their morals in danger, should the poop deck be available? Marianne Manchester recorded in 1870 that she and other single women were allowed on the poop by specific permission of the captain for special purposes — to practise dancing, to speak to another vessel, and so on. That this was a potential source of trouble was recognised in the official instructions: 'The single women are entitled to the use of the poop when on deck, or so much of it as may be set apart for their use, and they are on no account to go into any other part of the ship. The Matron is

Both mistress and servant often found the colony's social relations different from the norm at home. Employers' accounts are full of indignant complaints about the temerity of servants (in this case captioned 'Call yourself a lady and a Christian, and expect me to do the washing?') as this extract from Dunedin Punch *1865 shows. (Hocken Library)*

expected to be on deck with them and to discourage communication and prevent familiarity with the cabin passengers, if there should be any.' Unmarried female immigrants were not allowed to act as servants to cabin passengers 'under any circumstances'.[33]

Nor were their tribulations over at the end of the voyage. They might be called to account for insubordination, and they were usually accommodated in immigrant barracks while they awaited employment. These barracks were often unsalubrious, and were the subject of complaint by male and female immigrants alike. Fortunately, the stay was usually not long. Officials of the immigration administration doubled as labour bureau staff, acting as go-betweens with prospective employers.* They tried as far as possible to ensure that needs were matched on both sides. and that the women newly arrived in the colony were not unduly exploited, During the mid century the demand for labour was sufficient to ensure that most arriving immigrants had embarked on their new life within a few days of arrival.

NEW CHUMS

To those of the middle class socialised to the expectations of Britain, the nature of the relationship with their servants in their new home came as something of a shock. Anthony Trollope found this vastly entertaining. He had often, he said, been called upon to sympathise with women who had been unable to get a servant at all and had thus been obliged to make their own beds and cook their own dinners. But he went on to point out that 'the maid servant's side of the question is quite as important as the mistress's' and that in a place where a young woman might earn £40 a year working in a comfortable home and have a good expectation of finding a decent man for a husband, New Zealand was a paradise:

> The very tone in which a maid servant speaks to you in New Zealand, her quiet little joke, her familiar smile, her easy manner, tell you at once that the badge of servitude is not heavy upon her. She takes her wages and makes your bed and hands your plate — but she does not consider herself to be of an order of things different from your order. Many who have been accustomed to be served all their life may not like this. If so, they had better not live in New Zealand. But if we look at the matter from the maid servant's side we cannot fail to find there is much comfort in it.[34]

---

* This association between the administration of immigration and the administration of employment matters remains a feature of government activity to the present time.

Lady Mary Barker, who had several years' experience of the New Zealand servant problem at the employing end in the 1860s, took it philosophically. She became used to servants who could neither cook nor handle a broom without being trained, although she did wonder 'who in England did the necessary things of daily cottage life for them, for they appear to have done nothing for themselves hitherto'. But she paid tribute to the cheerfulness and willingness to work of all the servants she encountered, 'and I hear no complaints of dishonesty or immorality, though many moans are made of the rapidity with which a nice tidy young woman is snapped up as a wife'. And she went on to generalise her comments:

> The look and bearing of the immigrants appear to alter soon after they reach the colony. Some people object to the independence of their manner, but I do not; on the contrary, I like to see the upright gait, the well-fed, healthy look, the decent clothes (even if no-one touches his hat to you) instead of the half starved depressed appearance, and too often cringing servility of the mass of our English population.[35]

Charles Money was very struck on his arrival in Christchurch in 1861 by 'the most entire civility shewn to all strangers on arrival; the welcome

Skilled workers newly arrived in New Zealand moved quickly to set up branches of the British unions with which they were associated. This banner is from a slightly later period. (ATL)

greeting given by tradesmen or others with whom we were brought in contact was perfectly sincere.'[36] And Samuel Butler echoed Lady Barker in remarking to intending immigrant settlers that

> [y]ou and your men will have to be on rather a different footing from that on which you stood in England. There, if your servant were in any respect what you did not wish, you were certain of getting plenty of others to take his place. Here, if a man does not find you quite what he wishes, he is certain of getting plenty of others to employ him. In fact, he is at a premium, and soon finds this out.[37]

It is from this period that we can date the first trade unions in New Zealand. Printers' unions were in existence in both Wellington and Auckland by 1864, and a Carpenters' and Joiners' Society as early as 1857. In 1863 an arriving engineer, Alexander Bruce, brought with him to Auckland a charter to establish a branch of the Amalgamated Society of Engineers. Typically these were small craft unions which followed the pattern of their English counterparts. They were designed primarily to protect skilled tradesmen against the watering-down of their skills in the new place, but they also ensured that from the outset limitations were placed on the hours of work. Although we know little of these early unions and their members, it is likely that some of the latter had their emigration subsidised by their union in their home country — quite a common practice among the trades noted in mid-century Britain.[38]

No doubt many immigrants were pleased enough to find themselves living well and plying their trade, but for as many more that was simply a first step. Alexander Bathgate, who has already been quoted as saying that the main motive of the immigrant was to improve their position, continued: 'It may be asked if most of those who emigrate, with the expectation of bettering their circumstances, really do so. I have no hesitation in answering this question in the affirmative. To say that all do so would be too sweeping an assertion, but this I will say, that as a rule if people do not, it is their own fault.' [39]

Reading the letters of those who had settled down in New Zealand it is sometimes hard to escape the impression that they could not quite believe their new situation. Mary Charleston wrote to her father in England from Kaikoura in October 1866:

> My husband and I have got a very comfortable home and I don't think I will see England once more. We have twenty head of cattle, ten horse, a team of bullocks and a dray, they are valued at one hundred and twenty pounds, and five miles from here we have got seventy three acres of freehold land, and the place where we are living is our own

property. We are keeping a public house but the business is not very large but we hope in a twelve months time it will be better as there is a great many people settling here every day.[40]

In April 1867 Mary Hunter, in Remuera (then a village outside Auckland), and four years in New Zealand, echoed her enthusiasm:

Mother keeps a grocers shop. I have been living at a place until lately and now I have come home, and go into town every day to learn the dressmaking as I am tired of being at service. Though from six shillings to twelve shillings is the common wage, I had nine shillings a week and I was three years in one place but the servants do not work half as hard

For many working-class immigrants, now comfortably settled in their new homes, news from England was always welcome, not least because it enabled them to compare their situations. (ATL)

here as they do at home, such a thing would never be thought of as a woman going out to work in the fields, and as for milking cows that is a man's job, and the women in general would be afraid of spoiling their fingers.[41]

This is not to say that there was no hardship associated with material success. Sarah Pratt, writing from New Plymouth in 1858, says of a friend in England who is hoping to emigrate: 'I should like John to know that there is nothing but manual labour for him — farm labour, cutting down trees, sawing, fencing, roadmaking etc.' And she remarked that those who were best off in her settlement were the small farmers from Devon and Cornwall 'who have made themselves more than independent *by the sweat of their brow*. They have little or no education, some can neither read nor write, but they can dig and delve and make butter and cheese.'[42] Three years later in Collingwood Elizabeth Curtis also struck a more sombre note while recounting her present good fortune to her sister: 'We have got a snug house of our own and a small piece of land. . . It is like beginning the world anew. The children and me are getting a nice garden. . . I am sure that you would like it better here than where you are.' But she had not seen her husband for 19 months because his work with his team of bullocks had taken him to the diggings 500 miles to the south. 'When he once comes home,' she concluded, 'it will be a long time before I let him go away again so far.'[43] And there were always those who suffered, as Alexander Bathgate said, through their own failings. Sarah Haslam, a seamstress living in Auckland, broke off the narrative of a letter to her mother in 1863 to remark: 'Mrs Pearce just now came down and told me that a young man named Tiddeman, who came out with us in the second cabin, one of those you took such a dislike to, a drunken fellow, has just gone by all in rags, for all his clothes are kept by a person he owes money to. He was going to do such wonders when he got to Auckland.'[44]

'A SET OF HORRIBLE FELLOWS'

The success of the working-class immigrants was not always welcome to those who preferred a less upwardly mobile and fluid society. While they could hardly cavil at the success which attended hard work and frugality without appearing churlish, they had nothing but bad to say of that rowdy and profligate crew, the gold miners. It has already been remarked that the respectable citizens of both Dunedin and Christchurch were scandalised by the opinions and behaviour of the miners. The original leaders of the Otago settlement in particular never lost an opportunity to point up the

Attracted by the opportunities, some Victorian diggers left quite lucrative areas in Australia for the new field of New Zealand. Miners gather at the Railway Pier, Melbourne, for the journey to Otago in 1862. (ATL)

moral lessons associated with rapidly gained wealth sometimes as rapidly lost, although this did not generally prevent them from profiting from the extra business opportunities the miners created. Canterbury society was similarly scathing in dismissing the miners and the social values they represented.

Caroline Chevalier, who visited Hokitika at the height of the West Coast rushes, was appalled by this 'set of horrible fellows' whom she characterised as 'many half drunk, some miserable, some wild'.[45] And at least one newspaper denounced a society in which 'a slipshod, slatternly, stockingless, insolent servant woman demands and obtains from two to three pounds a week as wages besides her keep, while a thoroughly competent lady who opens a school for the education of girls, cannot get a sufficient number of pupils at four shillings a week to support her'.[46] Archdeacon Henry Harper was less ready to condemn. Although he thought the conversation of his western parishioners lacked a certain refinement and was too much taken up with the trivialities of daily living, he saw them as a young and hopeful community, devoid of social envy, enjoying 'a life in which, barring accident and misfortune, anyone may rise'.[47] Charles Money, who spent much of his seven years in New Zealand on the goldfields, thought that among the labouring men he encountered, the human mind, dwarfed and stunted at home by a sense of inferiority, was here 'enlarged and healthily braced'.[48]

The miners themselves cared nothing for the opinions of those who presumed themselves to be their social betters. The Hokitika-based *West*

Coast Times, which spoke for them, scoffed at the pretensions of Canterbury as a province from which 'everything approaching to Californian and Victorian elements had been so carefully eliminated, that the incursion of diggers was looked upon with the same feeling as we may suppose to have belonged to the old civilisation when it witnessed the invasion of the Goths'.[49]

Many of the miners were well-educated and highly skilled men who had joined the international workforce because they chose to, not because necessity had forced them to it. At Okarito Julius von Haast, on a geological expedition, had 'once more occasion to observe the fine character of the real miner; and those who were camped around me were, as far as enterprise, knowledge of their trade, and power of endurance is concerned, the finest set of men one could meet'.[50] Archdeacon Harper noted with some surprise that whereas 53% of the men in the Lyttelton and Christchurch gaols in 1866 could read and write, the comparable figure for Hokitika was 77%.[51] Court records give a figure of 2% in Christchurch and 10% in Hokitika for those with higher education among committals in 1867. They were certainly a different population from that which had arrived in New Zealand through the usual processes of immigration. Younger, predominantly male,

The gold miners, skilled workers, often with Californian and Victorian experience behind them, were often disliked or even feared by respectable middle-class immigrants. They added a particular egalitarian flavour to the new society. (ATL)

and already tempered in many ways by the colonial experience in Victoria or California, with a higher proportion of Irish among them, they formed a very distinctive community.

Harper also paid tribute to the miners' 'generous spirit of comradeship'. Their attitudes were both democratic and egalitarian. They wore a distinctive dress of blue flannel shirt, moleskin trousers, high boots and a tall 'wide awake' hat — one with a broad brim that did not require the wearer to squint his eyes against the sun. Anyone who appeared on the diggings in frock coat and top hat was roundly barracked. They did not thank the local governing class for criticising their social habits, and when local publicans imported the music-hall entertainer and comic singer Charles Thatcher from Bendigo and Ballarat to tour New Zealand in 1862 and 1863, the miners turned out in their hundreds to hear him and boisterously to applaud his celebration of their democratic point of view:

> At home aristocracy seems all the go;
> In New Zealand we're all on a level, you know.
> The poor man out here ain't oppressed by the rich
> But, dressed in blue shirts, you can't tell which is which . . .
> There's no masters here to oppress a poor devil,
> But out in New Zealand we're all on a level.[52]

When Edward Cargill, a member of the Otago Provincial Council, criticised the mining influx on the grounds that it would swamp the unique identity of the province, Thatcher, then in Dunedin, so effectively satirised him that his song became almost instantly a classic of the New Zealand music-hall repertoire and turned the expression 'the old identity' into such a pungent criticism of the pretensions of Dunedin's originating middle class that Cargill must have long regretted ever defending their interests and handing the miners' champion such a stick to beat him with.

Behind what some saw as an open and democratic spirit, and others saw as bumptious impertinence, lay the miners' right to vote, an apparently curious anomaly in a society which made this the only exception to the original property qualification of the Constitution Act for over two decades. Any miner possessed of a miners' right, which could be purchased for £1, need not even register to vote but only turn up on election day and produce it to be accorded a voice in choosing a representative.

The origins of this right go back as far as 1858, when a select committee of the House of Representatives resolved that 'it is desirable to make specific provision for the representation of the gold-digging population, under convenient regulations to be enacted for this specific purpose'.[53] Instead of this, a Miners Franchise Act was passed in 1860. Moving its second reading

*Alarmed by what had happened in Victoria where the gold miners had
rebelled in the famous Eureka stockade incident, the New Zealand
authorities extended the right to vote to all those who held a miners' right.
(Hocken Library)*

in the Legislative Council on 29 October, the Hon. Henry Tancred,
gentleman, of Canterbury, alluded to the Ballarat riots 'as an instance of
the evil resulting from withholding the franchise from this class'.[54] This
allusion, which would not have been lost on his audience, was a reference
to the Eureka stockade.

By 1853 some 80,000 miners were working the Victorian goldfields.
Many of these men were Chartists and nursed a fierce democratic spirit. A
favourite anecdote of the time recounts that a wealthy gentleman who
asked a miner to carry his bags was made a counter-offer of sixpence to
clean the miner's boots. What irritated the miners more than anything else
was a requirement to pay £3 a month to renew their miners' right. In
Ballarat, where the influence of the Chartists was particularly strong, they
held a mass meeting at which they not only reaffirmed the six points of the
charter including universal manhood suffrage, but conducted a general
burning of miners' licences. When the authorities retaliated by massing
police on the field, the miners retired to a stockaded hilltop in the Eureka

diggings, where they raised their own flag and defied the authority of Governor Hotham. Hotham was nothing loath to accept their challenge. Their stockade was attacked and overrun by some 400 troops and armed police, and 30 miners were killed. The ensuing public outrage forced the government of Victoria to reduce the cost of the licence to £1 a year and to grant miners a vote on production of it.[55]

The government in New Zealand, presumably wanting no stockades here, followed suit four years later. As a symbol of miner radicalism, this right to vote was deeply resented, and there was rarely a debate on a matter of voting until the achievement of manhood suffrage without some slighting reference to it. Speaking to the Qualification of Electors Bill in 1871, for instance, G. B. Parker, the member for Gladstone, called it 'manifestly unfair to property owners', accused the miners of illegal multiple voting and expressed the fear that 'if something were not done, those who could afford to take out miners' rights would rule elections'.[56] What he really feared was democracy. But no parliament ever dared overturn it before it was subsumed in the more general right in 1875. The miners were both feared and respected by those who liked to consider themselves their betters.

None of this is to say that life on the goldfields could not be harsh, brutal and degraded. It often was, especially for women. But the egalitarian mateship which developed among men was a response to this harshness, and became a means of integrating the working relationships of a largely itinerant and immigrant population into the broader community.[57] Those who stayed in New Zealand after the gold was done contributed this significant dimension to the developing culture of the new society.

Disrespect for or at best scepticism towards the motives of the authorities and others who might otherwise have had pretensions to social and political leadership in Britain, and who claimed a similar position in the new colony, seems to have been widespread in mid-century New Zealand, and was by no means confined to the miners. Mary Hunter, in Auckland in 1867, writing home that her father had been waiting for some time for a job on the railways, said that 'the head men squander the money so that I do not know when it will be finished, but everyone out of pure selfishness thinks only of themselves and not of the affairs of the province'. She gave every impression of stating a generally accepted truth rather than a personal opinion.[58] Over the next two decades, working people were to have proof that this scepticism was well founded.

CHAPTER NINE

THE DECLINE OF BRITISH AGRICULTURAL EMPLOYMENT 1870–1885

When Arch beneath the Wellesbourne tree
His mighty work began
A thrill of hope and energy
Through all the country ran
The farmer, parson, lord and squire,
Looked on with evil eyes
Some looked with scorn, and some with ire
And some in dumb surprise.[1]

By the final quarter of the nineteenth century Britain had developed a unique economy. During this period, and up to the First World War and beyond, Britain always imported more commodities than it exported, the deficit reaching as much as a third of the overall value of commodity trade in the 1890s.[2] That this economy worked can be attributed to two factors. The first was that the balance was more than made up from 'invisibles' — internationally traded services such as banking and insurance, shipping and returns on investment in overseas territories, and ownership of the infrastructures such as railways, docks and processing facilities of the countries supplying imports. The second was the ability, either directly or indirectly, to command the activities of countries trading with Britain through the assertion of economic or political power. This power was used to ensure that these countries took British goods and kept others out, and that Britain was the primary recipient of the imports it needed. New Zealand was an integral and dependent element in this system, became increasingly so as the century progressed and remained so until after the Second World War.[3]

The most significant category of commodities imported by Britain was foodstuffs — grain, meat, dairy produce, and fats in particular. By 1875 these constituted about half of all Britain's imports,[4] and far outweighed in value the imports of raw material for such industrial purposes as cloth manufacture. The most important of the imported food commodities were grains (predominantly wheat) and flour, worth £56 million by 1875.

Wheat is the most efficient grain available for human consumption.[5] A kilogram of bread a day — about half a standard loaf — can deliver enough energy to support a hard day of physical work. Other grains — rye, maize, millet and rice — cannot match this. But in the nineteenth century Britain found it difficult to produce enough wheat to support its burgeoning population. Northwestern Europe, and especially Britain, the Low Countries and Germany, is one of the largest grain deficit areas of the world. By 1870 Britain had to import grain in large quantities if it was to survive. This simple fact lies at the root of most emigration to New Zealand in the 15 years after 1870.

Economic historians debate the nature of the period from 1870 to the mid nineties. Mostly it has been characterised as a period of depression, both in Britain and in its dependent economies. That there was widespread social distress and hardship in many countries during those 20 years seems undeniable, although some historians have tried to deny that there was any depression at all.[6] This viewpoint is sustainable only in terms of statistical indices, which present a variety of opportunities for interpretation.

From a base of 100, prices fell almost continuously from 1871 to 1900, and had still not reached anything like the 1870 level by the outbreak of the First World War.[7] But a fall in prices even of this magnitude does not always betoken a depression. During the same period real wages maintained their level, and even rose to 1890, although by how much is not clear.[8] Whatever may have been the extent, if any, of wage growth, it was not accompanied by much general economic growth, and this tended to squeeze profit margins and forced some businesses into bankruptcy. It does not, however, seem to have led to the widespread unemployment which classical economics would have predicted in such circumstances. Available figures suggest that although unemployment was higher overall between 1874 and 1895 (7.2%) than it had been in the preceding two decades (about 5%) and the two which followed (5.4%), the reasons for this were sectoral rather than general.

Was this a period of depression? One of the drawbacks of statistical indices is that on their own they cannot account for human experience. People seemed to *think* that what they were experiencing was a depression. The period to 1890 is replete with descriptions of social hardship as severe as any which disgraced the 'hungry forties'. To account for these it is necessary to look more closely at what the figures cannot tell us. Contemporary observers, and in particular Charles Booth and Beerbohm Rowntree, did precisely that. Their subsequent published reports, which painted a picture of a large underclass living in miserable circumstances, greatly shocked the less complacent of their readers. Their efforts were seconded by a widely read radical press, and what they found has since been confirmed by historical research.[9]

Most cities contained large areas of ramshackle, unhealthy and overcrowded slum housing, a legacy more often than not of 50 years' too-rapid expansion of towns to accommodate industries, and their masses of workers. The sanitary officer for the London parish of Shoreditch, for example, drew attention in 1868 to the severe overcrowding in his area, which he attributed to the widespread demolition of dwellings to build factories, workshops, railways and other constructions. 'Numbers of the working classes,' he reported, 'are by these means driven from their houses to seek shelter elsewhere, whose occupations compel them to live near their daily employment. They are therefore obliged to get into almost any place, often places totally unfit for many to reside in, frequently they are underground dwellings, contrary to the public health act.'[10] This situation worsened significantly by the eighties.[11] Housing densities of nine persons to a small dwelling were not uncommon, and in the worst areas of some cities might rise to as high as 13.

One of the more popular middle-class responses to working-class distress was the distribution of soup, as here in Limehouse, one of London's poorest districts in 1868. (Illustrated London News)

In the case of Jennings Building in London's Kensington, a group of 81 two-storey tenements grouped around five courts which was almost continuously the subject of investigation by the authorities between 1856 and 1873, nearly 1500 people lived crammed together in a space designed for 200. It had only 49 privies, and until 1866 no source of drinking water. The pigs in another slum nearby, said the local medical officer, were better accommodated.[12] Shortly thereafter the pigs were removed, ironically not because they were a hazard to human health but because the state of the human dwellings was a danger to the pigs, which could not be passed as fit for human consumption because of it. These were extreme cases but they were not unusual of their kind. Many people slept casually in the streets, and as late as 1912 workhouses were the only home for nearly 300,000 people.

Even those in work were often in a precarious situation. William Booth, giving evidence to the Royal Commission on Labour in 1892, presented statistical information to show that in East London and Hackney fully a third of the workforce were employed on a casual, day-to-day basis, and nearly another third, although in regular work, received very low pay for what they did. Fewer than one in 10 of the more than 100,000 workers he sampled could be described as in regular work and receiving reasonable wages. Many families could only survive if wives also worked. Usually this work was menial and miserably paid. Booth and other researchers discovered it was a significant mark of status among married male workers if their wives did not have to work — it showed they were earning sufficient to keep a family on their own.

Understandably in these circumstances many workers were ill-fed as well as ill-housed and underemployed. Poorer workers continued to live principally on bread and potatoes, and, Rowntree found, regarded even peas and beans as luxury foodstuffs. A recent researcher on nineteenth-century diet comments: 'In reality, consumption of vegetables (mostly onions, cabbage or turnips) was limited to about one quarter pound per person per week, especially in urban areas. . . Fruit consumption was usually limited to a small amount of dried currants used for making the "roly-poly". Fresh milk was almost unknown, particularly in the towns, where small amounts of tinned condensed milk were used to whiten tea.'[13] The working-class diet was high in carbohydrate and fibre, but deficient in energy, protein, fat, calcium, and vitamins A and C. Rickets and beriberi were not uncommon among the poor in the nineteenth century; their presence was casually recorded along with other health statistics by the registrar general in his *Statistical Review of England and Wales* in 1901.

This situation was worsened with the widespread introduction of steel rolling mills for flour milling in the eighties. Although this was more efficient from the point of view of flour production, and the price of bread fell as a result, the new technology produced a flour deficient in fibre, thiamine and iron. As late as 1890 it was possible for a man to faint in St James's Park, to be taken to hospital and there to die shortly thereafter, and for a coroner's jury, without any sense of irony, to bring in a verdict of death from starvation.[14] This particular unfortunate, it transpired, had walked from Liverpool in search of work and had been without food for five days.

These depressed social groups were not generally those from whom emigrants, particularly to the antipodes, were drawn. But the knowledge of the widespread existence of such groups contributed significantly to the social fear of falling into the underclass, and motivated much emigration to colonies and territories where, it was believed, this was much less likely to happen. The developing lower middle class was particularly prone to such anxieties.[15] Between 1870 and 1885 it was not this, however, but another group within the British economy which contributed the bulk of New Zealand immigrants — agricultural labourers.

Even for those with work the conditions were often appalling. Whole families, including children, were involved in scraping a living, as this depiction of matchmakers at Bow in 1871 illustrates. (Illustrated London News)

THE AGRICULTURAL CRISIS

The price falls which began in the 1870s affected British agriculture more severely than any other part of the economy. Domestic wheat which had sold for 55s a quarter in 1870 was, by the turn of the century, selling for 27s. This fall was continuous. Although one economic historian has remarked, 'it would be excessive to talk of a catastrophe',[16] the consequences of this were serious enough, especially for those working on the land. The interesting question is why this had not happened two decades earlier, following the repeal of the Corn Laws.

The simplest answer to this complex question is that three sets of factors were in play in mid century.[17] The first was that the vast available lands of the American mid-west, of the Argentine and of Australia were not yet in full cultivation. Secondly, the infrastructure so necessary for a viable international export trade in grain was not in place either. The building of railways had not yet been completed; the reception and dispatch centres had not yet been created; and the necessary international financial and shipping arrangements had not yet been set up, although they existed in embryo. All of these things had to be in place before it was economic to dispatch grain from the centre of America or the bottom of the southern hemisphere, and to deliver it to British millers and bakers at a price which seriously undercut the domestic product available often just a few miles away. And thirdly, as surpluses began to flow onto the international market, they were initially absorbed by demand in other places, at first by the Crimean War, then by the American Civil War, and finally by the development of the great meat markets centred on Chicago which demanded large quantities of grain for fattening purposes before thought could be given to exporting the grain itself. By the 1870s these considerations no longer applied. Between 1860 and 1900, for example, the cost of transporting wheat from Chicago to Liverpool fell by 72%, most of this between 1875 and 1884.

British grain producers could not cope with this competition. Wheat acreages in Britain had peaked in the 1840s, and in 1870 were still close to this maximum, at 3.8 million. By 1904 this was down to 1.37 million.[18] With this went a sudden and catastrophic (for those working in it) decline in agricultural employment. Figures for this loss of jobs vary, but even the most conservative suggest that 3 million agricultural workers in 1870 had become 2.3 million by 1911. Again, most of this happened during the period from 1870 to 1880. A minimum of several hundred thousand surplus workers was many more than an economy which was slowing down could possibly absorb.

But paradoxically, this was also a period in which British agricultural productivity increased by about 0.3% a year — about the same rate as the economy as a whole. British agriculture itself was a very complex industry. The apparent easy prosperity it enjoyed between 1850 and 1870 was partly a mirage: the state of the industry was quite fragile. The narrow profitability of British farming was based on very careful producer assessments of domestic markets and the ability to switch quickly from one product to another to meet changing demand. While grain consumption rose overall with population growth, it remained constant per capita. The real area of growth in demand was in animal products. To meet this demand farmers had to increase production from lighter soils by increasing stock-carrying levels. This was the factor which lay behind the development of mixed farming, in which the animal-carrying capacities of the farms were raised by growing root fodder crops on a heavily fertilised and intensely cultivated basis. This required high levels of both capital and labour input. It also entailed a complex set of relationships between input and output prices — grain, fodder, meat, labour, fertiliser — with very little room for manoeuvre. When the price of grain was high, farmers sold it and fed their livestock root crops; when it was low, they fed grain to their livestock and held back on root cultivation until the price rose again. Similarly, when the price of livestock fell, they did the same in reverse until the market recovered. Cheap imported grain brought this delicately balanced structure tumbling down.

Farmers moved out of grain production and either shifted into other commodities such as vegetables where the climate and soil was suitable, or they stayed completely in animal production and stopped growing their own root crops and wheat, and instead purchased imported cattle cake and fertilisers. This made economic sense. Between 1875 and 1895 the cost of purchased feeds fell by 40% and the cost of fertilisers by 55%. This significantly reduced the cost of horse power. Profit margins were squeezed ever harder as this transition took place, and many farmers were put out of business altogether. Those who survived did so by cutting their largest and most inflexible input of all — labour. Wages for agricultural labour rose marginally over the period from 1870 to the First World War (although this was not uniform, and they fell either temporarily or permanently in some regions), but employment fell steeply, and became much more casualised and precarious for those remaining in the industry. The areas which took this change particularly hard were those surrounding London to the south, and to the immediate north and east of the capital — areas in which mixed farming had been most prevalent for the previous two decades.

What appeared to be a significant crisis in agriculture so alarmed Britain's rulers, many of whom were landowners, that they appointed two separate royal commissions to inquire into it. The first of these, sitting from 1879 to 1882, reported the decline in agricultural employment; the second, in 1895, analysed its cause. 'The first great cause of the reduction of labour is the diminution of arable land,' noted the report of this second commission. 'In many instances farmers themselves informed me that they had reduced their staff of men, and were still reducing it. As an instance, a farm of 700 acres in South Norfolk is worked with twelve labourers whereas a few years ago a similar farm half the size, would have employed as many.'[19] With labourers accounting for nearly two-thirds of the rural workforce, it is hardly surprising that the total agricultural wages bill fell by 15% between 1871 and 1891, notwithstanding any increase in real wage levels.[20] With the decline in employment the general misery level of agricultural workers rose sharply.

THE LABOURERS' LOT

Some economic historians claim to detect an improvement in agricultural wages during the prosperous times of the mid century, but the statistical evidence, to the extent that it exists at all, is inconclusive. Even if there were increases, a minor improvement on nothing much at all continues to constitute very little. There is a wealth of anecdotal evidence besides, some of which has been cited, to illustrate that no one would have seriously chosen the life of a British agricultural labourer in the nineteenth century if they had had the option. After 1870 this option became even less attractive.

Francis Heath, one of those indefatigable Victorian collectors of statistical data whose energy and efforts continue to amaze later generations, studied the annual budgets of rural labourers over several decades. In 1874 he found that a typical young married labourer might earn a little under £32 a year. After adding up his annual expenses (which included church tithes and a contribution to a friendly society to help him in sickness and his family in the event of his death), he was left with a surplus of 2s 9d for the year. His budget included no meat, and by way of food items only bread, potatoes (which he grew himself on a small rented plot), tea, butter and treacle.[21] Some rural workers kept a pig, but by the time the cost of the meal advanced for feeding by the corn chandler had been repaid, and a weaner bought for the next year, they saw little more than a couple of hams for their trouble.

The Rev. Edward Girdlestone was so shocked by the poverty of the labourers in his rural parish in Devon that he publicised their plight in *The Times*: 'The labourer breakfasts on tea-kettle broth, hot water poured on bread and flavoured with onions; dines on bread and hard cheese at 2d a pound, with cider very washy and sour; and sups on potatoes or cabbage greased with a tiny bit of bacon fat. He seldom more than sees or smells butchers' meat.'[22] He went on to describe a typical working life in which toiling in wet clothes because there was no fire to dry them brought on premature rheumatism and an old age cursed by the shade of the workhouse.

In the final chapter of his book *The English Peasantry*, Francis Heath had piously hoped for a better future for the rural labourer. Largely this hope was to be disappointed until well into the nineties, and even then rural workers enjoyed few luxuries. In *Lark Rise to Candleford*,[23] her famous account of a rural childhood in the period up to the First World War, Flora Thompson described the main meal of the day, eaten in the evening after the men had returned from the fields and the children from school:

> Everything was cooked in the one utensil; the square of bacon amounting to little more than a taste each, cabbage or other green vegetable in one net, potatoes in another, and the rolypoly swathed in a cloth . . . for other meals they depended largely on bread and butter, or more often bread and lard, for butter was too costly for general use, although a pound was sometimes purchased in the summer, when it cost ten pence.

This might just as well have been a description of a meal of 30 years previously. Those who were lucky might occasionally enjoy an egg or two, but if they cared to supplement this diet with a rabbit or bird, it was as well to recollect that the game laws were still in force for most of the century, notwithstanding that Joseph Arch, a principal architect of the rural labourers' unions of the period, told the Select Committee on the Game Laws in 1873 that in his opinion ground game was wild and therefore belonged to no man and that he saw no harm in knocking over a rabbit. The arguments advanced in favour of the game laws — that they prevented idleness and dissipation on the part of labourers — were unlikely to appeal to men, in the words of one historian of social reform, 'whose families starved on one side of the road while fatted birds slumbered on the trees in the plantation opposite'.[24] At least landowners could no longer set spring guns and mantraps for poachers, as had been common until outlawed in the face of vigorous opposition in 1827.

They still prosecuted men who objected to particularly bad working conditions or cavilled at the rate of pay offered to them, however, by bringing charges under the Master and Servant Act. As late as July 1900 five men were haled into court by a farmer who had refused to pay extra for handling wet hay, whereupon the men had walked off, with the resulting loss to the farmer of some £20 in all. In 1872 there were 17,000 convictions under this law, and although this was the high point, more than 6,000 were convicted in 1885.[25] This was class legislation at its worst. A worker who broke a contract committed a criminal offence, was subject to pursuit and arrest by the police, and might be sentenced to up to three months in gaol. If an employer broke a contract, however, it was a civil matter and had to be pursued by the plaintiff through the courts in the same way as any other alleged breach of contract. It is interesting to note that with all the impediments this presented, labourers increasingly turned to it as a remedy during the sixties and seventies. That the law operated unfairly was well known. In July 1875 representatives of farm labourers met the Home Secretary to seek to have both sides to the dispute made civil matters. Their request was bluntly rejected on the quite open grounds that farmers would be disadvantaged at harvest if workers broke their contracts and the farmer was unable to have them arrested and arraigned but had to wait until the appropriate sessions for redress. This, thought the Home Secretary, would have placed altogether too much power in the hands of workers.

The labourers harboured significant resentments against their farmer

Rural working conditions were often exploitative. Workers had few if any rights and were often treated like cattle. This depiction is of a Warwickshire hiring fair in 1872. Here farmers came to engage labourers and householders to seek servants, as in the foreground. (Illustrated London News)

employers on a range of matters beyond those of wages and hours of work. Farmers, who had previously, and often within living memory, lived a life very similar to their men, worked alongside them and sympathised with their concerns, had by the latter part of the century distanced themselves from them socially, and now related much more clearly in their class sympathies and standard of life to the landowners of whom they were tenants. This was particularly resented when the declining profitability of farming forced economies by way of a reduced labour force which was expected to undertake tasks which had previously engaged the full workforce.

Nor did the accommodation available to the labourers improve much until the turn of the century. The Royal Commission on Housing of 1885 was replete with instances of rotting thatch dropping unimaginable filth on the heads of those sleeping beneath it. William Little reported in 1893 of the cottages of rural labourers that 'the sanitary condition and the water supply are lamentably deficient generally, and require amendment'.[26] Successive acts of parliament, designed to improve the housing of working people, seem to have passed many rural areas by, although the comprehensive Public Health Act of 1875 slowly began to make a difference in those areas in which the authorities insisted upon its enforcement. Evictions following dismissals for no particular reason continued to be common.

And the problem of the elderly remained, for, as Flora Thompson remarked, they

> had no homes at all, for as soon as they got past work they had to go to the workhouse, or find accommodation in the already overcrowded cottages of their children. A father or a mother could usually be squeezed in, but there was never room for both, and one child would take one parent and another the other . . . [and] it was a common thing to hear aging people say that they hoped God would be pleased to take them before they got past work and became a trouble to anybody.[27]

Naturally, they continued to stay in work as long as possible. One later reminiscence recalls a harrowing contemporary scene in which a man of 74, having been casually advised without warning by a farmer on horseback that he was too old and his services were no longer required, clutched at the farmer's boot and implored him to keep him on the payroll. His pleas were ignored.[28]

Other pressures were also coming to bear. Farm income had always been a family affair. Children worked from an early age, and were often organised in gangs which were contracted for simple tasks, especially at harvest time. In 1869 the employment of children under eight in this way was forbidden by law, and in 1873 their employment was outlawed entirely. The introduction of compulsory school attendance under the Education Act of 1870 also significantly reduced the contribution of the younger children to the family budget, although finding children as young as 10 carrying out quite physically demanding tasks during harvest remained common enough until the First World War, if the horrendous accident reports are anything to go by.[29] At the same time the practice of gleaning or leezing, in which the wives of labourers were traditionally permitted to pick up the ears of wheat lost to the sheaf during the reaping process, became a bone of contention. Farmers, aware that the amounts involved might be substantial enough to represent a number of bags of wheat for each field, began to assert their rights of ownership over this wheat, sometimes in the courts. At the same time the introduction of mechanical reapers and binders significantly reduced the quantity of wheat a gleaner might collect. Combined with a growing unwillingness to allow the labourers plots for cultivation of household vegetables, all these developments reduced the family income of labourers, sometimes seriously.

The farm labourers were not uncomplaining beasts of burden who dumbly accepted their lot. As with urban workers during the nineteenth century, they responded to their circumstances in a variety of ways, including collective self-help and co-operative activity. Many were members of friendly societies of one sort or another, the purpose of which was to provide financial and medical help during periods of sickness, and a pension in old age, and most particularly to cover the cost of a proper funeral and burial, rather than interment in a paupers' mass grave or, worse, a journey to the medical schools for dissection.[30]

These friendly societies became particularly important to labourers following the enactment of the 1834 Poor Law Amendment, and by the last part of the century they had developed into a national network of organisations, almost a form of co-operative welfare state. The Manchester Unity, for instance, had 31 rural branches in Dorset and 96 in Norfolk by 1875. By the end of the century, and encouraged by the passage of the Friendly Societies Act of 1875, the co-operatives had commonly extended their activities into the provision of clothing and coal as well. Often these groups were supported or subsidised by landowners and farmers who saw them as a much cheaper alternative to the payment of the parish poor rate.

Even more interesting was the development of groups whose avowed purpose was to encourage migration of workers from areas where there was a surplus of labourers and wages were low to areas where wages were higher. William Girdlestone, whose indignation at the depressed condition of his own rural parishioners at Halberston in Devon has already been noted, took practical steps in 1867 to remove 38 labourers and their families to new jobs as far away as Yorkshire and even Ireland. This was not a popular move with his landowning neighbours, and he was the subject of a torrent of abuse both locally and nationally, the accusation being, as is commonly the case with practical social reformers, that he was stirring up discord where none had previously existed.[31]

However, his example was followed by a number of others. In 1871 the North Hertfordshire and South Shropshire Agricultural Labourers' Improvement Society was established for the same purpose, and at its height claimed 30,000 members and a modest success in redeploying workers to less depressed areas. Similar societies existed in Leicestershire and Lincolnshire.[32] It was a short step from migration to emigration. One of these societies had as its slogan 'emigration, migration, but not strikes'. Despite this eminently moderate focus, these societies continued to be frowned on by the local elites.

Since the suppression of the Captain Swing protests of 1830, and the transportation of the Tolpuddle labourers in 1833 for daring to essay the establishment of a combination, the rural workers had put up with their lot, if not without complaint, certainly without concerted protest. Assiduous surveyors of the court records of the 1860s would, however, have noted what subsequent research has confirmed: a rising tide of protest in the form of actions for recovery of wages arbitrarily denied and conditions of work arbitrarily imposed by farmer employers.[33] A surprising number of these were successful, given the class composition of the bench, and these may have encouraged rural workers to go further. When they did, they caught landowner, farmer and parson unawares, if the genuine outrage of these groups is anything to go by. From the early seventies workers began to set up rural unions.

THE REVOLT OF THE FIELD

The 'revolt of the field', as it came to be known, should have astonished no one. This was the period of what has since been described as 'the new unionism'.[34] Trade unions had existed for decades, but they had tended to be combinations of skilled trades workers, founded primarily to maintain control over entry to these trades. Originally, combinations of workers of this or any other sort had been declared illegal, and were rigorously suppressed. Until the 1850s trade unions had led something of a hunted existence, part way illegal but growing in respectability. Many of them functioned mainly as friendly societies.

The end of the 1860s had seen the creation of a national body, the Trades Union Congress, and a successful agitation for a royal commission to inquire into the legal position of unions.[35] This recommended the repeal of the legislation of 1825 which had severely restricted where it did not actually suppress the activities of unions, and its replacement with what became the Trade Union Act of 1871. This recognised the legitimacy of collective bargaining, and in so doing encouraged the formation of unions. Many previously unorganised groups, including in particular unskilled and semi-skilled workers, took the opportunity the establish unions for themselves. The same period saw the passage of the first of a series of extensions of the franchise which were eventually to lead to universal male suffrage by the end of the century.

Rural workers were no more immune to and no less aware of these developments than most other groups of workers. They were, however, notoriously difficult to organise because of their relative isolation in small workplaces spread out over large areas, their dependence upon their employer for their housing, and their daily personal contact with the farmer who was in a position carefully to monitor and influence their views. There had been unsuccessful attempts to set up small local unions, in Buckinghamshire in 1867, and in Kent in 1866 with the Agricultural Labourers' Protection Association — the latter interesting because of its perception of itself as a purely defensive organisation. These were mainly responses to combined attempts by employers to reduce wages. There was also a brief burst of activity in Lincolnshire in 1871, led by the Methodist lay preacher Thomas Strange, which rapidly spread across six counties and at its height created an organisation with an estimated membership of 30,000.

In 1872, following a bad harvest, always the source of discontent because of the reduced demand for labour, these and other initiatives came to a focus after a local dispute at Harbury in Warwickshire over wages and the supply of beer. The upshot was the calling of a general meeting of labourers from several villages at the central point of Wellesbourne on 7 February. Those responsible for calling the meeting, not wishing to take the platform for fear of victimisation, asked the Barford hedger, Joseph Arch, to do so.

The choice of Arch was significant for several reasons. He had for the past two decades also been a Primitive Methodist lay preacher, and had travelled the district and preached regularly to crowds of labourers who often detested the established church which, with good reason, they associated with the local landowners and employers. They also bitterly resented the payment of tithes for the support of parsons who bullied them and told them that their lot was divinely ordained, and whose wives patronised them. This made Arch well known and trusted, as well as a practised public speaker. He was also widely respected for his work as a hedger, one of the most skilled of rural occupations and one which did not require a contractual relationship with any single employer or confinement to a specific locale to earn a good living. But perhaps most important of all, Arch had inherited a freehold cottage from his grandparents, with a large kitchen garden attached. He was therefore remarkably difficult to threaten or to victimise.[36]

By his own account Arch reluctantly agreed, and with many misgivings went to Wellesbourne where, to his astonishment, he found many hundreds of labourers awaiting him. Mounting a stool to address them, he looked out across a sea of faces, a scene which he later described in his autobiography in the almost biblical terms suitable to a lay preacher:

> In the flickering light of the lanterns I saw the earnest upturned faces of these poor brothers of mine — faces gaunt with hunger and pinched with want — all looking towards me and ready to listen to the words that would fall from my lips. These white slaves of England with the darkness all about them, like the children of Israel waiting for someone to lead them out of the land of Egypt.[37]

The men, inspired by what Arch had to say, voted to set up a union, and within two months the Warwickshire Agricultural Labourers' Union had 64 branches and 5,000 members. By June it had reconstituted itself as the National Agricultural Labourers' Union, which by 1874 had 86,000 members and had successfully exerted pressure on employers to raise wages in many counties, in some cases by as much as 25%. Although Arch's organisation was by far the largest, it was seconded by a number of other local unions, raising the combined membership to an estimated 120,000.

These unions, thanks partly to the shrewd use of sympathetic newspaper backing, were able to draw on widespread urban support from other trade unions and from middle-class radicals, many of whom donated funds. The radical wing of the Liberal Party was also very sympathetic, particularly when the unions showed interest in the Liberal land policy which called for the widespread distribution of smallholdings to the landless and the entrenchment of tenant rights. The Liberals were not, of course, motivated entirely by altruistic concern for the plight of the labourers. The sight of social conflict in the heartlands of their Conservative political enemies was balm to their spirit, and leading radical Liberals were quick to appear on platforms with Arch.

The rural unions were anything but revolutionary in either their demands or their tactics, rarely having resort to strikes, for instance. The landowners and employing farmers, on the other hand, after an initial period in which they did nothing, mainly from astonishment, reacted with fury to what they saw as a fundamental challenge to the social order. Possibly they also took heart from the defeat of the Liberals and the return of a Conservative government in 1874. All over southern England union members found themselves threatened with eviction for daring to join such combinations. Some of the actions of farmers, usually abetted by the local clergy, were vindictive in the extreme. In one case a man was refused a coffin for his dead child by the local Poor Law commissioners simply because he was a member of the union. And one boy whose father was secretary of the local branch of the union later recalled: 'I was in the choir when I was thirteen or fourteen. . . it was Christmas morning and the parson told the choir to stay after service. He gave all the men five bob, he give the boys half a crown, and he give me sixpence.'[38]

Farmers and landowners, convinced that 'their' men would never take

The response of many rural labourers to the economic downturn and social distress was to set up unions. Here in 1876 labourers join up en masse to an agricultural union. (Illustrated London News)

such actions on their own, determined to stamp out the unions, and in early 1874 commenced a policy of planned lockouts of union members. By March over 10,000 men in East Anglia had been locked out for refusing to abandon their union membership. *The Times* sent one of its senior correspondents, Frederick Clifford, to cover events, and his reports make fascinating reading. It is clear from these and from handbills and circulars sent around districts by local landowners that it was the challenge the union represented to their 'natural' leadership that they found profoundly shocking, and most deeply resented. To them it was inconceivable that labourers should look to their own union leaders, usually men from outside the district, rather than to those who had traditionally exercised hegemony within it, sometimes for generations. When what they thought of as their reasoned arguments failed to make any impression on their employees, they turned to the coercion of evictions and lockouts until 'the men came to their senses'.

This was a battle the unions could not win. Not only did they suffer from the disadvantages already noted — an isolated and dispersed workforce, omnipresent employers, a rural police force at the beck of the local landowning magistracy — but, more to the point, even at their height the unions could not muster more than one in 10 of the farm labouring workforce to their side. By a combination of the widespread use of non-unionised labour, the vigorous prosecution of those who tried to discourage this practice by picketing and 'rough music', a well-conducted publicity campaign and the threat of eviction, the employers forced the labourers to capitulate. By 1881 the membership of the NALU was down to 15,000. It struggled for some time as a benefit society, but in 1896 it was forced to dissolve from lack of support.

More than anything the revolt of the field was a great collective, existential cry of despair by the rural labourers at the intolerable nature of their situation. When it failed, and despite echoes and local revivals from time to time, they mostly lapsed into a state of apathy. Nevertheless, their revolt had a significant impact, not least in concentrating political attention on the inequities of landholding and agriculture in England. The Agriculture Holdings Act of 1875, notwithstanding that there was a Conservative administration in power, entrenched the rights of tenants (although this was of more use to farmers than those they employed). And it is fair to say that even some Conservatives had their consciences tweaked by the obvious desperation of the rural workers. This was followed by the Ground Game Act in 1880 which began the process of dismantling the game laws, and in 1887 by an Allotments Act which permitted local authorities to set aside areas for lease to small tenants and landless labourers. In combination with the extension of the franchise to rural workers and a slow improvement in wage rates, such initiatives gradually contributed to the amelioration of the living and working conditions of the labourers and their families, although they have always remained a relatively depressed group within the broader workforce, even in prosperous times.*

To most of those writing subsequently on English union or agricultural history, the revolt of the field has been a minor curiosity, of interest but of little relevance. It would have had no relevance at all to New Zealand but for an important happenstance. Among the hundreds at the meeting at Leamington that created Arch's county union in March 1872 was Charles Carter, the New Zealand immigration agent, recruiting immigrants for New Zealand. Following the meeting he interviewed Arch, and was sufficiently impressed to discuss the question of emigration with him at length on two occasions. At this juncture Arch was not enthusiastic about this expedient as a remedy for rural poverty. But as the tide turned against the unions over the next two years he altered his views. From the point of view of New Zealand immigration, this meeting between Carter and Arch was to have important consequences.

---

* This continued to be true when the author was working in association with the United Kingdom Forestry Commission in the 1970s and had many dealings with agricultural workers. The problem of tied accommodation remained a central issue even a century on.

CHAPTER TEN

VOGEL AND THE
IMMIGRANTS 1870–1885

B y 1870 the New Zealand economy was beginning to exhibit one of the most significant of its abiding characteristics — its vulnerability to external forces. Any trading economy is dependent on its market. If it has few markets and a narrow range of commodities for sale, then the effects of this dependence are greatly magnified. As a trading economy with a single significant commodity, wool, and largely a single customer, Britain, New Zealand was particularly vulnerable. As the British economy became increasingly fragile in the late sixties, so did that of New Zealand. By 1869 the value of wool exports was down by a third in relation to 1861, and the value of gold exports was entering a decline. For the next 20 years New Zealand passed through a period labelled 'the long depression' by most economic historians.[1]

Recently, at least one major economic historian has thrown doubt on this orthodoxy, remarking that 'the nature of the "depression" is very indistinct'.[2] He suggests that the only genuine test of the existence of a depression is a decline in real incomes, and that this was not characteristic of the period 1870 to 1890; rather, this was a period in which import prices fell more than export prices, to the significant benefit of consumers. Specific groups may have suffered, he says, particularly in relation to their previous position — for example, fixed assets shifted from their previous owners to lenders as international prices fell. Banks, it is true, found themselves overextended, and some subsequently failed or required government assistance; local manufacturers, too, had problems coping with the competition of cheap imports. But these were the inevitable effects of an economy adjusting to change, and overall New Zealand's economy was sound enough. To call this a depression is to make too much of it.

There is some justification in other statistical data for taking this view over the longer term. It is certainly true that in the two decades after 1870

New Zealand developed comprehensive infrastructures in both telegraphic and rail communications, trebled the *quantity* of wool exported, increased the area of land under cultivation sevenfold, and increased the factory workforce from 7,000 to 25,000. This was also roughly the period which saw the commencement of a trade in frozen meat, butter and cheese which by 1890 had reached an overall value for meat alone of more than £1million, establishing the basis of an export industry which was to carry New Zealand's international trade to high levels of prosperity (interspersed with periodic crises) for the next century.

Nevertheless, the suggestion that there was no depression in the 1870s and eighties is unconvincing for a variety of reasons. In the first place this is an argument about terms. If there is to be a depression only when both import and export prices fall, and the latter less than the former, then there was no depression in the eighties. But this is a rather limited definition of a depression. Secondly, the assertion that import prices fell more than export prices in New Zealand during this period is controversial. Some data suggest that this was not the case, particularly in the seventies.[3] Thirdly, most economic historians would argue that there are other relevant factors to be taken into account besides the simple relationship between commodity costs and the value of exports in assessing whether there is a depression.

One of the best indicators of the level of prosperity within a society is the relationship between disposable income and size and structure of the group spending it (usually families). How they spend this income is an indication of the relative level of prosperity within the economy. The evidence available for the two decades from 1875 suggests that while individual wages for some occupations may have risen, and purchasing power theoretically increased because falling prices meant that the same income bought more, disposable income in fact declined significantly.[4] This is because the circumstances in which people find themselves is more than simply a question of aggregated wage rates.

Recent research cited earlier[5] has shown that the labour market in nineteenth-century New Zealand operated at two levels. A core of permanent employees was supplemented by a large group of temporary employees whose periods of employment varied with the state of the economy, the weather and the harvest. During the eighties in particular the second group increased in size as the time spans between employed periods increased. At the same time the numbers of women and young people employed at significantly less pay than men also expanded as a proportion of the overall workforce. Although we do not know what proportion of the male workforce was unemployed until a census asked this question for the first time in 1893, it is apparent from the statistics available thereafter that what the employment patterns of the two previous decades had meant was a significant decline in family income. The unit doing the spending, in other words, had less money to spend, and this effect was by no means offset by lower prices.

Another set of data supports this conclusion. These are the figures for government revenues from taxation. It is necessary to be aware in reading these figures that there was no income tax until 1891, and that although there were small land taxes from 1879, most government revenue came from flat-rate commodity taxes, usually in the form of *ad valorem* duties on imported items. Between 1874 and 1886 the value of this tax per head for the non-Maori population fell by about 20%.[6] This meant that expenditure by individuals and families declined significantly over that period, for such a drop in value is almost invariably a sign that incomes have fallen and that people are reducing their household expenditure accordingly.

Underlying this is another factor. Human experience alone validates the conclusions drawn from the data. People at all levels of society said at the time that they were finding life difficult and that contrary to their expectations the standard of living they were able to afford fell. It was they who perceived themselves to be experiencing a depression. If they thought so, then very likely they were. Nor were they very pleased to have their aspirations upset in this way. They looked to their politicians to do something about it. The most creative and imaginative of those who tried to deal with this crisis was Julius Vogel, and it was his plan for recovery which was adopted.

THE VOGEL PLAN FOR RECOVERY

Vogel remains one of the most interesting and controversial of all New Zealand political leaders. It seems that no one who knew him was able to remain neutral about him. At about the time of his death in 1899 two histories of New Zealand were published, both written by politicians who had known Vogel well. William Pember Reeves described him in *The Long White Cloud* as 'one of the short list of statesmen whose work has left a permanent mark on the Dominion, and of whom it may be said that almost all he did or tried to do was wise.'[7] The other, Alfred Saunders, in his *History of New Zealand*, describes him in quite different terms as 'a common, ambitious, self-seeking man, who valued no popular rights, no national safeguards, [and] no bulwarks to constitutional freedom'.[8] As a follower of the pseudoscience of phrenology, Saunders went on to say that he thought that the shape of Vogel's cranium showed that he lacked bene-volent moral sentiments. In retrospect Vogel emerges as something of an opportunist. Even his most recent, and sympathetic, biographer has des-cribed him as 'a political adventurer'. But she also adds that he 'contributed more to the development of New Zealand and possessed a greater vision of its place in the Pacific, and in the world, than any other politician of his time,'[9] and there is little doubt that his effect on New Zealand was profound.

Vogel came from a wealthy London Jewish middle-class family. But he had little money of his own, and went out to Victoria in 1852 at the age of 17 to see what he might make of his prospects. In 1861 he followed the gold to Dunedin, not as a miner but as a journalist, a skill he had developed in Australia where he had also tried, unsuccessfully, to enter politics. Later that year he founded the *Otago Daily Times*, which he edited until 1868,

Premier Julius Vogel at the height of his powers and influence in 1874. Without him there would have been no mass immigration in the seventies, and New Zealand would not have the unique culture it has today. (ATL)

gaining a local reputation for his sometimes uncontrolled attacks on local and national governments. In 1863 he entered local politics as the member on the provincial council for Waikouaiti, and eventually became provincial treasurer. In the same year he was elected unopposed as member for Dunedin North in the General Assembly. Six years later he became a minister when William Fox invited him to join his government as colonial treasurer or, as we would now term it, minister of finance.

Vogel was a robust and forthright man, but he had given no previous indications that he was a particularly original or innovative thinker in financial matters, and it was probably his reputation as a responsible treasurer for Otago, and the need for representation in the cabinet from the South Island, which commended him to Fox. However, he had obviously given careful thought to the financial and developmental problems of New Zealand. This much at least was clear when he presented his budget statement to parliament in 1870. In a pre-Keynsian age, his was a bold approach.

What New Zealand needed, he told his parliamentary colleagues, was public works and people. He proposed, therefore, to borrow £10 million over 10 years on the international financial markets, and to use this money to build railways, roads and bridges, and to encourage immigration. The new immigrants would be employed on the public works until they were able to fend independently for themselves. The public works would create prosperity in the short term by spending money within New Zealand and in the longer term by opening up land to settlement and development. The loans and the cost of the interest on them would ultimately be repaid because the government would set aside land reserves in the areas through which the new railways would pass. This land would enhance in value as the area opened up for settlement, and in due course could be sold.

When Vogel resumed his seat, some of his colleagues were quickly on their feet to condemn what he was proposing. The orthodox response of the day to economic downturn was retrenchment, not further borrowing. He had 'never heard of a scheme so wild, so unpractical, and so unpracticable', cried Reader Wood. Others went even further. H. J. Tancred described it as 'the last throw of a desperate gambler' and Thomas Gillies said it would be 'the signal for any man who had any respect for himself or property, to make preparations, as soon as he could, to raise a reasonable amount of money, to get quit of his property, and to go out of it.'[10] Others, however, were enthusiastic, and the heat of Vogel's critics was cooled by the subsequent election which made it clear that the voters substantially agreed with him.

By 1875 £2 million of borrowed money had been spent on railways alone. By the end of the decade a total of £20 million had been borrowed to finance these and a variety of other schemes. By then there were 1,136 miles of operational railway in place where there had been virtually none in 1870. This included a trunk line of 400 miles between Christchurch and the Bluff.[11] Large sums had also been spent on the acquisition of Maori land for settlement. Along the way to these achievements, Vogel had become premier in 1873; successfully abolished the provincial governments in 1876 as an unwarranted impediment to his schemes; and been knighted for his accomplishments, notwithstanding his rather shady personal involvement in at least one of the railway ventures.

But if these achievements seem spectacular, they pale beside Vogel's endeavours in the field of immigration. Between 1870 and 1885 the non-Maori population of New Zealand increased from 248,400 to 575,226.[12] Much of this increase was attributable to incoming settlers. More than 200,000 people entered New Zealand as immigrants between 1870 and 1880. The peak year was 1874, when an astonishing 43,965 arrived.[13] This outcome occurred not only because large sums of money were spent on assisting emigrants to come to New Zealand; it was also because of the relationship which had developed between the New Zealand immigration agents engaged by the agent-general, Isaac Featherston, and Joseph Arch's agricultural union.[14]

The Immigration and Public Works Act of 1870, through which Vogel enacted his programme, made provision for the first time for the appointment of an agent-general to represent the New Zealand government in Britain. This was not a particularly innovative move; the Australian colonies had done the same some years previously. But it was clear that if immigration was to be one of the cornerstones of policy, there had to be someone in Britain in overall charge of it. This did not necessarily mean that the provinces should not continue with their own initiatives. Although an amending Act of 1871 incorporated the existing provincial offices into the new office of the agent-general, Canterbury, Otago and Taranaki still appointed agents from time to time, although they usually ended up working for the agent-general. After some debate the government chose the long-serving Wellington politician Dr Isaac Featherston for the new position, and he took up his duties in August 1871.[15]

Featherston was initially to have access to £1 million for immigration purposes, but he quickly discovered that his was no enviable task. Baldly instructed by Wellington at the end of 1871 that he was to dispatch 8,000 emigrants for railway construction purposes, he consulted Vogel, who was in London negotiating further loans, and they engaged the services of John Brogden and Sons, international railways contractors, to send skilled navvies to New Zealand at a fare of £15 a head. This money would be recovered from the men after their arrival in New Zealand. As it transpired, this was not a simple matter, and two years later, after sending only about 2,000 labourers, Brogdens abandoned their contract.

In August 1873, James Billings, the deputy manager for Brogdens in New Zealand, explained his company's actions to an inquiry into immigration set up largely by Vogel's enemies in the Legislative Council.[16] The Brogdens labourers had been indiscriminately mixed on the emigrant ships with other emigrants recruited directly by officials working for Featherston. The navvies quickly discovered that the others had been required to contribute £5, and in the case of single women nothing at all. Understandably irritated by this differential treatment, many of the navvies refused to honour their contracts when they arrived in the colony. To compound the problem, said Billings, the work they had been promised was often not immediately available, so they had to make other arrangements until it was. Once settled in a job, they could see no reason to return to railways construction. This was especially so in respect of those who were not navvies at all but rural labourers who were neither trained for nor suited to railway construction work, a highly specialised occupation. The upshot had been that many of the men — in the case of one group sent to Otago, 95 out of 100 — no longer worked for Brogdens, but had become permanently engaged in farming and other work. When the contractors attempted to sue the men for the passage money, they discovered that it cost more to do this than the money they were able to recover.

Billings went on to give some more general evidence as to the reasons why many emigrants were unwilling to choose New Zealand in preference to other destinations. In particular he instanced a report, sourced from Melbourne and widely carried in London and provincial newspapers two months previously, 'respecting a threatened Maori outbreak', with the result that many people who had indicated a wish to come to New Zealand had withdrawn and had given as their reason 'that they were not going out to that country to be murdered by a lot of niggers'.[17] Billings was, in fact, identifying a problem which Featherston's immigration agents had encountered again and again in trying to recruit settlers for New Zealand. The country was little known; there was a temporary labour shortage in Britain; and those who would emigrate preferred the shorter journey to the better-known United States. The government, becoming desperate, even gave favourable consideration to Chinese immigration, but abandoned the idea in the face of vigorous opposition from the provinces and from workers already in New Zealand.[18] The agent-general then turned more fruitfully to Germany and Scandinavia, and some thousands of immigrants from those countries entered New Zealand over the next few years.[19]

Notwithstanding, Featherston was not having much success in fulfilling Wellington's requirements. By June 1872 he had been able to send only 2,758 immigrants, and for the full year 6,292. The colonial secretary, Lord Kimberley, aware that New Zealand was trying to recruit large numbers, was scathing in his sarcasm. 'It is curious,' he minuted to Governor Bowen on 27 March 1872, 'to compare hypothesis with fact: the hypothesis being that there are a vast number of half starved Englishmen who would make good colonists; in fact paupers are utterly unfit for colonists, and those that are fit are generally well employed at home, and don't want to go abroad.'[20] Events were, however, shortly to confound his lordship.

If his initial results were disappointing, Featherston had not been wasting his time nor the government's money. He had, indeed, gone to considerable trouble to find ways not only to reduce the cost of transporting immigrants but to improve the arrangements on board the vessels. One of the difficulties he had encountered from the outset was the virtual monopoly of shipping to New Zealand held by the Shaw Savill Company. Although he tried as much as possible to use the New Zealand Shipping Company as an alternative, its operation was too small for the mass emigration he was being asked to arrange. In the end Featherston fell back on the expedient of chartering ships as he needed them. This arrangement was more flexible, but in having to deal with a multiplicity of owners his work became more complex and he had to keep a close eye on the accommodation arrangements for steerage passengers in particular, because these could vary widely depending on the owner of the vessel.

Featherston set out comprehensive arrangements in the contracts he drew up with shippers. These were in general somewhat better than the provisions of the Passenger Acts. On top of the water supplied for cooking purposes, steerage passengers were to get 3 quarts a day (4 in the tropics together with 6 oz of lime juice a week). They were to have each week 3 1/2 lb of meat, 2 lb 10 oz of biscuit, 2 lb of potatoes, a quantity of oatmeal and of flour, and specified minimum amounts of butter, carrots, peas, onions, salt, raisins, tea and coffee.[21] Special additional rations, including eggs and preserved milk, were provided for children on a scale according to their ages. This scale was further improved after 1875.

Featherston and his staff often found on inspection of the vessels that although the steerage compartments complied in strict terms with the legislated minimum requirements, they had inadequate ventilation, were overcrowded, lacked adequate toilet and washing facilities, and seemed to have made arrangements for the sick on the assumption that everybody would be healthy. As early as 1872 New Zealand officials had alerted Featherston in very blunt terms to the existence of problems:

> Under the present system it would appear evident that the contractors endeavour to work to the greatest possible economy of space, layout and provisions, satisfied if they can manage to keep within the letter of their contract and the Passenger Act, and give a bare or superficial compliance with the regulations of the Emigration Commissioners. This course naturally results in what has been justly complained of — insufficient ventilation, overcrowded space, incomplete working apparatus, incompetent cooks, badly placed hospitals, ill fixed fittings, and many other defects which do not become apparent until the actual experience of the voyage shall have discovered what is wrong, but any one of which may . . . inflict much discomfort or produce great mortality during the voyage.[22]

Consequently, a system was instituted by which the fitting of the ships was subject to daily inspection by a staff member from the agent-general's office. Aware of the many complaints made about the standard of the depots at which the emigrants were assembled prior to embarkation, Featherston also hired a separate emigration barracks at Blackwall near the Shaw Savill dock for the New Zealand immigrants.

All in all, his efforts were considerable. This did not, of course, stop people from criticising him, particularly about the numbers he was able to send. Among those who gave evidence to the same 1873 inquiry which had taken evidence from the aggrieved Mr Billings was James Macandrew, the superintendent of Otago province, who may well still have been smarting from the general government's supersession of his province's immigration activities. If the government had stayed with the previous system, he said, they would have trebled the number of immigrants by now. Instead, he claimed, the agent-general had dismantled the arrangements his province has so painstakingly put together, and significant numbers of prospective Scottish immigrants had been lost as a result. He differed entirely from the view expressed by the colonial secretary; in his estimation there were plenty of available emigrants. Regrettably, the agent-general was attracting the wrong type. What were needed were self-made men, 'living epistles of the doctrine they are preaching'. As to the Brogdens immigrants, 'I remember feeling in my mind,' he told the Hon. Mr Waterhouse, who had asked him how he compared present immigrants with those of the past, 'that I could almost rather have dispensed with the immigration policy altogether than have had such a ship-load in the country.'[23]

His views were shared, up to a point, by William Rolleston, the superintendent of Canterbury. If the central government had not interfered and had left matters in the hands of the provinces, there would have been fewer problems, Rolleston thought. In particular the recruitment of immigrants should have been based on the previous practice of recommendation. This was a system whereby any person who was living in New Zealand could nominate a person known to them in Britain for emigration to New Zealand and, if they wished, guarantee the passage money. Local authorities knew best what sort of people they needed, Rolleston told the committee, and handing the responsibility to the central government ensured only that those who came were not the best available.

As it happened, Featherston was highly critical of the nomination system. Often his agents found that the person nominated had no desire to emigrate, or had already done so to some other destination. In many cases they could not find the person at all. All this wasted a good deal of his office's time. Rather than rely on nominations, Featherston had set up a comprehensive network of more than 200 resident agents throughout Britain both to publicise New Zealand and to recruit would-be immigrants. He had been criticised for this too by Macandrew, who thought that peripatetic agents were much more suitable. Otago had consistently used this method, sending men to Britain who had, themselves, successfully made the transition to the new life, who knew the colony well and were known in the localities they visited. Whether Macandrew's view was correct was by that time no longer relevant, because by 1873 Featherston's methods had begun to bear fruit.

In the middle of 1873 he had heard from a Dr Bakewell who had travelled not only to New Zealand as a surgeon but to Trinidad as well. Bakewell pointed out that one of the disadvantages the most distant colonies experienced in attracting immigrants was the additional expense of the outfit for a much longer journey than to the Americas. Trinidad had grasped the nettle and offered free immigration and free outfitting for the voyage. From that time it had experienced no difficulty in finding the number of immigrants sought. Others had pointed out that most of the sorts of people New Zealand needed to attract could not, by themselves, save up the money required even for a subsidised passage. Featherston was moving inexorably to the conclusion that to get the number of settlers the New Zealand government was demanding, free passages would have to be offered.

In New Zealand, Vogel, premier from April and minister of immigration from October, had arrived at the same conclusion. He instructed an astonished Featherston to send a further 20,000 immigrants, and authorised him to give them free passage if he thought it appropriate. That Featherston was able to comply was partly because reports of a depression in the United States and Canada were having an effect on emigration to North America. But the crucial factor in New Zealand's reaping the benefits of this was the relationship Featherston's agents had developed with Joseph Arch and the rural unions in Britain. Arch and his colleagues, faced with the developing intransigence of rural employers who had begun their locking-out campaign, were now more favourably disposed towards emigration than previously.

In the middle of 1873 the executive committee of the National Agricultural Labourers' Union addressed itself to the government of New Zealand. In their letter they set out the plight of the rural labourers, their poor expectations in Britain and the desirability of emigration as a means of improving their situation. But the letter also went on to point out emigration was impossible without the means. Should the government of New Zealand feel able to extend assistance, then the union would do all in its power to assist at the British end.[24] There was not much response to this in the first instance, but when Vogel became minister the change was immediate. 'Suggest try obtain cooperation organisation Joseph Arch connected with', he cabled Featherston. He also wrote to Arch confirming the availability of free passages. This letter, especially after it was published in the union newspaper in November, must have had a significant impact. That same month the *Labourers' Union Chronicle* carried an editorial which began, 'Not a farm labourer in England but should rush from the old doomed country to such a paradise as New Zealand,' and ended, 'Away, then, farm labourers, away! New Zealand is the promised land for you; and the Moses that will lead you is ready.' Where previously Featherston had been struggling to dispatch a few hundred emigrants, between December 1873 and February 1874 he sent 4,973 in 16 ships. For the next several years the stream of emigrants headed for New Zealand was almost continuous.

The New Zealand authorities also paid for Christopher Holloway, an executive member of the union, to travel to New Zealand with a party of emigrants he had recruited, and to travel throughout the country to report back on the desirability of New Zealand as a destination. Holloway spent most of 1874 touring New Zealand and speaking extensively to those who had come out as immigrants in the previous few years. His reports appeared regularly in union publications in England, and after his return in mid 1875 he took up employment with the New Zealand agent-general as principal peripatetic recruiter, a position he filled most effectively for the next five years. In 1874 over 11,000 emigrants received assistance to come to New Zealand; in 1875 this rose to 28,580. Nothing like these levels could have been achieved without the active support of the unions, which naturally ensured that it was largely their members who took advantage of the subsidised passages.

Some British newspapers were initially inclined to scoff at these efforts. *The Times* reminded its readers in November 1873 that organising large parties of emigrants required some skill, and rather sniffily wondered if this was perhaps beyond the capabilities of those such as Arch. The same newspaper also questioned the ability of farm labourers to adapt to new circumstances in the colonies, and warned both the government and farmers of New Zealand against too enthusiastically welcoming such people.[25] Then, as 1874 passed and the numbers leaving continued to climb, farmers and landowners began to become alarmed. Their best and most skilled workers were leaving their districts. In at least one case, that of the Cullimore family, the employers enlisted the help of the police to chase after the departing workers, and had them arrested and returned in the hope of preventing them from going, although to no avail in the event.[26] Employers, landowners and in some cases the local clergy gave currency to reports that all was not as had been painted in New Zealand, or arranged for the publication of accounts of the loss by fire of the ship *Cospatrick* in 1874. Sometimes their actions were petty in the extreme. These included refusing permission for the use of village halls for emigration meetings or declining to issue certificates attesting to good character. But the leakage of skilled labourers continued, possibly because of as much as despite this opposition.

The government agents also made a special effort to recruit in Ireland. This was a period of considerable political ferment in that country, of the Fenian agitation and the Irish Home Rule League, leading to the passing of the Land Act of 1881 which finally gave Irish tenants some security of tenure. A decade earlier, with no clear indication of how it all might end, many Irish men and women preferred to leave. In the 1870s over half a million people left Ireland for good and Featherston was determined to capture some of these emigrants for New Zealand. Ironically, in the light of his being, as provincial superintendent, the target of a protest meeting a decade earlier for allegedly instructing the provincial immigration agents that they were not to recruit Irish settlers, it was Featherston who was responsible for opening an office in Belfast in mid 1872, and another in

Dublin towards the end of the year. In all, Ireland contributed about 25,000 immigrants to New Zealand during the 1870s.[27]

In 1875 Vogel again visited England to raise more loans, £1.5 million of which would be devoted to further immigration. He took the opportunity, rather to the irritation of Featherston as the two men did not get on, to reorganise some aspects of the immigration work of the agent-general's office. Characteristically he also prepared a comprehensive report on some shortcomings he had identified in the arrangements for emigrants.[28] Among his detailed concerns about nomination, shipping arrangements, the need to establish an agency in Scotland, and the undesirability of German and Scandinavian immigrants when so many English were available, he particularly dwelt on two matters.

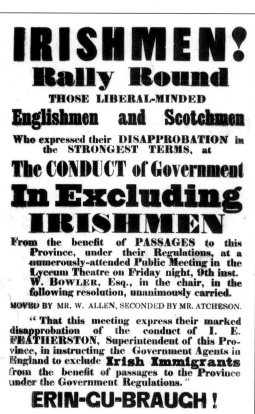

The pressure to recruit was sufficiently great for the agents to seek Irish immigrants, something they had avoided hitherto except in the Protestant north. This was an embarrassment to the agent-general Isaac Featherston, who as superintendent of Wellington province had opposed Irish immigration in earlier decades. (ATL)

The first was the adequacy — or, in the light of some recent disasters, inadequacy — of the medical arrangements prior to embarkation, and especially the danger of disease in the emigration barracks. Places in the Blackwall barracks were not always available, so many emigrants were allocated to general emigration barracks or specialist boarding establishments while they awaited the departure of their ship. Here they mixed with others who were bound for a wide range of destinations. Just how loathsome the conditions in these barracks could be is apparent from a later report by F. D. Bell who was agent-general in the 1880s. Writing to his friend William Rolleston in 1883, he remarked:

> I don't suppose you ever saw an arrival day of a cargo of men, women, girls, and children assembled for a ship. Some of 'em swarm with vermin and have never known what it is to be without lice in their life: others come with itch from head to foot; others smelling of every conceivable ordure. Don't imagine for a moment that these things are 'contracted' in the Depot; they are brought there. Yah! it is at times horrible beyond words.[29]

The medical examination which intending immigrants were required to undergo prior to being accepted for a passage was often perfunctory, to say the least. From time to time there was an inquiry; in the course of one, evidence was taken that as many as 400 passengers might be seen by a doctor in the space of an hour. A doctor who had travelled on a number of American emigrant ships was so disgusted by this that he wrote to the *New York Times*, describing how two doctors 'stand behind a little window, and when the people come before them they say "Are you quite well? Show your tongue", and in the meantime their ticket is stamped.' [30] This was in mid century and the conditions of emigration to America were notoriously lax, but matters had not improved much one or even two decades later.

The spread of infectious disease was as likely to happen on ships bound for New Zealand in the 1870s as on those bound for the Americas in 1850s, as an article in the *Lancet* in 1873 made clear. [31] Indeed, long sea voyages remained dangerous and unhealthy long into the age of steam. Although it was not necessary to go to the lengths demanded by, say, an insurance company before a policy was offered, Vogel nevertheless considered that more careful medical examinations needed to be undertaken immediately prior to boarding, to supplement those already insisted upon before an immigrant was accepted. These would ensure the earlier examinations had been properly carried out and would identify any problems which might have subsequently arisen. If there were any problems, then the passage should be refused, although this could be very harsh on the would-be emigrant family who had abandoned their previous life, and who would then be cast adrift without access to the new one for which they had hoped. It is understandable in such circumstances that emigrants often tried to conceal illness, especially in children.

Vogel's second concern was with cost recovery. Possibly he was already aware of the developing criticism of his policy of bringing more and more people to New Zealand when unemployment was becoming a worrying problem. 'I believe the time has come,' he minuted, 'when immigrants should pay some portion of their passage money. The colony has incurred expense for the immigration to such an extent as to make it reasonable to suppose that those who have had their passages paid have left behind them a number of relatives or friends, who, on their representations, should be glad to follow.'[32] But he was also aware of the difficulties associated with demanding money sums prior to departure from those who could not pay. Instead he suggested a system of promissory notes for £7, payable after arrival in New Zealand.

This was the same system as the provinces had operated, and it is interesting to learn how much of this money the government expected to recoup, particularly as the authorities in New Zealand might easily lose track of a new arrival. Rolleston had been asked about this in 1873 and had given some figures. Up to 1870, Canterbury had paid out well over £200,000 in passage money for immigrants. About a third of this had been recouped by payments prior to departure from Britain. Of the rest, about £26,000 remained uncollected and the province had more or less written this off as a bad debt. If this was typical, then something like nine out of 10 immigrants repaid the money invested in their passage — quite a high level of recovery. Rolleston calculated that if all the money had been collected, the average cost of bringing an immigrant to Canterbury had been £4 14s 9d. This was quite a bargain if the earlier calculation of the Otago authorities that an immigrant added £2 or more each year to the revenue through consumption taxes was still valid.

From 1876 the government began to demand fewer immigrants, and then to confine the numbers to about 5,000 a year. But the agent-general found that the tap, once turned on, was not so easy to turn off. In the year to June, 16,607 were sent. In the following year a further 13,000 assisted passages were given, and in 1878–79, 8,000. This may have had something to do with the fact that in mid 1876 Vogel moved to Britain to take up the coveted position of agent-general following the death of Featherston. His principal motive to do so was ostensibly to negotiate a new series of loans in a market which was growing unresponsive to the demands of the New Zealand government. He also said that he could most effectively oversee further immigration initiatives from London rather than Wellington. Most commentators are agreed, however, that his real reason was the growing unpopularity of his policies at home. The frantic spending and the arrival of thousands of immigrants had not had quite the effect Vogel had hoped. New Zealand remained in the doldrums; export prices continued to fall; and unemployment continued to rise. By 1876 public debt had doubled to £18 million; the government account was showing a significant deficit, despite revenues having more than doubled in the previous five years; and the electors were beginning to look more kindly on Vogel's critics. It was time to be off.

Vogel remained committed to his immigration policy and found encouragement from James Macandrew who had become the responsible minister in the Grey government of 1877–79. This was ironic in the light of his criticism of the Vogel schemes to the 1873 committee. But the period of mass migration had peaked and except for another short period of enthusiasm in 1883 there was little for Vogel to do in respect of emigration except to vet applications and follow up on nominations. From 1880 the emigration administration in the agent-general's office was wound down. This is not to suggest that the Vogel policy was a failure. But a policy which had looked so straightforward as a formula for getting the country back on the move in 1870 had proved to be more complex than its author had imagined.

In retrospect, it is clear that many of the problems encountered by Vogel's policies were beyond his control. He could neither determine export prices nor anticipate the effects of a British domestic downturn on one of its dependent economies, although a more prudent politician might have weighed these factors more carefully before he leaped. And in one area he was thwarted by his political opponents. It was crucial to his policy that lands should be retained in reserve for later sale to pay back borrowings and meet interest charges. But the landowning and speculative interests which mostly controlled the upper house, the Legislative Council,[33] and the provincial assemblies where control of land policy was mainly located, had prevented this by refusing to pass legislation to effect it. They did this from one of the oldest of all human motivations. If any profit was to be made from the land which was opened up by the new roads and railways, then they wanted it for themselves. They certainly did not intend the government to have it.

The means were at hand for them to achieve this. The expansion of credit at relatively low interest rates, the consequence of the borrowing policies which Vogel initiated, encouraged the banks to respond liberally towards those who wanted to borrow, even when this was patently for speculative purposes. Indeed, the owners of the Bank of New Zealand, the largest bank in the colony, maintained special facilities for precisely this purpose and extended the same privilege to their Auckland friends.[34]

In 1870 an important legal case had established the rights of banks to take title over property held as security, and they began either to compete with the loan and mortgage companies which had hitherto carried out most of the borrowing and lending or to set these up themselves. These offered premium interest rates and attracted significant overseas investment, usually through London holding companies set up for the purpose. This served to perpetuate artificially the boom initiated by Vogel's borrowing programme beyond the retrenchment upon which the government had now embarked. The economy appeared prosperous enough, and business confidence was buoyant, but the reality was rather more fragile than appearances suggested. By 1878 the banks had extended their credit by £10 million over the level it had reached in 1872. The management of these loans and advances has been described by at least one study as '[betraying] in many cases utter recklessness. The commonly accepted checks were disregarded. The banks became largely land mortgage companies, advancing with the utmost liberality on fixed securities as though the need of liquid assets in banks had passed away.'[35]

During the 1870s, and especially as it became increasingly apparent that the provinces would soon be abolished, the provincial councils hastened to divest themselves of their landholdings, particularly in the south, and often at virtual giveaway prices. Those who had money or could borrow it on easy terms bought land, and land values accelerated. A subsequently developed index of these values shows a progressive increase from 1872. Values had doubled by 1875, and by 1878 had increased eight times.[36] This was paralleled by a concentration of ownership. By 1882 about 1% of landowners were in possession of 32% of the assessed values of landholdings. About 250 people or companies owned seven and a half million acres.[37] This concentration of ownership had already caused protests as the depression deepened, not only from those who were unemployed but from those who wished to move onto smallholdings and found that much of the suitable land was already owned by someone else. When it was available, its price had often been so inflated that they could not afford to buy it.

These values could not be sustained by the productive capacity of the land itself — always the final arbiter of what land is worth financially. This tended to be hidden during the seventies by such factors as an increase in production of some commodities, the development of some new exports such as wheat (although this did not last much beyond 1882), and a steep and permanent fall in international freight rates (always an important consideration for a dependent economy such as that of New Zealand).[38] Many landowners continued to borrow to cover the difference between their income and their outgoings in the optimistic expectation that this situation must improve sooner or later. But in 1879 there was a banking crisis in Britain when the City of Glasgow Bank collapsed. Thanks both to this and to an expansion of economic activity in Victoria which made that a more attractive field for investment, credit in New Zealand collapsed about the same time. Strenuous efforts, especially in Auckland, to replace this lost credit in the early 1880s were ultimately unsuccessful. Many landowners, finding that they could not go on, then discovered that their assets could not be realised at a level which enabled them to repay their loans, because the security upon which these were based — the land itself — was overvalued. Nor, when they defaulted on their loans, could the banks afford to repossess them without heavy loss. Much of the financial activity which had stimulated the economy was thus brought to a standstill, with consequential rising levels of bankruptcies and unemployment.

Business and governments responded in various ways. Between 1880 and the turn of the century, for example, manufacturing expanded significantly. But this was largely on the basis of depressed wages and sweated conditions. Vogel, who returned briefly to government in the mid eighties, tried to create employment through new public works schemes and the organisation of labour bureaux to assist the unemployed to find jobs. These efforts were not effective, especially as there was retrenchment in government expenditure, particularly following the election of the Atkinson government in 1887.

One of the most significant responses, as it turned out, was that of William Davidson, general manager of the New Zealand and Australian Land Company. Although this company was directly affected by the British banking collapse of the late eighties, Davidson, who knew New Zealand well from some years' practical experience as an estate manager here, set about trading out of the company's financial difficulties by identifying a new export commodity — frozen meat and dairy produce — and organising its preparation and shipment. Recognising the immense potential for this trade in the British market, he reorganised the British end of the transport system to cope with it. He was, of course, inventing a whole new basis for the New Zealand export trade, but that was in the longer term, and had to wait for the breaking up of the big estates into smaller farms, the development in particular of dairying technology and the creation of state-based farming credit in the nineties to bear fruit fully.[39]

In the meantime, many of those who had come to New Zealand as immigrants in the confident expectation that they would improve their prospects were finding their hopes sadly disappointed. In 1880 the government had instructed Vogel as agent-general that he was to offer no more free or assisted passages to New Zealand. The country could not absorb any more workers, and nothing should be done to encourage them to come. This effective halt to the initiatives of the previous decade showed up at once in the immigration figures. In 1881, total immigrants entering New Zealand fell to 9,688. Although nearly 150,000 immigrants entered New Zealand in the decade to 1890, a new phenomenon appeared. Almost as many left as came. In some years, notably 1888 when the net outflow reached 9,175, these exceeded those arriving. Net immigration for the decade was actually closer to 30,000. [40] This was a very different situation from that which had greeted incoming settlers between 1850 and 1880. The response of those settlers to changing times, and the response of those who came in the decade to 1890, was to have a significant influence on the subsequent development of New Zealand's political culture. And all of those who came between 1870 and 1885 — in many ways the most significant period of emigration to New Zealand, certainly in terms of numbers — were to contribute their motivations for coming and their collective experience of immigration to that development. We should therefore turn, penultimately, to that experience.

CHAPTER ELEVEN

THE LAST FAREWELL

Speaking of the emigrant vessels of the later part of the nineteenth century, one of the principal historians of New Zealand immigration has said, with considerable understatement, '[a]t the best the ships were not attractive'.[1] We are able to judge conditions on ships in this period more completely than during any other because, as already noted, when the central government took over the principal responsibility for immigration, government immigration officers met every incoming ship and filed reports, many of which were subsequently published as parliamentary papers. Undoubtedly the bulk of these were written to a rote formula to suggest that all was as might have been hoped. That of Daniel Pollen, reporting the arrival of the *Parsee* in Auckland on 8 May 1873, is fairly typical:

> The ship was found clean and in good order, and everything had been done for the comfort and health of the passengers; the compartments for the married people, as for the single women and men, were well ventilated. The condensing machine which was on board was not required to be used, there having been sufficient fresh water on board for all purposes; the provisions were examined, and proved to be of excellent quality. There was not a shadow of complaint on board; all the immigrants spoke in the highest praise of the captain, surgeon, and ship's officers.[2]

But if there had been an obvious serious problem during the voyage, or the immigration officer was confronted with a barrage of complaints from the passengers, there would be an inquiry. Even when this was not the case, some officials could be quite waspish in their observations. There are sufficient reports of this type extant to make it clear that all was not always well on board. Pollen's colleague Maurice O'Rorke, for instance, in passing his report to the agent-general in London in June 1873, described the *Wild Duck* on its arrival as manifestly unfit for the conveyance of emigrants, and fitted and provisioned with that strict regard for economy, and carelessness for the health and comfort of the passengers, which distinguish Messrs Shaw Saville and Co. The leakage of the top sides to be expected in so old a vessel kept the beds in the married people and single women's compartment almost constantly wet; and with regard to the hospital arrangements, no-one who has inspected them can avoid agreeing with Dr Driver when he says (*vide* his report herewith) that he was 'quite disgusted with them' and that 'they were not fit for the purpose at all'.[3]

O'Rorke went on roundly to criticise those responsible for the arrangements, and concluded: 'I would impress upon you the fact that letters written home by immigrants who have been made miserable throughout the passage

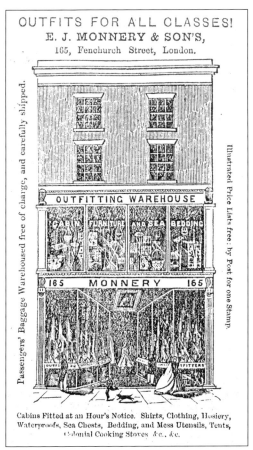

By the seventies emigration was a well-organised business, with its own specialist outfitters, as this shop in Fenchurch Street, London, demonstrates.
(ATL)

by causes entirely remediable, do more to retard emigration than all the costly advertisements, peripatetic lecturers, and highly paid agents do to advance it.' Whether passengers sailed on a satisfactory or an unsatisfactory ship was still very much a lottery.

In this regard the letters and diaries of emigrants make fascinating reading a century and more later. It is clear from these that many emigrants — and not only those in the steerage — continued to find the voyage a disillusionment and an ordeal. This process often began before the vessel put to sea. Writing from Plymouth in 1879, Charlotte Couchman told her family how 'we were rather surprised when we got to the depot, they had hundreds more like us waiting to embark but oh, how different to our nice little home at Hastings.' Three days later she complained that they had not been allowed outside the barracks except to go to church, and, worse, 'not allowed any beer nor get the chance to buy any. So now we know what it is to be mixed up with all sorts of people and no means of getting away . . . so we are obliged to make the best of it.' [4] Her complaints seem to have been well founded. A previous inquiry into the condition of the *Scimitar* on arrival in 1874 had found that 'the depot at Plymouth is said to be damp, the bedding in many cases being damp. The situation is not a healthy one. The accommodation in the way of fireplaces is too limited, and the front of the stoves usually occupied by babies' clothes drying. The depot at the time was overcrowded. The weather was very rainy and the emigrants going in and out got wet. Colds and catarrhs were prevalent in consequence.' [5]

Regular inspections more often than not revealed the depots to be filthy and damp, but there was little the officers of the agent-general could do, except complain to the management or owners. This was obviously to little avail. In 1883 in the course of an inquiry into an outbreak of infectious disease on the *Oxford,* there was again an inspection of the depot at Plymouth. This found that: 'The establishment was faulty in various respects: the sleeping accommodation was described by the married witnesses as being absurdly small, and the filthy condition of the bedding almost incredible; vermin appear to have abounded; a proper supply of bed clothing for the existing cold weather was not forthcoming; and a considerable amount of unnecessary harshness displayed in the management, more particularly of the women and children.' [6]

Nor were conditions at sea much better during the seventies and beyond. There was still little privacy. Elizabeth Allbon, travelling steerage to Sydney with her husband in 1879, found to her disgust that 'our bunks are all fitted up between decks not private at all side by side and just a curtain hung in front'.[7] Vermin, including lice, were commonly present,[8] and rats were endemic to all ships at all periods. Charlotte Couchman noted that '[the men on watch] say the rats do run at such a rate that it is fun — but not for us. I laid in bed and found something running about over me and when I looked out of the clothes there was a great rat jumping from one bunk to another.'[9] And the absence of adequate water closets made the stench almost indescribable. James Badland, a cabin passenger, in his evidence to the inquiry into the *England* in 1872, was one of the few to make an attempt. 'The emigrants themselves were very dirty,' he said of his fellow passengers in the steerage, and their quarters emanated 'a very unpleasant smell so bad I do not wish to meet the same again — it often reached the poop cabin and was so bad that I was obliged to go on deck. I do not know what the smell came from, and it continued throughout the whole voyage more or less.'[10]

Food standards also continued to be a problem, despite the theoretical improvement in the scale of victualling. There were so many complaints when the *Halcione* berthed in Wellington in 1872 that there was a full inquiry. Ralph Crawford, speaking on behalf of the complainants, deposed that 'on five occasions the pork served out to the single men's compartment was putrid and unfit to eat'.[11] He had complained to the captain to no avail. Other standard supplies such as molasses were not available, and food was returned uncooked if the passengers refused to tip the cook regularly. His evidence was confirmed by two other steerage passengers, Robert Porteus and Edwin Hibbett, the latter complaining that food was often burned and that his children had been denied the dried milk to which they were entitled. This evidence was vigorously denied by the doctor on board, who claimed to have eaten the meat himself and found it 'perfectly wholesome' although he admitted that it was 'slightly tainted'. The purser, Henry Innis, thought the complaints exaggerated, and he endorsed the evidence of the doctor, but he was obviously bound to do this as an employee of the company. This inquiry ended inconclusively.

It is also clear that some emigrants could be exasperating to those charged with the unenviable task of moving hundreds of people confined in a very small space over long distances and with no chance to revictual. Anne Timpson on the *Langstone* in 1886 refused to eat or allow her children to eat salt meat (which was a staple item), and was indignant when the cook refused to bake bread especially for her as a replacement without an additional payment. When she complained to the captain of the food, 'he says we are all too dainty'.[12]

Most passengers put up with hardships as part of the price exacted by the journey, merely noting them as an inconvenience in their journals or letters. Charlotte Couchman found the water distilled from sea water unpleasantly salty to drink, and 'we don't get any beer only the women that have children sucking have a pint of stout in two days and a glass of port if they are not well'. But like most passengers she continued to think the hardship was worth it. Half way through the voyage, and despite her misgivings at the point of embarkation, Couchman described herself (she was 50 — an unusually advanced age for an emigrant) as 'a foolish old woman to go from England, but I don't wish myself back again yet.'[13]

Sea voyages also continued to be hazardous. The *Surat,* bound for Otago in 1873 with 270 immigrants aboard, struck a rock on the inhospitable coast near Catlins and began to sink. Luckily she could be run ashore, so no one aboard was lost, although they suffered considerable privation until they were discovered and rescued. Sometimes hazards were created by the passengers' own unfamiliarity with the requirements of a sailing vessel. Mary Brooke, travelling with her husband Edwin on the *Piako* to Lyttelton in 1879, recounted how '[o]ne of the passengers in the main hatch where the third class married people are, opened one of the port holes to let in a little fresh air, and the sea being somewhat rough when the ship gave a dip on the side it came in and nearly flooded that part of the vessel.'[14] The captain, understandably perturbed, called the passengers together and informed them that a ship had been lost off the English coast not long before for this reason. If anyone did it again he would put them in irons and they would be prosecuted on arrival in New Zealand.

FIRE AND DISEASE

The two great fears of those travelling by sea at this period were, however, fire and disease. Such worries were very real. In 1882 while Frances Thomson was travelling with her surgeon husband to Rockhampton, there was a cry that fire had broken out.

> At once panic took place, men, women and children rushed madly about, shrieking and crying. The noise was deafening, women fainting on all sides, little children neglected by their mothers, went about with their little hands clasped begging someone to save them. About fifty of the single men at once tore the covers off the lifeboats and got into them, ready to save themselves.[15]

This turned out to be a false alarm occasioned by the mainsail collapsing onto the deck, but the captain was so annoyed he held a shipboard inquiry and put the passenger who had started the panic in irons for a week.

Unfortunately, not all alarms were false. In October 1878 the *Piako* left Plymouth with 281 emigrants on board, bound for Timaru and Lyttelton. On 11 November, 200 miles from the nearest landfall, the port of Pernambuco in Brazil, the ship was discovered to be on fire. Captain William Boyd ordered the beating to fire drill, played the hoses on the affected areas of deck, flew his distress flag and sent a man aloft to see if any vessels were nearby. By good fortune, in those pre-radio days, the *Loch Doon* was not far away, and was able to take the passengers off while Boyd and his crew continued to fight the fire. Both vessels sailed in company to Pernambuco and the fire was extinguished. The vessel was extensively damaged, however, and the passengers had to be kept on shore for some time and transferred to other ships bound for New Zealand as they were diverted to the port for the purpose.[16] The subsequent inquiry pointed out that but for the prompt action of Boyd and the proximity of another vessel, this might easily have ended in a terrible disaster.

The *Piako* seems to have been particularly accident prone. Mary Brooke was on its next voyage and noted especially that fire drills were practised every Saturday at 12.30. Notwithstanding, there was a fire on this voyage too, on Christmas Day 1879. Alerted by the cry of fire, she

> soon bundled the children up in blankets and hastened up on deck and never shall I forget the sight which greeted our eyes. Large volumes of smoke were issuing from the second class hatchway and the sailors were busily engaged with the fire hose attempting to put out the fire. Several of the second class passengers were in bed and so quickly did the fire spread that it was with difficulty that they escaped with their lives.[17]

She described how a child was rescued by the heroic persistence of a sailor, who several times fought his way into the cabin through dense smoke and got the child out, and the coolness of Captain Boyd. After about half an hour the fire was extinguished. The subsequent inquiry established that fireworks, carried for celebrations during the voyage, had got loose in a rough sea, and their rolling about had eventually ignited them by friction. The captain told Brooke that had the fire taken hold he would have made a run for the coast of Australia not far off, and abandoned the ship at the last moment if necessary.

One fire did end in disaster. On the night of 11 September 1874 the *Cospatrick* caught ablaze in the south Atlantic off the Cape of Good Hope. All 429 immigrants on board died; only three of the crew survived. At the inquiry conducted by the British Board of Trade, evidence made it clear that the stores carried had been easily broachable from the steerage quarters.

They had been broken into and pillaged for food and alcohol. Unfortunately the ship also carried large quantities of oils, varnish, turpentine and other inflammables. As far as could be established, a carelessly dropped candle or a lighted match had set this ablaze, and with such a cargo there was no hope of stemming the flames.[18] It also became clear that no fire drills had been held, and that only two boats were carried — obviously far too few for the number of emigrants. These boats were not fit for use; although they were got away with 62 people on board, one was never heard of again, presumably because it foundered. By the time the other was picked up, all but four of its occupants were dead, and one of these died subsequently.

There is little doubt that many other emigrant vessels were in a similar precarious state and that providence alone brought them safe to New Zealand. Vogel, in a letter to the colonial secretary, the Earl of Carnarvon, in 1875, took the opportunity to convey his general concerns about the state of the ships.[19] It is impossible to say whether this had much immediate effect, but it is noticeable that mention of fire drills became much more common in emigrant letters and journals from this point.

Fires which ended in disaster were mercifully rare. Disease on the other hand was rife. It was, indeed, a common expectation of passengers, Mary Brooke remarking that 'there has been no sickness of any serious nature on board during the excessive heat which is a cause of much thankfulness. Very frequently fever breaks out where there are so many people in such a small space, but so far we have gone on without it.'[20]

All ships continued to carry doctors but the tasks they performed and the conditions under which they worked still did nothing to attract good professionals, unless they had some other personal motive such as their own emigration. A cabin passenger writing anonymously to the *Lyttelton Times* in 1873 at the completion of a voyage described the doctors' tasks as encompassing 'the unwholesome duty of inspecting the various "closets" and prompting his assistants during the removal of unavoidable collections of filth, while dispensing medical comforts necessary to cases of indisposition and sickness. It was the doctor's task also to provide ventilation and warmth, to superintend the examination of food, to record the imperfections of the ship's officers, and exercise jealous espionage over his own servants.'[21]

Some doctors were conscientious men who tried their best to ensure that their charges were delivered safe and sound. Charlotte Couchman recorded the surgeon on her ship as saying 'that when he sailed around this coast with the last lot of immigrants he brought out three years ago he lost forty women and children with diarrhea (*sic*), so it makes him rather fidgety about what we have to eat and drink, and they give us a certain portion of lime juice to drink every week.'[22] But given their standard of skill, the crowded conditions in the steerage and the state of contemporary medical knowledge, ships' doctors were virtually helpless when disease broke out. Their best protection was to ensure that inspections were rigorously carried out so that no disease was brought aboard in the first place.

What might easily occur if this was skimped or wilfully ignored is clear from the report of the inquiry of the special commission set up to investigate an outbreak of infection aboard the *England* in 1873.[23] This small vessel carried 102 immigrants, of whom 81 were adults. A significant proportion of these were Norwegians and Danes. There were some cabin passengers besides. By the time the ship arrived in Wellington, 16 of the emigrants were dead and many others had been ill of a disease which can only have been smallpox. Why this was not detected prior to departure is unclear. George McDonald, a steerage passenger, two of whose children came down with the disease and one of whom died, saw the Scandinavians come on board and said that some had bad coughs and one was badly scabbed. This had been widely remarked by other passengers, but he never saw the doctor visit the passengers or inspect them before leaving. The surgeon himself agreed that the required medical inspections had been 'loosely conducted', and put this down to 'the confusion on board prevailing just prior to departure'. The captain had obtained no clearance to depart and professed his ignorance as to the need to obtain one, claiming that he thought this was the responsibility of the owners.

When the disease became apparent on board a few days after departure, with the death of the first child on 28 December 1872, so did the incapability of the doctor. It transpired at the inquiry that although well qualified, he had been in poor health, was subject to epileptic fits and had undertaken the voyage to improve his own health. That he 'laboured under a defective memory' is abundantly apparent from the transcript of evidence which shows that he forgot who he had treated and gave different diagnoses to the same patients on different days. When Christopher Erickson's wife fell ill, it took the doctor six days to respond. Mrs Erickson died. The doctor's incompetence, in fact, quickly became so notorious on board that after only three weeks at sea a number of steerage passengers wrote the captain a formal protest that concluded: 'having witnessed the carelessness and inhumanity shown by the ship's doctor to those who required his aid — we have determined after mature deliberation to have nothing whatever to do with him, leaving ourselves with the greatest confidence to your care for the rest of the passage.' The doctor responded by attempting to resign his post but was ordered by the captain to continue with his duties.

The passengers' decision to rely on the captain may not have been a good idea either. The inquiry evidence established that there were inadequate medical supplies on board, the hospital space was occupied with stores which the captain refused to move because he had placed them there to trim the ship, and the single women were forced to use a lifeboat covered with a tarpaulin as an isolation facility. The pathos of the situation and the anguish of bereaved parents is apparent in the letter which James Burness addressed to the captain after arrival: 'I beg leave to state to you the charge I brought against the ship doctor or surgeon of gross neglect towards my son Alexander Burness aged four years and four months who died at sea.' It did him little good. The commission recommended that although the surgeon had failed to discharge his duty properly, he should be exonerated on the grounds that his illness had affected his temper.

This was not an isolated case. On 24 December 1873 the *Scimitar* left Plymouth for Port Chalmers with 430 emigrants on board. On the fourth day measles and scarlatina broke out. There were 150 cases during the voyage; 25 children and an adolescent girl died. The subsequent inquiry[24] found that, despite claims that medical inspections had been adequately carried out in respect of the adults, 'it is doubtful whether the children were very carefully examined. To do this properly more time was necessary than was given, and the parents, being afraid of losing their passage, concealed any incipient illness.' Unbelievably, the surgeon said in evidence that he had detected the presence of disease, but after consulting two colleagues who had advised him that the passengers were as likely to succumb on shore as at sea, he had allowed the ship to depart.

The commissioners found themselves 'unable to concur in this opinion' and went on to say that 'the circumstances then existing should have induced a more stringent and careful examination, and that all suspected cases should have been detained for treatment ashore.' Vogel, in passing the report to Featherston, was less restrained, writing that 'the ship went to sea with the seeds of infection notoriously on board; fever broke out a few days after leaving port; and under exceptionally favourable circumstances as to the character of the vessel itself, the conduct of her captain and officers, and the supply of water and provisions, she became a floating pest house.'

In the case of the *Mongol*, reported in the same year, disease which led to the death of a number of children was compounded by bad provisions. Much of the biscuit had to be thrown overboard, and Vogel, again writing to Featherston, reminded him 'in dealing with the immigrants on board ship that the class from which they are drawn are not ready of resource in novel situations and consequently it becomes the duty of those under whose charge they are placed to suggest and enforce good arrangements.'[25]

This view was probably unwarranted. The emigrants were, after all, those self-selected among the British population who had had the initiative

Arrival at the other end was by now well organised. Immigrants arriving in Lyttelton as this group in the 1870s were initially accommodated in purpose-built barracks, although these could be quite grim and daunting, as in the case of Dunedin (below). By the time this photograph was taken the Dunedin barracks had been turned to other use. (Both ATL)

to make the break with a former life and face the prospect of a new, usually unknown, land. They had, simply, a reasonable expectation that the voyage would be properly conducted by professionals who knew their business.

A WONDERFUL COUNTRY FOR A WORKING MAN?

If the travails of the journey during the later part of the century were not so different from those of earlier decades, there was a difference upon arrival. The government acknowledged that it had a responsibility to the assisted immigrants at least, and new or extended barracks were constructed at the main points of disembarkation to provide for the accommodation of immigrants until they could be settled. Some of these could hold several hundred people. Mostly their stay was confined to a few days, but some, and particularly the single women, stayed longer, although they could find the regime irksome.

During the first part of the seventies the response of the immigrants to their new land was little short of ecstatic. 'My master and mistress are like father and mother to me,' wrote Henry Kaill of his new employer. 'No working man in England has any idea what a good master is, or what good living is.'[26] 'This is the country for living,' wrote another, ' — beef, mutton, butter and eggs, and everything else that is good. . . We are as happy as the day is long. I would not come back on any account, for we can get something to lean over, no water broth, but a good belly full of beef . . . '[27]

And John Traves, writing from Canterbury in 1875 where he was working as a farm labourer, told his sister:

> We are busy getting the harvest in; we turn out about 9 o'clock in the morning, home again at 7 in the evening. That's not like your old grumps. The 'boss' is with us working, and sits down and smokes his pipe and chats like yourself. There is no bowing and scraping here, to Mr Woolley, as you do, and when you are worn out from old age, sent to the slaughter house, as my poor old father was at that accursed union, where he pined to death.[28]

These and many such letters flowed back to rural England, no doubt encouraging others to follow in the wake of family and friends.

A cooler view was taken by 'Hopeful', the anonymous woman author of *Taken In, A Sketch of New Zealand Life*, written in the 1880s. Disappointed by the experience of emigration, she remarked upon the low standards of many commodities such as meat, and rather tellingly noted that 'a great many of the class of people in the Colonies are those who in

England rarely taste meat, or if so of the commonest cuts, [and] they naturally think it beautiful, and can't understand if the "new chum" is not loud in its praise; but a great deal depends from what class the "new chum" comes!'[29] Hopeful went on to distinguish between those who should and those who should not come to New Zealand. Among the latter she counted 'ladies and gentlemen who have been well brought up', particularly if they were in straitened circumstances, or anyone who was 'sympathetic, imaginative, poetic and refined'. On the other hand, if they were prepared to rough it, labourers, skilled rural workers and those of good business habits would be sure to prosper. 'Those who love money-grubbing to the depth of their souls, and care not what hardness or trouble they go through to attain this much wished for goal, and those who have little softness or refinement in their nature, will get on well,' she concluded.[30]

By the mid eighties disaffected or disappointed voices of this description were rather more common than they were a decade earlier. As the money for assisted emigration dried up, and with it the money available for public works schemes, the voices of the unemployed began to be heard more

Most of the incomers continued to make their way, at least in the first instance, as rural workers, a job they had been well used to in England. But they soon discovered that their prospects were much brighter in the new land. Threshing the harvest in Nelson in the 1870s.
(Nelson Provincial Museum)

often, and those of the new immigrants, thrilled to be in such a bounteous place, rather less.

In October 1875, a time of year in which work was usually relatively plentiful, a Dunedin meeting of about 1,000 unemployed passed a resolution to be forwarded to the House of Representatives recording that it viewed with 'increasing alarm the action of the Government of New Zealand in bringing emigrants to this country which is already crowded with unemployed workmen who are utterly unable to find work of any kind.'[31] They asked the government to stem the tide of immigration, and to concentrate on finding work for the unemployed. When the government failed to respond, and instead voted more funds for immigration, a further meeting denounced this as 'a wicked and abominable policy', and announced an intention of 'acquainting the people of Great Britain with the real state of the country, and the miserable fate which such as intended to emigrate will have to encounter on their arrival in this much belauded, but corrupt and misgoverned corner of the Queen's dominions.'

They were not alone in their outrage. Over the next decade meetings of this kind became such a regular feature of urban life that they were lampooned by some unsympathetic writers.[32] In 1877 a mass meeting of Christchurch labourers petitioned the government for assistance in leaving the country, claiming that if there was any money available this might be a better use for it than bringing in further workers for whom there was no work. An upturn in the economy proved temporary, and in 1879 and into the following year there were further protests which extended well beyond the unemployed. A pamphlet circulating at the time quoted a settler as writing: 'We send home expensive emigration agents and when small capitalists or labourers, with a few pounds in their pockets, come out in response to our invitations, we turn the cold shoulder to them and let them bewilder themselves with our incomprehensible land laws, or wander about the streets without a friend and without employment until their little store of money and their patience are exhausted.'[33]

By 1880 these protests were spilling over into a broader context. Letters home by disappointed emigrants were appearing in local newspapers in Britain. A hundred colliers, brought out on the promise of work in the mines at Westport, wrote bitter letters home when the work failed to materialise on arrival. One of these appeared in the Durham *Daily Chronicle* in January 1880:

> There are hundreds of men travelling the country, and where there is one days's work to be got, there are ten men for it. What is wanted here is not labouring men or miners, but men with capital. I would therefore

strongly advise all men who are intending emigrating thither to stay where they are, for I believe the Old Country is better than this at present. Now that they have got us here they have made complete fools of us.[34]

The governments of the day proved singularly unsympathetic to the plight of the unemployed. They feared the encouragement of what newspapers were pleased to call the 'growth of a spirit of dependence' if they did.[35] The premier, John Hall, speaking to a deputation of Lyttelton unemployed in 1880, was typical enough in firmly refusing to provide regular relief work because it was

> not a function of government to find continuous employment for men. Indeed, no government could do such a thing. Where any working men have been out of employment for a considerable time, and are in distress, a government may well help them to tide over bad times; but it would be most mischievous if, in doing this, a government were to pay such wages as would not act as an inducement to the men to go into other employment as soon as they can possibly obtain it.[36]

Most local and central authorities engaged men seeking such relief as was available in stone-breaking in the first instance, to establish if they were 'really' in need. It is easy to see why in such circumstances a group of the unemployed, incensed by the attitudes of the New Zealand authorities, petitioned the president of the United States in 1880 to pay for their re-emigration to his country.[37] Some, not waiting for the outcome of such initiatives, took ship for Australia which, particularly in Victoria, was experiencing a boom not unlike that which had taken place in New Zealand in the early 1870s. In the six years from 1886 to 1891, nearly 100,000 people left New Zealand for better prospects elsewhere. In folklore this period became known as 'the Great Exodus'.[38]

This was not an option available to everyone. For many rural labourers, the long depression meant reduced wages or going 'on the swag'. Nineteen-year-old Charles Smith took to the road in 1880 after the Christchurch bakery in which he had been working went bankrupt.

> What could I do. Steal. No. Only the road. I paid my fare to Ashburton and became a swagger. I walked into the country, called at a large station. I was allowed to sleep in a wood-shed overrun by rats with the promise of a job in the morning but I did not get the job. On the road again.[39]

He subsequently suffered the indignity of being threatened with having dogs set on him by a station owner, but still could not find work, and like many others tramped from station to station getting only his food on the way.

Some observers saw in this only laziness and loafing. The *Illustrated New Zealand News* in 1885 characterised the swagger as '[c]ool as a cucumber, thoroughly stoical, full of quaint anecdotes, thankful for small mercies, averse to labour of any kind'. The reality was rather more grim. Josiah Claridge, who walked from Wellington to Napier and back in 1886 in a vain search for work, reported that upwards of 1,000 men were roaming

As the depression of the eighties deepened many men were obliged to go 'on the swag' or found themselves as seasonal workers working for their keep and living in rough barracks. This was not what they had come to New Zealand to find. (Both ATL)

the roads in a state of semi-starvation looking for work which did not exist.[40] The situation in the towns was as bad. It was not for this that men and women had endured the ordeal of a passage by steerage to their new country.

The 1880s was also a period during which there was an upsurge of unionism, especially among unskilled workers. Those who unionised included seamen, watersiders, miners, shearers and railway workers, and by the end of the decade the first unions of women workers had been formed, in the clothing industry. The eighties also saw the creation or revival of trades councils, groups of unions which came together in the main urban areas for mutual support and, increasingly, to sponsor candidates for parliament. They were encouraged by the election of the first working man to parliament in 1879, a plasterer, S. P. Andrews. In 1884 the first national conference of the trades councils took place in Dunedin, and in 1889 some of the larger unions combined in the Maritime Council, New Zealand's first attempt to create a national trade union federation. A leading historian of the labour movement has calculated that in 1888 there were perhaps 3,000 organised workers in New Zealand in 50 unions; by 1890 there were in excess of 50,000 in more than 200 unions.[41] After initial successes most of these unions collapsed, destroyed by unemployment and the concerted action of employers during the maritime strike of 1890.[42] But the longer-term effects of these organised responses to the economic distress of the long depression should not be underestimated.

At the end of the decade the colony was also horrified by the revelations of the Sweating Commission which investigated exploitation of workers in a wide range of industries, and not just women in the garment industry as is often supposed. Time after time the commission heard evidence of long and irregular hours, overcrowded workrooms, boys and girls displacing older workers and being worked in conditions which abrogated such labour laws as existed, and unsafe and unsanitary working environments.[43] Perhaps even more shocking to the conscience of the many middle-class people who were aghast at this evidence was the action of some employers who sacked their workers for giving it. This was not, it seemed, the 'wonderful country for a working man' of popular imagining.

NO CAPPING OR BOWING GOES ON

By now the immigrants had largely ceased to come in large organised groups. The typical immigrant was more likely to be a self-motivated individual or small family, often coming out to the new country to join relatives or friends.

Certainly the heroic age of migration to New Zealand was over. Nevertheless, the experience it had entailed had significant consequences. Before turning to these, however, we should note a change in the nature of the emigration experience as the nature of the immigrants changed. This change becomes increasingly apparent in the journals and letters of the immigrants as the eighties progressed. No longer were people willing to accept whatever conditions they were given in their haste to escape to new chances and a new life. This is attributable in part to the ending of assisted immigration, and in part to the introduction of steam as the common means of ship propulsion. The former meant that all passengers now paid their way and expected this to be recognised in the treatment they received. There were usually fewer people on board each vessel, and it was possible to arrange for the erection of a private space below decks by paying a small premium. The term 'steerage' dropped out of general use to be replaced by 'third class'. Steam propulsion not only shortened the journey by almost a month but also ensured that there was a break in the voyage for coaling and reprovisioning at Cape Town.

Attitudes also seem to have experienced a sea change. There were still class distinctions on vessels, but the lines began to soften. First-class passengers still generally imagined that they might come into other classes of accommodation whenever they pleased. Elizabeth Herd noted that separate church services were still held for different classes of passengers.[44] But there was a rising level of resentment at this. 'After dinner one of the ladies of the saloon came and held church etc in our cabin, much to the disgust of many passengers,' recorded Joseph Sams in 1874.[45] His view of this sort of class distinction was blunt and to the point: 'There are a lot of humbugs on board,' he wrote indignantly in his diary. Protests of the first class notwithstanding, captains were also more likely to allow access to the poop deck, particularly for women, and the classes increasingly mixed rather than remaining exclusive during the passage.

Mary Brooke recorded with obvious pleasure that although they were second-class passengers, her husband Edwin had been invited to join the choir got up in first class. A Miss Binks who travelled first class on the *Rimutaka* in 1887 also inadvertently revealed the nature of this change. 'A most fussy, bumptious, individual from the second class came along and said they were getting up another concert for Thursday and could we help, so we had to promise to as we could not get out of it.'[46] In previous decades the response to such presumption would more likely have been a cold refusal. The other classes were also much less inclined to put up with slights and snubs from the first-class cabin. On Elizabeth Herd's ship the second-class passengers were very much affronted by the attitude of the captain who 'is certainly restrained in his manner towards all classes but the First, and he wished his officers not to speak with the second class passengers which is mean of him to say the least.'[47] The second class retaliated towards this discourtesy by refusing to join in social activities organised by the first-class passengers, even when begged to do so by the ship's doctor, until the captain mended his ways.

Passengers travelling to New Zealand for the first time also began to record encounters with longer-term emigrants who had been on a home visit to England. The new settlers were sometimes surprised, even distressed, by the views of their fellow travellers. The anonymous author of *Taken In* described one such as 'a rough sort of diamond, good at bottom, but a red-hot radical, and never happier than when employing his tongue in running down Church, State, aristocracy, clergy, and all time-honoured institutions'.[48] Another of her travelling companions she called 'the colonial spitfire' characterised by 'hatred and jealousy of the English and their little sea-girt isle'. This surprise persisted after landfall. The same writer went on to remark on there being 'no respect of class. Your ears will rarely be greeted with the customary home greetings of sir, madam, miss or master. No capping or bowing goes on, in fact, no respect is shown to position, birth, or anything in that way. Esquires are very cheap out here; any one who has a small banking account is sure to be an esquire.'[49]

What this betokens is an emigrant experience which had begun to fashion a distinctive and not-quite-British perspective on the world. It was, as the poet Alan Curnow was later to remark, 'something nobody counted on', but it was to have a profound influence on subsequent events.

CHAPTER TWELVE

EXPERIENCE AND OUTCOMES: A CONCLUSION

It has already been noted that in *The Making of the English Working Class*,[1] his magisterial account of the popular response to the immense changes the British people endured during the first half of the nineteenth century, social historian Edward Thompson observed, '[t]he working class community of the early nineteenth century was the product . . . in a high degree of conscious working class endeavour.'[2] By this he meant that the popular culture which sustained the resistance of working people to many of the changes visited upon them was not just something which developed naturally or by happenstance from the objective circumstances of their lives, but was largely their own self-conscious creation.

Confronted by changes which deeply offended their most cherished beliefs, they strove to refashion their social structures and recreate a 'moral economy' which they believed to be not only their fair and proper entitlement but also the natural condition of a society which had existed in the past, and which had only recently been corrupted by the takeover of the political system by a commercial elite.

By this moral economy they broadly meant one which respected their traditional rights; treated them in a just and equitable way; paid them fair wages; kept the price of food, and especially their staple, bread, within reasonable bounds; and ensured that they had decent housing, with a small plot of land attached if possible. They also wanted a society which negotiated change with them rather than imposed it willy-nilly upon them, and which did not then insult them when they protested against this imposition by suppressing their protest, and telling them it was for their own good into the bargain. These seem modest enough requirements; but together they formed a deeply held and interlocking pattern of expectations, legitimising a political consent which might be withheld if these expectations were disappointed. When they were, workers developed a culture of resistance with its own significant characteristics.

Thompson instances political activism, radical journalism, Chartism, trade unionism, various collective endeavours directed to individual improvement, and the co-operative movement as pre-eminent examples of the defining characteristics of this process of self-creation as a class.[3] But he ignores emigration, surely one of the boldest of all the workers' responses to the pressures brought to bear on them by the industrialisation of Britain. This absence seems an oddity.

Many of those who were the authors of the changes which workers struggled to come to terms with were enthusiastic proponents of the remedy of emigration. This did not discourage or prevent large numbers of working people seizing opportunities to emigrate when they presented themselves. Sometimes they had little choice, but most went voluntarily. They did not, however, necessarily perceive emigration in the same light as their putative betters. While Britain's rulers were largely interested in solving Britain's problems by getting rid of what they saw as surplus population, those workers who took or made opportunities to go elsewhere to create a new life did not see themselves as a surplus. Nor were they interested in solving any problems but their own. They saw themselves as immigrants going to something, rather than as emigrants leaving something.

Specifically they were seeking a new beginning in a new place where the moral economy which they felt had been theirs in the past, and to which they felt they still had an entitlement, could be recreated in new

Educated but middling immigrants such as Robert Stout and John Ballance were deeply shocked by the appearance of old-world social problems in the new. Both entered politics as liberals and, eventually, radicals to change this. In their way both succeeded in doing so. (Both ATL)

circumstances. Not only is this difference in perception dramatised by the opposition of the rural authorities to the departure of workers in the 1870s, when it became clear that in some cases those who wished to go were not those of whom the authorities wished to be rid. Appreciation of it is crucial to an understanding of what the immigrants who came to New Zealand in the nineteenth century thought they were doing, what they made of their experience, and the political culture which they created as a result. That many of those who came here brought with them a radical political orientation, or even a specific political agenda, seems incontrovertible when their actions in their new environment are considered. That this was a significant element in the popular culture that resulted seems equally clear.

POPULAR CULTURE AND THE EMIGRANTS

It is sometimes possible to trace the emigration of individual working-class radicals to this part of the world. Robert Booley, for example, a founder member of the Ipswich Working Men's Association and its delegate to the Chartist National Convention in 1838, emigrated to Australia in the late 1840s. There he founded the Geelong Peoples' Association and continued to agitate for the Chartist programme, parliamentary democracy and the eight-hour day. There were many others like him who contributed to the creation of the unique flavour of Australian democracy.

Closer to home, George Binns, joint proprietor of a successful Chartist book and magazine shop in Sunderland, emigrated to New Zealand in the 1840s, although he died in 1848 of the tuberculosis he had contracted during his imprisonment for sedition in 1840 for his Chartist opinions, before he could make his political mark.[4] William Griffin, noted as the Auckland painter who led a successful campaign in 1851 for shorter working hours, who founded the first workers' newspaper in New Zealand, the *Auckland Independent and Operatives' Journal*, and who was subsequently elected as a working man's representative to the Auckland Provincial Council, was also a Chartist leader who had emigrated to New Zealand in 1845.

Irrespective of whether these individuals had a particular influence, the popular culture of the moral economy which Chartism articulated among working people in early and mid nineteenth-century Britain was clearly widespread. Certainly the refusal of some steerage passengers to submit to the deference demanded of them by the cabin and poop, and the attitude taken by tradesmen and skilled artisans in particular towards wages and working conditions once they arrived in the new colony, are consistent with the notion of a moral economy, and suggest that the emigration experience had reinforced adherence to the popular culture the Chartists represented. The arriving gold miners added their own peculiar supportive flavour to it.

It was further buttressed by arriving trade unionists, some of whom moved to set up branches of their unions in the new land. These unionists shared in the popular perception that they owned their own labour, and if necessary were prepared to act to protect that ownership and the fair wages it implied. They had behind them the experience of the industrial revolution, the worst excesses of which were well within living memory, and were determined not to see them repeated in the new community they had joined. Neither had they endured the horrors of a journey in the steerage to be confronted by experiences similar to those they had fled. Their agendas were straightforward enough: they insisted upon fairness and autonomy in the workplace, and they were prepared to combine to achieve this if necessary.

Such attitudes were reinforced again in the 1870s and eighties with the arrival of thousands of immigrants fleeing the hardship and unemployment which the agricultural unions had been unable to ameliorate. They not only brought with them an adherence to trade union perspectives, but also strengthened the popular view that land was a community asset and it was inequitable that it should be owned by the few. The rural labourers who came to New Zealand in the 1870s in particular also had an agenda. It too was simple, although its implications were profound. They wanted access to land, the availability of smallholdings and allotments, a home from which they could not be evicted on the whim of a landlord, and some hope of security in their old age far from the shadow of the hated Poor Laws and the workhouse. And like all the rest who had come, they wanted autonomy in their lives, and a future for their children which promised more than it had for them.

Those who had preceded this last great mass migration had already moved to extend the franchise beyond its original limitations. The establishment of self-government in New Zealand under the provisions of the Constitution Act of 1852 conferred the franchise upon all men over 21 who had freehold estates valued at £50, or who leased estates worth £10 per annum, or who occupied urban or rural houses at low annual values. While this was generous by contemporary standards, it was by no means democratic, even leaving aside the exclusion of women and of most Maori.[5] The Chartist conventions had endorsed a specific programme of electoral reform. This included annual parliaments elected on the basis of universal

manhood suffrage, the secret ballot, an end to the property requirement
for standing for parliament, the payment of members, and equal electoral
districts. These are now so taken for granted as the foundations of any
democracy that it is hard for us to understand or appreciate the frisson of
apprehension they created in the minds of the British middle class, and the
vigorous opposition they engendered. By the latter part of the century they
had long broken from their Chartist origins and become the commonplaces
of liberal political reform.

In this guise they travelled to the antipodes, where they were enacted
step by step in both Australia and New Zealand. By 1860 the New Zealand
franchise had been extended to include any miner who held a miner's right
to prospect, although when it was soon after followed by the gold rushes
with their mass influx of miners some of those responsible for the extension
of the franchise regretted it. In 1875 the vote was extended to anyone
living in unfurnished lodgings worth more than £10 a year. In 1879 the

*To achieve the socially oriented notion of a 'moral economy' that radicals,
Chartists and trade unionists had brought with them required popular
mobilisation. One of the most effective means of doing this was in mass
unions rallying to particular causes, as with this group in the early nineties.*
(ATL)

Qualification of Electors Act conferred the franchise on all men who had lived in New Zealand for a year and in an electorate for six months. Agitation for the secret ballot began as early as 1858 and was achieved by 1870. Payment of members, equal electoral districts and ultimately votes for women followed in due course.

Working people made their presence felt in elections early in New Zealand, if the responses of landowners are anything to go by. The pastoralist J. D. Lance complained in 1866 that he had lost an election because '[the] pothouse influence was too strong for us'.[6] Like Sidney Smith's Mrs Partington he was opposing the tides with a mop. The intensely egalitarian culture which was delivering such political outcomes was not to be gainsaid. From the outset those elected on a broader franchise used its extension to achieve the radical reforms denied them in Britain. The radical popular culture of the moral economy was not just a movement for political reform. Rather, its proponents saw political reforms as the prelude to the creation of a society which was decent for all, and not just the privileged few. Their goals involved key social areas such as land, education, work, sickness, housing and old age.

As well as the right to organise through trade unions and the imposition of limitations on the number of working hours in a day, those sympathetic to working people did not hesitate from the outset to use the lawmaking powers of the community to create an environment within which their objectives could be attained. Through factories legislation and through such enactments as the Employment of Females Act 1873 which imposed limits on the maximum working hours of women, they circumscribed the power of employers in the workplace, despite the opposition of those employers who claimed that restrictions such as creating Boxing Day and Good Friday as holidays, or requiring regular breaks from work, would have a damaging effect on the economy and on employment.[7] But they were also sufficiently sophisticated in their approach to be aware that the real basis of security was full employment, particularly when it became apparent that during the long depression widespread unemployment had allowed employers to evade the legislation. In 1888 a powerful alliance between manufacturers and the trades and labour councils forced a comprehensive protective tariff on the unwilling Atkinson government in the face of bitter opposition from landowners. The unions at least were quite clear as to their motivation. Protecting local industry created and protected jobs.

Similar considerations were at work in the fields of health and education. There was never any resort to the workhouse as the focus of the relief of distress in New Zealand. Nor were there the networks of local wealth upon which the charitable relief of distress relied in Britain. The tradition of friendly and mutual benefit societies transplanted easily to the new colony, but from the outset immigrants looked to the wider community acting collectively to undertake general social responsibilities. These undertakings might look rudimentary in retrospect, but they were ahead of contemporary welfare arrangements in England.[8] The 1868 Sick and Destitute Act of the Auckland Province, which imposed a poll tax on all non-Maori adult males for the relief of the sick, the destitute, lunatics and orphans, is fairly typical.

In the field of education New Zealand may fairly claim to have been an international leader. Radical reformers had long recognised that access to equal educational opportunities was fundamental to the creation of an egalitarian society. In Nelson province, dominated by working people almost from its origins, universal free and non-denominational education at primary level was established as early as 1856. In 1871 Canterbury followed suit, and with the abolition of the provinces in 1876 these principles were established on a national basis. Within two decades secondary education was being similarly opened to talent.

THE MORAL ECONOMY AND POLITICAL CULTURE

It was the practical experience over time of colonising a new country which quickened the pace of these developments. Many of the immigrants of the 1850s and sixties believed that being an immigrant in a new country was of itself sufficient to assure them a comfortable life for the future, provided they were prepared to work hard and accept pioneering conditions for their first few years in the colony. This notion was underpinned by another widespread belief that while old Europe corrupted those who lived there, and more particularly those who lived in cities, those in the new country would be free of this corrupting influence, more especially if they took up a rural life.[9] By the 1870s people were not so certain about this, and by the end of the eighties, with the experience of the long depression to ponder, they had arrived at the conclusion that creating the sort of society which reflected the moral economy they had hoped to achieve by emigrating was by no means an automatic process which could be left to the self-improving efforts of individuals.

It is interesting to watch this point of view working its way to the surface among those such as John Ballance and Robert Stout, who were to be the 'intellectuals' of the reforming Liberal governments of the nineties.[10]

Both began as orthodox *laissez-faire* Victorian liberals; both were converted to an interventionist approach by the social distress of the eighties. In particular Stout, influenced by Herbert Spencer, had long believed that poverty and suffering were simply part of the process of weeding out the unfit in life's struggles and a punishment for moral shortcomings. But by 1878 his tune was changing. In that year, his first as a member of a government, he brought forward a Trade Union Bill to recognise and legalise trade unions in New Zealand. Significantly, this passed into law without opposition. By 1885 he was going much further, supporting eight hours legislation on the basis that '[t]he state must protect those who require protection. If you have strife between labour and capital, which is the stronger of the two? Of course capital is the stronger, and the state must come in and assist labour whenever it can.'[11] By now he was a supporter not only of labour legislation but of protective tariffs for industry to create jobs, and of education as the key to the advancement of working people. He went on to say: 'It is only a question of time. As soon as the labourer is educated he will have his rights; he will have his rights though all the capitalists in the world declare he should not, because he will organise, and if he is faithful to his fellows the battle is won.'[12] This is a very long way from *laissez faire*.

Many middle-class people, horrified by the outcome of a Commission into Sweated Labour in 1890, were prepared to lend their active political support to Liberal reformers such as Ballance and, later, Seddon. (ATL)

What changed the minds of men such as Ballance and Stout was the evidence they saw of the classless society they had hoped for in New Zealand eluding them. If it was to be achieved, they recognised that it would require positive political action. In 1889, in the course of a speech in response to the report of the infamous conditions of exploitation uncovered by the Sweating Commission, Stout made his position crystal clear: 'It was with great sadness he saw such a meeting. When he left the old land he had felt as others had — that in coming to a new land he was coming to a country that would be rid of the evils that had tormented the land of his birth; and yet before this colony was fifty years old these troubles were affecting its inhabitants.'[13]

Such views were widely shared. People were profoundly shocked by the social conditions which had arisen as a result of economic depression, and they tried to puzzle their way through the reasons why this had happened. The conclusions they reached were of a piece not only with those of Stout and Ballance but with the proponents of the moral economy. The problem, many people decided, was to do with labour and with land, and with the need clearly to establish who might own the right to what these produced. When Stout, who was temporarily out of parliament, was attacked by George Beetham in the House of Representatives in 1888 as an enemy of capital, Ballance leapt to his defence. Stout, he said, had never denounced capital. But what he had denounced was the application of capital without restriction to the acquisition of a monopoly of the public lands. In saying this he was stating a widespread popular view.

In 1887 Ballance had published a collection of earlier essays as a pamphlet entitled *A National Land Policy Based on the Principles of State Ownership*. As a New Zealander by adoption and an Irishman by birth, Ballance might well be expected to have been interested in the land question. In arguing as he did for a comprehensive land tax and the state repurchase of land in private hands, he was reflecting views which were in common currency in New Zealand and in many other places as well. Those who were interested in the land question in mid to late nineteenth-century New Zealand — and there cannot have been many who were not — were taking part in a debate which had also been the source of much political controversy in the Britain of Arch's agricultural union, and which continued to bedevil British politics in the period up to the First World War. No doubt much of this controversy had entered New Zealand with the agricultural immigrants of the seventies. Those arguing for the more equitable distribution of land as the basis for a fair society were able to find their ideological justification in the works of Henry George.

Henry George is now largely forgotten in New Zealand,* but in the 1880s his name was familiar to all. Reading his *Progress and Poverty*, first published in New York in 1879, it is easy to see why. Its crisp and compelling prose, and the radical substance it contains not only make it an exhilarating read; the message it conveys is also entirely consistent with the perception of the moral economy which many immigrants had brought to New Zealand. 'The ownership of land,' said George, 'is the great fundamental fact which ultimately determines the social, the political, and consequently the intellectual and moral condition of a people.'[14]

George's response to what he saw as this central fact was premised on the belief, shared with the moral economists, that labour was the source of capital and not the other way around. Thus, the owners of land might have a moral right to enjoy the fruits of any improvements they made to land they owned. But they had no right to appropriate the increase in the unimproved value of the land, because this increase (which George denominated 'rent') had been created by the general state and progress of the economy and society. It therefore belonged to the larger community, which was entitled to levy a charge on it to meet whatever general social needs existed. This levy, the single tax, would serve to pay for all of those needs; no other taxes would be necessary.

In New Zealand of the 1880s this theory, grounded in aspects of popular culture widely familiar and accepted, had immense appeal to all of those who could see that the pattern of land ownership was unfair and inequitable. This belief served as the moral dynamo driving the radical agendas of the Liberal governments of the nineties, first under Ballance and then under Seddon. These governments first moved to establish clearly that they were now in political command;[15] then they set about implementing wide-ranging land reforms designed to break up monopoly landholding and to settle large numbers of small proprietors on the land thus released. Unfortunately, they also effectively sequestered many millions of acres of the Maori estate, dispossessing its owners, and creating problems of equity and redress which continue to haunt the New Zealand community.

While it is important to be aware of this, it is also important to appreciate that in so doing the Liberals created a basis of political support which gave them a platform on which to erect many of the other social structures implicit in the moral economy over the next two decades — labour laws, education and health reform, the first worker housing built by the state,

---

* Although not, interestingly enough, in Australia, where the Henry George League maintains a presence and a bookshop in Melbourne.

*Given the origins of the immigrant population, it is hardly surprising that
pensions and decent housing in old age were high on the list of social
objectives pursued by the Liberal governments of the nineties and beyond.
Two pensioners 'at home' in Onehunga in 1898. (ATL)*

and pensions for the old. Underpinning all of this was the gradual emergence
of full employment as the role of New Zealand as a principal supplier of
foodstuffs to Britain crystallised.

A community of immigrants, largely driven from their homelands by
social adversity, had, it appears on any sober assessment, brought with
them the notion of a society based on a popular perception and a programme
of what equity and natural right for all entailed. Confirmed in their beliefs
by the experience of both emigration and of their new country, they enacted
first a political, and then a social and economic programme in realisation
of that notion. What that subsequently was to mean in the daily lives of
citizens and their families has been very adequately limned by others.[16]
Those who have sought to argue that the development of New Zealand in
the nineteenth century proceeded on some other basis remain unconvincing
in their analyses. This is partly because the facts cannot adequately sustain
these alternative interpretations, and partly too because such explanations
are discontinuous with the nature and experience of New Zealanders in
the twentieth century.

The political culture which grew out of the nineteenth-century experience of emigration to New Zealand has continued to lie at the root of most of the social attitudes of New Zealanders and the political actions which have flowed from them. The experience of the depression of the 1930s reaffirmed these attitudes, and numerous subsequent studies have shown that they continue to underpin the most cherished beliefs of most of those who live here.[17] These beliefs in the importance of accessibility to education for all; the availability of community-funded assistance during periods of unlooked-for or unavoidable adversity such as sickness, accident or unemployment; affordable and decent housing; and support in old age do not differ in any material way from the programmes espoused by the Chartists, trade unionists and others in nineteenth-century Britain who endeavoured to recover the moral economy they believed had been denied them by the changes through which they had passed. The political culture which grew out of the nineteenth-century experience of New Zealand's British immigrants is appropriately perceived as one of the richest and most prolific flowerings of that economy and its culture.[18]

REFERENCES

ABBREVIATIONS
AJHR Appendices to the Journals of the House of Representatives
ATL   Alexander Turnbull Library, Wellington
BPP   British Parliamentary Papers
NZJH New Zealand Journal of History
NZPD New Zealand Parliamentary Debates

INTRODUCTION
1   Official figures are available from a number of sources, British, Irish and colonial. For New Zealand there are the *Official Yearbooks*; for Ireland the *Commission on Emigration and Other Population Problems* (Dublin 1954); and for Britain to 1873 the annual *General Report of the Land and Emigration Commissioners*. Higher estimates must remain just that. Richard Douthwaite in *The Growth Illusion* (Dublin 1992), p.44, gives 9 million but does not cite his source.
2   *New Zealand Official Yearbook* for 1892, pp. 60-1.
3   For a fascinating and detailed account of the shortcomings of the statistical data on nineteenth-century immigration to New Zealand, see D. H. Akenson, *Half the World From Home: Perspectives on the Irish in New Zealand 1860–1950* (Wellington 1990), *passim*.
4   op.cit., Vol. VII p.243 cited and explored further by Akenson, op.cit. pp.35-53.
5   The works of New Zealand history expressive of these two schools have burgeoned exponentially in recent decades. The basic works remain: W. P. Reeves, *The Long White Cloud* (London 1898); K. Sinclair, *A History of New Zealand* (London 1959 and subsequent revised editions); W. B. Sutch, *The Quest For Security in New Zealand 1840–1966* (Oxford 1966) and *Poverty and Progress* (Wellington 1969); and W. H. Oliver and B. R. Williams, *The Oxford History of New Zealand* (Wellington 1981 and 1992).
6   Reeves, op.cit. p.237.
7   Sutch, op. cit. (1969) p.121.
8   Miles Fairburn, *The Ideal Society and its Enemies* (Auckland 1989).
9   Interestingly, although this particular call for a new approach has produced a number of Maori proponents presenting in European academic or popular mode — most notably and recently Ranginui Walker in *Ka Whawhai Tonu Matou* (Auckland 1990) — the process was commenced by Pakeha historians at least two decades ago and may probably and ultimately be traced to K. Sinclair, *The Origins of the Maori Wars* (Wellington 1957).
10   See, for example, *NZJH* Vol. 25 No. 2, October 1991, which is devoted entirely to this topic, and R. Arnold, 'Community in Rural Victorian New Zealand' in *NZJH* Vol. 24 No. 1, April 1990.

11 See J. Phillips, 'Of Verandahs, and Fish and Chips, and Footie on Saturday Afternoon' in *NZJH* Vol. 24 No. 2, October 1990, and J. G. A. Pocock, 'Tangata Whenua and Enlightenment Anthropology' and E. Olssen, 'Where To From Here? Reflections on the Twentieth-century Historiography of Nineteenth-century New Zealand' both in *NZJH* Vol. 26 No. 1, April 1992.
12 Olssen, op.cit. p.69.

CHAPTER ONE
1   B. Tuchman, *The March of Folly* (London 1984), p.159.
2   For an analysis of the part such naval considerations played in the establishment of a British presence in the south Pacific region, see A. Frost, *Convicts and Empire: A Naval Question* (Melbourne 1986).
3   For an account of this, see D. McKay, *In The Wake of Cook: Exploration, Science and Empire 1780-1801* (Wellington 1985).
4   Those interested in following up this grisly topic are referred to D. Hay, P. Linebaugh, J. G. Rule, E. P. Thompson and C. Winslow, *Albion's Fatal Tree* (London 1975).
5   A. G. L. Shaw, *Convicts and the Colonies* (London 1966), p.29.
6   Included by Robert McNab in his *Historical Records of New Zealand* Vol. 1 (Wellington 1908) at p.55. This work, although published so long ago, is a treasure trove of early papers relating to New Zealand.
7   Frost, op.cit. p.137
8   McNab, op.cit. p.120.
9   McNab, ibid. p.432.
10 For a detailed exposition of the development of these trading patterns, see S. E. Morrison, *The Maritime History of Massachusetts 1783–1868* (Boston 1921), this figure at p.71.
11 V. T. Harlow, *The Founding of the Second British Empire 1763–1793* (London 1964), p.55.
12 D. C. North, *The Economic Growth of the United States 1790–1860* (New York 1966), p.20.
13 McNab, op.cit. p.239.
14 C. Wilkes, *Narrative of the United States Exploring Expedition During the Years 1838–1842 with Illustrations and Maps* (London 1845) Vol. 5, p.485.
15 John Savage, *Some Account of New Zealand, particularly the Bay of Islands and Surrounding Country* (London 1807; ed. C. R. H. Taylor, Wellington 1939), p.91.

CHAPTER TWO
1   C. Barnett, *Britain and Her Army 1509–1970* (London 1970), p.270.
2   J. H. Clapham, *An Economic History of Modern Britain* Vol.1 (London 1932), pp.66, 113.
3   D. Defoe, *A Tour Through Great Britain* Vol. III (London 1724), p.135.
4   The classic study of this friction and its consequences is that of E. P. Thompson in *Whigs and Hunters* (London 1875). This has been updated and extended in Thompson's essay 'Custom, Law, and Common Right', in *Customs in Common* (London 1991) at pp. 97–184.
5   H. Newby, *Country Life: A Social History of Rural England* (London 1987), pp.27–8.
6   See, for instance, M. Beresford, *The Lost Villages of England* (Gloucester 1954). The classic work on Scotland has become John Prebble, *The Highland Clearances* (London 1963). For Ireland, see R. Douthwaite, *The Growth Illusion* (Dublin 1992), pp.249–60.

7   Douthwaite, ibid. p.24.

8   A detailed case study of the arrival of the industrial revolution in a single area is to be found in P. Hudson, 'Proto-industrialisation: The Case of the West Riding Wool Textile Industry in the 18th and early 19th Centuries', in *History Workshop Journal* No. 12, Autumn 1981, pp.34–61.

9   R.J. White, *Waterloo to Peterloo* (London 1968), p.21.

10   C. R. Fay, *Life and Labour in the Nineteenth Century* (Cambridge 1945), p.184.

11   *Hansard Parliamentary Debates 1820* House of Lords Vol.1, p.421, cited by White, op.cit. p.24.

12   For a more detailed account of the theories of Ricardo and the ideologists of the classical free market, see J. K. Galbraith, *A History of Economics: The Past as the Present* (London 1989), p.82.

13   Cited in the classic work by J. L. and B. Hammond, *The Town Labourer 1760–1832* (London 1919), p.34.

14   Vol.5 cited by J. C. Drummond and Anne Wilbraham in *The Englishman's Food* (London 1957), p.327.

15   Parliamentary Papers 1824 No. 392 p.47, cited by J. Burnett, *Plenty and Want* (London 1979), p.20. Another work containing much valuable information on this topic is S. Freeman, *Mutton and Oysters: The Victorians and Their Food* (London 1989).

16   Newby, op.cit. p.30.

17   William Cobbett, *Rural Rides* (Edinburgh 1853). This from the entry for 7 November 1821.

18   James Walvin, *Victorian Values* (London 1988), p.68.

19   E. Hobsbawm and G. Rudé, *Captain Swing: A Social History of the Great English Agricultural Uprising of 1830* (New York 1975), p.78.

20   The classic study in this field is A. G. L. Shaw, *Convicts and the Colonies* (London 1966). See in particular the chapter entitled 'Who Were the Convicts?' commencing at p.146.

21   Those interested in pursuing this grisly subject are referred to 'A Treatment for Treason, in E. S. Turner, *Roads to Ruin: The Shocking History of Social Reform* (London 1966) and Hay et al, *Albion's Fatal Tree* (London 1988).

22   Shaw, op.cit. *passim.*

23   See, for instance, W. Stafford, *Socialism, Radicalism, and Nostalgia: Social Criticism in Britain 1775–1830* (Cambridge 1987); G. Claeys, *Citizens and Saints: Politics and Antipolitics in Early British Socialism* (Cambridge 1989); and I. McCalman, *Radical Underworld: Prophets, Revolutionaries and Pornographers in London 1795–1840* (Cambridge 1988).

24   These and successive figures from R. Williams, *The Long Revolution* (London 1965), pp.157, 186. Williams does not, unfortunately, cite his sources. A more recent and fascinating account of the extent and use of working-class literacy is to be found in Patricia Anderson, *The Printed Image and the Transformation of Popular Culture 1790–1860* (Oxford 1991).

25   These have been the subject of recent study. In particular there are the works of G. Rudé, notably *The Crowd in the French Revolution* (Oxford 1959) and *Ideology and Popular Protest* (London 1980), which includes information on the custom of *taxation populaire*. There are also the essays 'The Moral Economy of the English Crowd in the Eighteenth Century' and 'Rough Music' in Thompson op.cit. (1991).

26   There have been many studies of the Luddites. The most recent and in some ways the most interesting is R. Reid, *Land of Lost Content: The Luddite Revolt 1812* (London, 1986).

27   Comprehensive accounts and analyses of these protests and their period are to be found in R. J. White, *Waterloo to Peterloo* (London 1968), and in what has become the classic work, E. P. Thompson's *Making of the English Working Class* (London 1963).

28   The standard work on this subject is E. Hobsbawm and G. Rudé, *Captain Swing, A Social History of the Great English Agricultural Uprising of 1830* (New York 1975).

29   Thompson, op.cit. (1963) p.212.

30   Hobsbawm and Rude, op.cit. p.255.

31   Newby, op.cit. p.44.

32   *Political Register* 27 November 1830, cited by C. Hampton (ed), *A Radical Reader: The Struggle for Change in England 1381–1914* (London 1984), p.451.

33   The passage of this Act was closely contested and it passed the Commons by a single vote. There is a dramatic eyewitness account in a letter by Thomas Macauley in P. Johnson (ed), *The Oxford Book of Political Anecdotes* (Oxford 1986), p.114.

34   There have been many books and articles written on the Chartists, and the subject remains controversial. A recent and comprehensive study, *The Chartists* by Dorothy Thompson (London 1984), covers most of the necessary background. One of the more interesting of the recent attempts to explicate what the Chartists signified is to be found in G. S. Jones, 'Rethinking Chartism' in his collection, *Languages of Class: Studies in English Working Class History 1832–1982* (Cambridge 1983).

35   The complexities of these governments, in an age before disciplined political parties, almost defy unravelling. They have been explicated nevertheless in P. Mandler, *Aristocratic Government in the Age of Reform: Whigs and Liberals 1830–1852* (Oxford 1990).

36   E. Bulwer-Lytton, *England and the English* (New York 1833), cited by G. Himmelfarb in *The Idea of Poverty: England in the Early Industrial Age* (New York 1984), p.172.

37   A. O. Hirschman, *The Rhetoric of Reaction* (Harvard 1991), p.30.

38   Drummond and Wilbraham, op.cit. pp.363–73. For a more comprehensive account of the working of the new Poor Laws, see Newby, op.cit. pp.47–51.

39   Thomas Carlyle, *Selected Writings* (London 1971), p.228.

CHAPTER 3

1   The theories of Malthus and Ricardo are wittily set in their context in J. K. Galbraith, *A History of Economics* (London 1989), p.78.

2   Hazlitt in his *The Spirit of the Age* (1825), and Cobbett in his *Rural Ride* for 28 August 1826. One of the most interesting recent studies of this critique is to be found in Ian Dyck, *William Cobbett and Rural Popular Culture* (Cambridge 1992).

3   For a detailed account of Horton and his influence, see H. J. M. Johnston, *British Emigration Policy 1815–1830* (Oxford 1972).

4   Charles Buller MP, *Hansard* 1843 lxviii col. 522.

5   A full account to the background and activities of these bodies is to be found in F. H. Hitchens, *The Colonial Land and Emigration Commission* (Philadelphia 1931), particularly pp.8–36.

6   Wakefield has found a number of biographers. For a summary of his career there is a biographical essay in M.F. Lloyd Pritchard, *The Collected Works of Edward Gibbon Wakefield* (Auckland 1969), pp.9–92. This title is misleading; it contains mainly works relating to New Zealand and omits significant others entirely. A bibliography of his writings relating to New Zealand and the works of others on the same topic is to be found in P. Stuart, *Edward Gibbon Wakefield in New Zealand* (Wellington 1971).

7   For some of the detail of this, see C. Woodham Smith, *The Great Hunger* (London 1965) from p.202, and J. Prebble, *The Highland Clearances* (London 1969) from p. 187.

8   For the detail of this, see Lloyd Pritchard, op.cit. from p.32.

9   BPP HC 1836 Vol XI, commencing at p.499.

10   Robert McNab, *Historical Records of New Zealand* Vol.1 (Wellington 1908) p.483.

11   ibid. p.516.

12   ibid. p.523.

13   In a letter to the Rev. Josiah Pratt from Parramatta, 4 June 1824.

14   Instruction from Earl Bathurst to John Bigge of 6 January 1819, printed in BPP for 3 July 1823.

15   His full report is carried in McNab, op.cit. pp.587–96.

16   This affair in which Te Rauparaha hired the *Elizabeth* to exact a horrible revenge on his Ngai Tahu enemies has been often written up. See, for instance, my *A Cargo of Flax* (Wellington 1991).

17   For a list of those who figured in this group, see P. Adams, *Fatal Necessity: British Intervention in New Zealand 1830–1847* (Auckland 1977), p.252.

18   A brief but revealing account of the nature of the New Zealand Company is to be found in M. Turnbull, *The New Zealand Bubble* (Wellington 1959).

19   ibid. p.14

20   Johnston, op.cit. p.167.

21   Cited by Turnbull, op.cit. p.19, but without a supporting reference.

22   Lloyd Pritchard, op.cit. p.113.

23   See, for example, the chilling effect of his intervention in 1836 in the military scandals surrounding the Earl of Cardigan in Woodham Smith, op.cit. p.53. There are a number of interesting accounts of the work of the Select Committee on Transportation and its underlying agendas. These include J. B. Hirst, *Convict Society and its Enemies* (London 1983), pp.76–7 and 199–205; D. W. A. Baker, *Days of Wrath: A life of John Dunmore Lang* (Melbourne 1985), pp.137–8; and R. Hughes, *The Fatal Shore* (Sydney 1987), pp.493–8.

24   The full report of the select committee, together with its notes of evidence, are to be found in BPP for 1838.

25   Extract from Molesworth's own notes cited by Hughes, op.cit. p.494.

26   BPP 1837 Vol.VII, commencing at p.1.

27   McNab, op.cit. p.628; the following extract, ibid. p.723.

28   The full story of the eventually successful attempts by the Wakefield colonisers to impose some sort of intervention leading to sovereignty of New Zealand by the British government is superbly detailed in Adams, op.cit.

29   BPP 1838 Vol. 21, commencing at p.329.

30   The full text is to be found in McNab, op.cit. from p.729.

CHAPTER FOUR

1   From *The Story of New Zealand* published in 1910 and cited in C. McGeorge, 'Learning About God's Own Country', *New Zealand Journal of Education Studies* Vol. 18 No. 1, May 1983.

2   A number of these are to be found in N. Colquhoun (ed), *New Zealand Folksongs: Song of a Young Country* (Wellington 1972); G. Huntington, *Songs the Whalemen Sang* (Massachusetts 1964); and R. Bailey and B. Roth (eds), *Shanties by the Way* (Wellington 1967).

3   H. Norton in *The Whale's Wake* (Dunedin 1982), p. 238, citing Charles Heaphy.

4   Col. William Wakefield, *Supplementary Information Relative to New Zealand* (London 1840), p.28.

5   Unpublished manuscript held by ATL. Heberley's account gives a rare insight into the situation on the New Zealand coast prior to 1840 from the point of view of

a working man.

6   The full depositions are published in R. McNab, *The Old Whaling Days* (Wellington 1907), chapter XII.

7   Maning's *Old New Zealand*, his account of life in pre-Treaty New Zealand, is also a perceptive and colourful account from an unorthodox source.

8   Wakefield's *Adventure in New Zealand*, often reprinted, contains a fascinating chapter 'Life on a Whaling Station', from which this extract is drawn.

9   Richard Hill in *Policing the Colonial Frontier* Vol.1 (Wellington 1986), p.52. Others have gone further. One particularly interesting revisionist view is to be found in S. Eldred-Grigg, *A Southern Gentry* (Wellington 1980). This writer has explored the dynamic tension between class groups in early New Zealand, including the pre-Treaty period.

10   Given the significance of this relationship, it is surprising it has not been studied more, although there have been numerous books of analysis and memoirs covering the period to 1840. The most comprehensive is one of the oldest, E. J. Tapp's *Early New Zealand, a Dependency of New South Wales 1788–1841* (Melbourne 1958). Other recent interesting works include J. Lee, *Hokianga* (Auckland 1987), and O. Wilson, *Kororareka* (Dunedin 1990).

11   From Customs Imports into Colonies by Country 1832-41, CUST 6, Public Record Office, London, cited in P. Adams, *Fatal Necessity: British Intervention in New Zealand 1830-1847* (Auckland 1977) as Appendix 1(b), p.250.

12   A good deal of research and writing has gone into explicating the reasons behind the dispatch of the *Tory*, but commercial interest seems the most likely explanation. This is the view of most recent historians, although others, e.g. Patricia Burns in *Fatal Success: A History of the New Zealand Company* (Auckland 1989), hark back to earlier explanations.

13   *First Report of the Directors* 14 May 1840, published as an addendum to *Supplementary Information Relative to New Zealand Comprising Despatches and Journals of the Company's Officers of the First Expedition* (London 1840).

14   There have been very many accounts of the problems encountered by the Wakefield settlers in Wellington and at other places. The best include J. Miller, *Early Victorian New Zealand* (London 1974), and more recently Rosemarie Tonk, ' "A Difficult and Complicated Question": The New Zealand Company's Wellington, Port Nicholson Claim' in Hamer and Nicholls (eds), *The Making of Wellington 1840–1914* (Wellington 1990).

15   The precise number of New Zealand Company settlers is hard to establish. In her *The Collected Works of Edward Gibbon Wakefield* (Auckland 1969), M. F. Lloyd Pritchard says that nearly 10,000 had come by 1848, but this excludes Canterbury (p.42).

16   Crown Colony Statistics of New Zealand cited by M.F. Lloyd Pritchard in *An Economic History of New Zealand* (Auckland 1970), p.36.

17   The tortuous negotiations and subsequent manoeuvrings of the company to obtain maximum benefit from it are set out in Burns, op.cit. from p.165 and Adams, op.cit. from p.181.

18   There is an interesting background article to this action of FitzRoy's in J. Adams, 'Governor FitzRoy's Debentures and Their Role in Recall', *NZJH* Vol. 20 No. 1, April 1986.

19   Lloyd Pritchard, op.cit. (1970) p.35.

20   For a detailed examination of the situation at New Plymouth, see R. Dalziel, 'Popular Protest in Early New Plymouth: Why Did it Occur?', *NZJH* Vol. 20 No.1, April 1986.

21   See P. Mandler, *Aristocratic Government in the Age of Reform: Whigs and Liberals 1830–1852* (Oxford 1990), from p.228.

22   Burns, op.cit. p.293.

23   BPP 1851 (1398), Vol.XXXV p.18.

24   W. B. Sutch in his classic work *The Quest For Security in New Zealand* (Wellington 1966) gives a list of occupations of the first Wellington settlers at p.12. The vast preponderance were unskilled or semi-skilled workers.

25   Historians have not spent much energy on the development of the early New Zealand economy. This is a pity, because it is the key to an understanding of the period during which most immigrants came to the colony. A recent attempt to repair this deficiency is W. J. Gardner's 'A Colonial Economy' in the *Oxford History of New Zealand* 2nd edition (Auckland 1992).

26   Samuel Butler was able to use this opportunity to turn his investment into a fortune, on the income of which he lived for the remainder of his life. His *A First Year in Canterbury Settlement* remains an important early source. Farming's loss was literature's gain.

27   BPP 1844 (566), Vol.22. See evidence of Earp and Kettle.

28   This is according to a despatch of Grey's in BPP 1850 (1136), Vol.37 from p.140.

29   BPP 1850 (1136), Vol.37 p.132.

30   Chapter 33 of Vol.1 of the 1887 translation of the third German edition by F. Engels.

31   For the best account of Wakefield's sojourn in this country, see P. Stuart, *Edward Gibbon Wakefield in New Zealand* (Wellington 1971).

32   ibid. pp.60–6, which contains a summary account of Wakefield's political impact among the working people of the Hutt Valley.

CHAPTER 5

1   Alexander Marjoribanks, *Travels in New Zealand* (London 1845), p.10.

2   The relationship between this source material, the culture of diary-keeping which surrounded it and what it can tell us, is canvassed in A. Hassam, *Sailing to Australia: Shipboard Diaries by Nineteenth Century British Immigrants* (Manchester 1994), and D. Charlwood, *The Long Farewell* (London 1981). Although both are primarily concerned with Australia, Hassam's book in particular also draws on New Zealand sources. I have relied on these sources, on contemporary published accounts (of which there is a substantial quantity), and the rich original holdings in the ATL as the basis for this and several other chapters which follow.

3   C. Warren Adams, *A Spring in the Canterbury Settlement* (London 1853), p.2.

4   For the detail of this, see John Ward, *Information Relative to New Zealand compiled for The Use of Colonists* (London 1840). Ward was secretary to the company.

5   Hassam, op. cit. p.71.

6   There are many accounts of the condition of the cabin passengers en route. One of the most interesting of those specific to New Zealand remains that prepared by Helen Simpson for the centennial publications of 1940 and contained in her *The Women of New Zealand*.

7   Alfred Fell, *A Colonist's Voyage to New Zealand Under Sail in the Early Forties* (London undated), p.98.

8   Fell, op. cit.

9   Ward, op. cit. p.141.

10   Cited by H. Miller, in *Race Conflict in New Zealand 1814–1865* (Auckland 1966), p.151.

11   Cited by Hassam, op. cit. p.187.

12 ATL manuscript collection, qMS BAN.

13 Hassam, op. cit. p.35.

14 Marjoribanks, op. cit. p.11.

15 G. F. Angas, *Savage Life and Scenes in Australia and New Zealand* (London 1847).

16 Dr Alfred Barker, ATL MS-0137 p.3.

17 Hassam, op. cit. p.151.

18 ibid. pp. 92, 97.

19 Fell, op. cit. p.13.

20 Mary McKain on board the *Olympus* 1841, ATL MS 1353.

21 Jane Bannerman, ATL qMS BAN, and Thomas Renwick who was surgeon on the *Thomas Harrison* bound for Nelson in 1842, ATL MS 2015.

22   ATL MS 1353.

23 ATL MS ADA.

24 Fell, op. cit. p.32.

25 Most particularly Charlwood, op. cit.

26 Cited by Hassam, op. cit. p.115.

27 ibid. p.119.

28 ibid.

29 ATL MS ADA.

30 ATL MS-0137, p.3

31 ATL MS-0137.

32 Both cited by a number of writers, e.g. John Miller, *Early Victorian New Zealand* (Oxford 1958), pp.63–4.

33 John Wood, *Twelve Months in Wellington, Port Nicholson* (London 1843), p.9.

34 Ward, op. cit. p.136.

35 Letter of W Bannister 14 April 1841, cited by Miller, op. cit. p.152.

36 ATL qMS BAN.

37 E. Dieffenbach, *Travels in New Zealand* Vol.1 (London 1843), p.5.

38 Angas, op. cit. p.234.

39 Adams, op. cit. p.74.

40 ATL MS ADA.

41 Cited by Alison Drummond (ed), in *Married and Gone to New Zealand* (Hamilton 1960), p.59

42 Emma Barker, ATL MS BAR, p.43.

43 ATL qMS BOW.

44 ATL MS 1353.

45 Cited by Miller, op. cit. p.151.

46 Ward, op. cit. p.159.

47 For an entertaining account of this, see B. Patterson's unpublished Wellington Historical and Early Settlers' Association 1994 annual lecture, *Early Colonial Society: Reflections on Wellington's First Anniversary Day.*

48 John Miller, in *Early Victorian New Zealand: A Study of Racial Tension and Social Attitudes 1839–1852* (Wellington 1974), chapter 9.

49 Marjoribanks, op. cit. p.11.

50 Charles Heaphy, *Narrative of a Residence in Various Parts of New Zealand* (London 1842), p.68.

51 Hon. Henry William Petre, *An Account of the Settlements of the New Zealand Company* (London 1842), p.15.

52 From the Company to Colonel Wakefield in New Zealand, 26 January 1843, and cited by Miller op. cit. p.119.

53 *New Zealand Gazette and Wellington Spectator*, 18 October 1843.

54   The full text of their petition is to be found in W. B. Sutch, *The Quest for Security in New Zealand* (Wellington 1966), p.17. This is one of the earliest published expressions of the subsequent demand for the 'fair go'. It is also hard to escape the impression that the New Zealand Company was an employment scheme for the Wakefield family

55   Miller, op. cit. p.124, citing the scandalised accounts of Tuckett.

56   For a detailed account of this affair and the preceding uproar on the *Timandra*, see R. Dalziel, 'Popular Protest in Early New Plymouth: Why Did it Occur?' in *NZJH* Vol. 20 No. 1, April 1986.

57   Cited unsourced by W. B. Sutch, in *Poverty and Progress in New Zealand* (Wellington 1969), p.45.

58   For an account of this and other early battles over hours and conditions of work, see B. Roth and J. Hammond, *Toil and Trouble: The Struggle for a Better Life in New Zealand* (Auckland 1981), and D. Scott, *Inheritors of a Dream* (Wellington 1969).

59   See Eric Olssen, *A History of Otago* (Dunedin 1984), pp.36–7 for the detail of this dispute.

60   *Official Handbook of New Zealand 1883*, pp.112–13.

CHAPTER 6

1.   The most significant of these assessments commence with P. Deane and W. A. Cole, *British Economic Growth 1688–1959* (Cambridge 1967), and have been modified both by Deane herself in 1968 and by C. H. Feinstein in *National Income, Expenditure and Output of the United Kingdom 1855–1965* (Cambridge 1972). The general debate is summarised in F. Crouzet, *The Victorian Economy* (London 1982).

2   See F. Crouzet, *Capital Formation in the Industrial Revolution* (London 1972).

3   Feinstein, op.cit. Table 20, also cited by Crouzet, op.cit. (1982), p.41.

4   P. Bairoch, *Commerce extérieur et développement économique de l'Europe au XIXe siècle* (Paris 1976), p.138.

5   H. Perkin, *The Origins of Modern English Society 1780–1880* (London 1969), p.420.

6   There are some interesting comparative statistics in J. Burnet, *Plenty and Want: A Social History of Diet in England from 1815 to the Present Day* (London 1983).

7   The best account of this disaster and the failure of the British administration to cope with it remains that of C. Woodham-Smith, *The Great Hunger* (London 1962).

8   ibid. pp.202–10, 278.

9   Crouzet, op.cit. (1982), p.47.

10   M. Nelson, 'Social class trends in British diet 1860–1980' in C. Geissler and D.J. Oddy (eds), *Food, Diet and Economic Change* (Leicester 1993), p.102.

11   BPP 1864, XLIX 618.

12   Cited in J. C. Drummond and A. Wilbraham, *The Englishman's Food* (London 1991, revised edition), p.369.

13   R. A. Church, *The Great Victorian Boom 1850–1873* (London 1980), chapter 5.

14   There is controversy about the relative effects of the policy of free trade, however. Such external considerations as the effects on American industry of the American Civil War also need to be taken into account.

15   Cited by E. J. Hobsbawm, *The Age of Capital 1848–1875* (London 1975), p.49.

16   ibid. p.50.

17   For an explanation of the relationships this entailed, see D. R. Mills, *Lord and Peasant in Nineteenth Century Britain* (London 1980).

18   B. R. Mitchell and P. Deane, *Abstract of British Historical Statistics* (Cambridge 1962), p.488.

19   It is impossible to overemphasise the importance of bread to working people during

this period. There is a fascinating study by C. Petersen, *Bread and the British Economy 1770–1870* (Aldershot 1995), which deals with this matter in depth. The figures cited come from p.5, Table 1.1. For information on the general political avenues of protest open to the disenfranchised poor, including the custom of *taxation populaire*, see G. Rudé, *Ideology and Popular Protest* (London 1980), and E. P. Thompson, *Customs in Common* (London 1991).

20   Cited by H. Newby, *Country Life, A Social History of Rural England* (London 1987), p.85.

21   F. G. Heath, *The English Peasantry* (London 1874), p.99.

22   See D. S. Morgan, *Harvesters and Harvesting 1840–1900* (London 1982), pp.140–3.

23   Return of convictions under the Criminal Law Amendment Act 1871, cited by Morgan, op.cit. p.125.

24   Appendix 6: Report of the Medical Officer of the Privy Council on the Food of the Poorer Labouring Classes in England (1863), p.232.

25   Cited by Anne Digby in 'The Rural Poor', in G. E. Mingay (ed), *The Victorian Countryside* (London 1981) Vol. 2, p.591.

26   Both these observations cited by Newby, op.cit. p.93.

27   Thirtythird General Report of the Emigration Commissioners 1873.

28   The information on conditions aboard immigrant ships is voluminous from contemporary sources to the present. A recently republished and excellent account of the Atlantic passage is to be found in T. Coleman, *Passage to America* (London 1972 and 1992).

29   ibid. p.228.

30   For a full account of this by no means untypical affair, see ibid. chapter 13.

31   Evidence of Dr W. O'Doherty to the Select Committee on Emigrant Ships 1854 Vol. 13.

32   Cited by John Prebble in *The Highland Clearances* (London 1969), p.197.

33   A. Hassam, *Sailing to Australia: Shipboard Diaries by Nineteenth Century British Immigrants* (Manchester 1994), p.9.

CHAPTER 7

1   *New Zealand Official Yearbook* 1915, cited by M. F. Lloyd Pritchard, *An Economic History of New Zealand* (Auckland 1970), from which most of the following statistics are drawn. Despite being 25 years old, Lloyd Pritchard's book is still the primary overview of the historical New Zealand economy, although it has been recently supplemented by G. R. Hawke, *The Making of New Zealand: An Economic History* (Cambridge 1985).

2   *Statistics of New Zealand 1877.*

3   *Official Handbook of New Zealand 1883.*

4   ibid. for 1861.

5   The low is that of R. J. Campbell writing in the *Australian Economic History Review* in 1976. The subject is well canvassed in John E. Martin, 'Unemployment, Government and the Labour Market', *NZJH* October 1995 from p.170.

6   From the *Official Handbook* for 1876. Of course, an official publication would be unlikely to publish a gloomy account.

7   *New Zealand Official Yearbook* 1893.

8   In the South Island this was generally by forced sale on highly unfavourable terms which were often not honoured in any event. See H. C. Evison, *Te Wai Pounamu: The Greenstone Island* (Christchurch 1993), and Waitangi Tribunal, *Ngai Tahu Report* (Wellington 1991) for two recent accounts of this. In the north the more direct method

was confiscation following war and the individuation of title on a basis which made it almost impossible for Maori land to remain in Maori hands.

9   From E. B. Fitton's *New Zealand,* and cited by D. Hamer in *New Towns in the New World* (New York 1990), p.77.

10   From *New Zealand: The Britain of the South* (London 1861), and also cited by Hamer, op.cit.

11   Trollope visited New Zealand in the winter of 1872 as part of a tour which also included Australia, and published his account of the outcome in *Australia and New Zealand* (London 1873). His observations are to be found extracted in Stone (ed), *Verdict on New Zealand* (Wellington 1959).

12   From *A First Year in the Canterbury Settlement*, in D. Stone, op.cit. p.34.

13   For the philosophical background to this school of thinking, see M. Francis and J. Morrow, *A History of English Political Thought in the Nineteenth Century* (London 1994).

14   Noted by W. D. Borrie in *Immigration to New Zealand 1854–1938* (Canberra 1991). Borrie's work was actually written in 1937 but remains the only comprehensive account of this subject. His subsequent work, *The European Peopling of Australasia* (1994), contains the same New Zealand information in summary.

15   For an account of this, see W. P. Morrell, *British Colonial Policy in the Mid Victorian Age* (Oxford 1969).

16   The background to the consequent initiatives prior to 1870 is very well summarised in R. Dalziel, *The Origins of New Zealand Diplomacy* (Wellington 1975), chapter 1.

17   Cited by Dalziel, op.cit. p.17.

18   C. Terry, *New Zealand: Its Advantages and Prospects as a British Colony*, cited by Borrie, op.cit. p.10.

19   W. Swainson, *New Zealand and Its Colonisation* (London 1859), p.192.

20   Cited by Borrie, op.cit. p.14.

21   Claire Toynbee, 'Class and Mobility in Nineteenth Century Wellington Province, An Exploratory Study of Immigrants Arriving 1840–1880', unpublished MA thesis, Victoria University of Wellington 1979.

22   *AJHR* 1862 A3.

23   Books on this are legion, particularly in the last two decades, and far too numerous to cite here.

24   *Statistics of New Zealand 1877.*

25   See L. G. Gordon, 'Immigration Into Hawkes Bay 1858–1876', unpublished MA thesis, Victoria University 1965. There are a number of theses dealing with aspects of immigration. Some of these, primarily reflecting as they do the need to meet the requirements of examiners, are more useful for the present purpose than others.

26   Again there is a thesis which is of some assistance with the detail of this, V. Ward, *Immigrants and Immigration in the Auckland Province 1792–1876* (Auckland 1943). Although much of it is simply a digest of earlier published works, this in itself constitutes a useful summary.

27   See in particular Fox's *The War in New Zealand* (London 1860).

28   As well as a fairly full treatment in Borrie, op.cit., there is a useful summary note of the failure of this scheme in a leaflet on the 'Waikato immigration' issued by the National Archives, and containing a comprehensive list of sources.

29   There are a number of works on the gold rushes. Westland is particularly well served by P. R. May's *The West Coast Gold Rushes* (Christchurch 1967).

30   Cited by May, ibid. p.460, but unsourced.

31   ibid. Appendix 1, p.491.

32   The most important and pioneering work done in this field has been by Charlotte

Macdonald, culminating in her *A Woman of Good Character* (Wellington 1990) which deals in particular with the immigration of single women to New Zealand between 1850 and 1880.

33   The social historian J. O. C. Phillips has suggested in his *A Man's Country?* (Auckland 1987) that the conjunction of the Victorian notion of the family as the basic unit of civilisation, and the response accordingly to the gender imbalance of nineteenth-century New Zealand, has been an important basis for the development of our popular culture.

34   Charlotte Godley Letters, cited by Phillips, ibid. p.48.

35   From the *Official Yearbooks*. Presumably some at least of the males found wives or partners among Maori.

36   From Otago's Immigration Department Report for 1863, cited by Macdonald, op.cit. p.26.

37   Marsham to Rolleston (Provincial Superintendent), 25 August 1864, cited by Borrie, op.cit. p.36.

38   Borrie, op.cit. p.37.

39   *AJHR* 1868, 15 October.

CHAPTER 8

1   Harvey McQueen, *The New Place: The Poetry of Settlement in New Zealand 1852–1914* (Wellington 1993), p.22. John Barr published two collections of his work.

2   Alexander Bathgate, *Colonial Experiences* (Glasgow 1874).

3   Quoted by D. Charlwood in *The Long Farewell* (Victoria 1983), p.56.

4.   Cited by A . Hassam in *Sailing to Australia: Shipboard Diaries by Nineteenth Century British Immigrants* (Manchester 1994), p.52.

5.   T. Capper, *Emigrants Guide to Australia*. This was originally published as *Philips' Guide* in 1852 but with the advent of the gold rushes Capper extended it into a new and very popular edition selling at a shilling.

6   Charlotte Macdonald, *A Woman of Good Character* (Wellington 1990).

7   ATL MS papers 1192.

8   Hassam, op. cit. p.59

9   Charlwood, op.cit. p.252.

10   ATL MS papers 383.

11   Cited by Macdonald, op.cit. p.79.

12   Hassam, op.cit. p.35.

13   Hassam, op.cit. p.52.

14   ATL MS papers 1192.

15   Hassam, op.cit. p.139.

16   There is a set of these regulations included in the Salmon papers, ATL MS 3657. Salmon, then Margaret Evans, was a matron on the *Oxford* at a slightly later period. There is a testimonial among the papers signed by the single women attesting to her good offices. This may or may not have been solicited.

17   The report was sent to Auckland, and published together with other official papers. *AJHR* 1865 D-3, p.13.

18   Macdonald, op.cit. p.95.

19   Charlwood, op.cit. p.101.

20   ATL MS papers 383.

21   For an almost unbelievable account of the state of some of these 'coffin ships', as they were rightly denominated by their crews, see E. S. Turner, 'Plimsoll Rules the Waves' in *Roads to Ruin* (London 1966).

22   Hassam, op.cit. p.103.

23 Quoted by R.J. Hickin in his privately published *Never Too Old to Dream*, an account of the lives of John and Jane Wilson, settlers in Otago in September 1858 and kindly made available by a descendant.
24 ATL MS papers 1192.
25 Cited by Hassam, op.cit. p.118.
26 He records this experience and makes this comment in *A First Year in the Canterbury Settlement* (Auckland 1964).
27 Hassam, op.cit. p.115.
28 ibid. p.121.
29 Macdonald, op.cit., canvasses some instances of this at pp.81–3.
30 A number of writers refer to this incident, e.g. Macdonald, ibid. p.91, and Hassam, op.cit. p.71.
31 Hassam, op.cit. p.71.
32 ATL MS papers 1192.
33 Salmon papers, op.cit.
34 From *Australia and New Zealand* by Anthony Trollope in D. Stone (ed), *Verdict on New Zealand* (Wellington 1959), p.44.
35 Lady Mary Barker, *Station Life in New Zealand* (London 1883), p.43.
36 Charles Money, *Knocking About in New Zealand* (Melbourne 1871), p.5.
37 From *A First Year in the Canterbury Settlement* (London 1863) in Stone, op.cit. p.34.
38 Most of what we do know is summarised in H. Roth, *Trade Unions in New Zealand, Past and Present* (Wellington 1973), and H. Roth and J. Hammond, *Toil and Trouble: The Struggle for a Better Life in New Zealand* (Auckland 1981).
39 Bathgate, op.cit. p.42.
40 ATL MS papers 496.
41 ATL MS papers 1297.
42 ATL MS papers 229.
43 ATL MS papers 1971.
44 ATL MS papers 3895.
45 Cited unsourced by P.R. May in *The West Coast Gold Rushes* (2nd edition, Christchurch 1967), p.296.
46 Both of these are cited in ibid. pp.296 and 297, unfortunately without attribution.
47 In ibid. p.296.
48 Money, op.cit.
49 *West Coast Times*, 23 September 1865.
50 ibid. p.299.
51 In May, op.cit. p.273.
52 For biographical notes on and the songs of Thatcher, see Hugh Anderson, *Goldrush Songster* (Victoria 1958), and R. Bailey and H. Roth, *Shanties by the Way* (Christchurch 1967).
53 *AJHR* 1858 F-1.
54 *NZPD* 1858-60, p.777.
55 There are many accounts of this celebrated event. See, for instance, Grimshaw et al., *Creating a Nation* (Victoria 1994), pp.99–102.
56 *NZPD* 1871, p.331.
57 There is debate on this point. J.O.C. Phillips in *A Man's Country?* (Auckland 1987) is sceptical of the positive effects of mateship. Others have celebrated its his egalitarian influence, particularly John Mulgan in his descriptions of the 2NZEF in *Report on Experience* (Auckland 1967).
58 ATL MS papers 1297.

CHAPTER 9

1   Quoted by Josiah Sage in his *Memoirs* (London 1951), p18.
2   This figure is the estimate of C.H. Feinstein et al. in *British Economic Growth 1856–1973* (Oxford 1982) but it is broadly supported by others.
3   Geoffrey Barraclough in his *Introduction to Contemporary History* (London 1967) attributes almost all of the international events of the twentieth century to the development of this economy and the bitter economic rivalries it engendered, particularly on the part of those such as the Germans and Japanese who were excluded from markets by it.
4   *Statistical Abstracts for the United Kingdom*, cited by A. Offer in *The First World War: An Agrarian Interpretation* (Oxford 1991), p.82.
5   For a detailed explication of why this is so, see C. Petersen, *Bread and the British Economy 1770–1870* (Aldershot 1995).
6   Most notably S.B. Saul in his *The Myth of the Great Depression 1873–96* (London 1969).
7   Board of Trade index, cited by F. Crouzet, *The Victorian Economy* (London 1982), p.59.
8   One of the earliest attempts at an estimate actually calculates real wages, on an 1870 statistical base of 118, to have risen to 166 over the next 20 years, although this is almost certainly an overestimate. See G.D.H. Cole, *A Short History of the British Working Class Movement 1787–1947* (revised edition London 1948).
9   In particular there is G.S. Jones' study, *Outcast London* (London 1971).
10   *13th Report of the Vestry Sanitary Officer 1868*, cited by Jones, op.cit. p.170.
11   See *Report of the Royal Commission on the Housing of the Working Classes 1884–5*.
12   Cited along with some other instances in J. Davis, 'From Rookeries to Communities: Race, Poverty and Policing in London 1850–1985', *History Workshop Journal* 27, Spring 1989 from p.66.
13   M. Nelson, 'Social Class Trends in British Diet 1860–1980', in C. Geissler and D.J. Oddy (eds), *Food, Diet and Economic Change* (Leicester 1993), p.103.
14   Cited by J. Burnett, *Plenty and Want: A Social History of Diet in England from 1815* (London 1979), p.206.
15   For an interesting account of a number of the dimensions of this development, see G. Crossick (ed), *The Lower Middle Class in Britain 1870 to 1914* (London 1977).
16   Crouzet, op.cit. p.167.
17   For the long answer, see F.M.L. Thompson, 'Free Trade and the Land', in G.E. Mingay, *The Victorian Countryside* Vol. 1 (London 1981) from p.103.
18   R.J.P. Kain and H.C. Prince, *The Tithe Surveys of England and Wales* (Cambridge 1985), pp.173–4.
19   Quoted by Alun Howkins in *Poor Labouring Men: Rural Radicalism in Norfolk 1870–1923* (London 1985), p.12.
20   Cited by Thompson in Mingay, op.cit. p.107.
21   F. G. Heath, *The English Peasantry* (London 1874), p.41.
22   Quoted by J. Burnett, 'Country Diet' in Mingay, op. cit. Vol. 2, p.562.
23   This book, first published in 1939, has been reprinted many times since, and remains a classic of the later nineteenth-century countryside.
24   For an account of this curiosity and its reform, see E.S. Turner, *Roads to Ruin* (London 1966).
25   Quoted by D.H. Morgan, *Harvesters and Harvesting 1840–1900* (Guildford 1982), p.128.

26   BPP 1893,4 XXXV 123.

27   Thompson, op.cit. p.76 of the 1973 edition.

28   This incident is described by Flora Thomson in *Lark Rise to Candleford*.

29   Morgan, op.cit., has some horrendous material concerning this.

30   This fate after death was the source of immense distress and controversy in the nineteenth century. See R. Richardson, *Death, Dissection, and the Destitute* (London 1988) for an almost unbelievable account of this.

31   Morgan, op.cit. p.123.

32   Pamela Horn, 'Labour Organisations' in Mingay, op.cit. Vol. 2, p.582.

33   Morgan, op.cit. chapter 8.

34   A phrase usually attributed to the Webbs, who a few decades later wrote a history of the development of trade unionism in Britain.

35   For the background to this, see L. Birch (ed), *The History of the TUC 1868–1968* (London 1968).

36   There are numerous accounts of Arch's life (including an interesting autobiography) and of his career as a trade union organiser and subsequently Liberal member of parliament for Norfolk. One of the best brief summaries is contained in H. Newby, *Country Life: A Social History of Rural England* (London 1987) from p.120.

37   From Arch's autobiography, and cited by Rollo Arnold in *The Farthest Promised Land* (Wellington 1981), p.32.

38   Cited by Howkins, op.cit. p.35.

CHAPTER 10

1   There are many accounts of this period, most of them covering the same ground or aspects of it. In particular there are R.C.J. Stone, *Economic Development 1870–1890* (Auckland 1967) and *Makers of Fortune: A Colonial Business Community and its Fall* (Auckland 1973); Chapter 4 of W.B. Sutch, *The Quest for Security in New Zealand 1840–1966* (Wellington 1966); W.J. Gardner, 'A Colonial Economy' in G.W. Rice (ed), *The Oxford History of New Zealand* (Second Edition Auckland 1992); and M.F. Lloyd Pritchard, 'Depression and Recovery 1877–1914', *An Economic History of New Zealand to 1939* (Auckland 1970).

2   G. Hawke in *The Making of New Zealand: An Economic History* (Cambridge 1985), p.82.

3   See the *Report on the Statistics for New Zealand* of 1890 which shows the value at least of imports per head consistently tracking above the value of exports.

4   Sutch, op.cit. pp.65–8, and in his essay 'The Long Depression' in M. Turnbull (ed), *Colony or Nation?* (Sydney 1966).

5   J.E. Martin, 'Unemployment, Government and the Labour Market' in *NZJH* Vol. 29 No. 2, October 1995.

6   Lloyd Pritchard, op.cit. Table 73 p.140.

7   W.P. Reeves, *The Long White Cloud* (Revised edition London 1942), p.239.

8   A. Saunders, *History of New Zealand* (Christchurch 1899), p.336.

9   R. Dalziel, *Julius Vogel, Business Politician* (Auckland 1986), p.313.

10   All of these reactions from *NZPD*, 28 June 1870.

11   For a more detailed account of this railways era and its scandals, see Chapter Two 'Railways and Rabbits' in my *Shame and Disgrace* (Auckland 1992).

12   *New Zealand Official Yearbook* 1899.

13   ibid.

14   This relationship and its import have been covered in great detail by Rollo Arnold in his excellent and groundbreaking book *The Farthest Promised Land* (Wellington 1981), to which I am greatly indebted for much of what follows here.

15   The detail of this is set out in R. Dalziel, *The Origins of New Zealand Diplomacy* (Wellington 1975), chapter 2.

16   *Appendices to the Journals of the Legislative Council* 1873 No.12 from p.38.

17   ibid. p.39.

18   See *AJHR* for 1872 D–12.

19   W.D. Borrie, *Immigration to New Zealand 1854-1938* (Canberra 1991), p.59.

20   Cited by Arnold, op.cit. p.40.

21   These quantities were set out on the ticket itself. See, for example, the extant ticket issued to 25-year-old Louisa Morton to make the journey on the *Helen Denny* in 1873 and held by ATL Ms papers 1108.

22   *AJHR* 1873 D-1, cited by Borrie, op.cit. p.88.

23   *Appendices to the Journals of the Legislative Council* 1873 No.12, from p.38.

24   Arnold, op.cit. p.45.

25   Cited by Arnold, op.cit. p.52.

26   ibid. p.54.

27   Dalziel, op.cit. (1975) gives these figures sourced to a report by Featherston October 1872. The standard work on Irish immigration to New Zealand is D.H. Akenson, *Half the World From Home* (Wellington 1990).

28   Subsequently published as an official paper in the *AJHR* D series for 1875, letter of 30 April 1875.

29   This letter is cited by Dalziel, op.cit. (1975) p.45.

30   Quoted by T. Coleman, *Passage to America* (London 1992), p.78.

31   *A report on emigrant ships by the Sanitary Commission of the Lancet* (London 1873).

32   *AJHR* 1875 Series D, letter of 30 April 1875.

33   For an analysis of the social composition of the Legislative Council at this period, see A.H. McLintock and G.A. Wood, *The Upper House in Colonial New Zealand* (Wellington 1987).

34   The detail of this is to be found in N.M. Chappell, *New Zealand Banker's Hundred* (Auckland 1961), and in K. Sinclair and W.F. Mandle, *Open Account: A History of the Bank of New South Wales in New Zealand 1861–1961* (Wellington 1961). It is placed in its context by Sutch, op.cit. (1966).

35   H.D. Bedford, 'The History and Practise of Banking in New Zealand' (unpublished thesis, Otago University 1951) p.169, and cited by Sutch, ibid. A number of subsequent studies have borne out this harsh judgement.

36   Cited by J.B. Condliffe, *New Zealand in the Making* (London 1930), p.489.

37   Stone, op.cit. (1967), p.18, unsourced.

38   The nature of New Zealand as a dependent economy and what this means has long and often been analysed, especially by C.G.F. Simkin in *The Instability of a Dependent Economy* (Oxford 1951).

39   There is a fascinating article about Davidson and his initiatives by M. Palmer, 'William Soltau Davidson: A Pioneer of New Zealand Estate Management', in *NZJH* Vol.7 No.2, October 1973 from p.148.

40   *New Zealand Official Yearbook* for 1899.

CHAPTER 11

1   W.D. Borrie, *Immigration to New Zealand 1854-1938* (Canberra 1991), p.87.

2   *AJHR* 1873 D-1.

3   ibid.

4   C. Couchman, *Journal of a Voyage of the Arethusa from Plymouth to Wellington 1879*, unpublished MS held by ATL, qMS COU.

5   *AJHR* 1874 D-1A p.8.

6   *AJHR* 1883 D-11.

7   A. Hassam, *Sailing to Australia, Shipboard Diaries by Nineteenth Century British Immigrants* (Manchester 1994), p.111.

8   D. Charlwood, *The Long Farewell* (London 1981), p.155.

9   ATL qMS COU.

10 *AJHR* 1972 G-3.

11 *AJHR* 1872 D-16A, Enclosure 8.

12 ATL MS papers 2039.

13 ATL qMS COU.

14 ATL MS papers qMS BRO.

15 Charlwood, op.cit. p.159.

16 There are fairly full papers on this matter in *AJHR* 1879 at D-6.

17 ATL qMS BRO.

18 The report of the Board of Trade is carried in *AJHR* 1875 D-1.

19 *AJHR* 1875 H-1.

20 ATL qMS BRO.

21 Quoted by Rollo Arnold, *The Farthest Promised Land* (Wellington 1981), p.239.

22 ATL qMS COU.

23 The full report is contained in *AJHR* 1872 G-3.

24 *AJHR* 1874 D-1A.

25 ibid.

26 Quoted by Arnold, op.cit. p.242. Arnold quotes numerous similar reactions from the seventies throughout his book, from which the following is a brief selection.

27 ibid. p.243.

28 ibid. p.156.

29 'Hopeful', *Taken In: A Sketch of New Zealand Life* (London 1887), p.111.

30 ibid. p.175. The chapter of the book entitled 'Who Should Venture Out' makes interesting reading. The 'whingeing Pom' syndrome has an apparently lengthy history.

31 *AJHR* 1876 D-2.

32 See, for instance, John E. Martin, 'Unemployment, Government, and the Labour Market', *NZJH* October 1995, p.176.

33 Hocken pamphlet 19/7 1880, cited by Borrie, op.cit. p.82.

34 Someone thought this letter of sufficient significance for it to be published as an official paper, *AJHR* 1880 D-4.

35 *Christchurch Press*, 16 September 1884.

36 Cited by Martin, op.cit. p.181.

37 Cited by W.B. Sutch in *The Quest for Security in New Zealand 1840–1966* (Oxford 1966), p.61, but without attribution.

38 ibid. p.64.

39 Quoted by J.E. Martin in *The Forgotten Worker: The Rural Wage Earner in Nineteenth Century New Zealand* (Wellington 1990), p.28.

40 ibid.

41 H. Roth, *Trade Unions in New Zealand, Past and Present* (Wellington 1973), p.10.

42 There are a number of accounts of this strike. See, for instance, H. Roth and J. Hammond, *Toil and Trouble* (Auckland 1981), p.38.

43 *AJHR* 1890 H-5.

44 ATL MS papers 1744.

45 Hassam, op.cit. p.116.

46 ATL MS papers 1154.

47 ATL MS papers 1744.
48 'Hopeful', op.cit. p.3.
49 ibid. p.119.

CHAPTER 12

1   E.P. Thompson, *The Making of the English Working Class* (London 1963).

2   ibid. p.457.

3   The working out of the praxis which this entailed during the reign of Queen Victoria in limned in James Walvin, *Victorian Values* (London 1987).

4   Both of these and others are noted in D. Thompson, *The Chartists* (London 1984).

5   There is a helpful summary of the progress of electoral change by Raewyn Dalziel, '100 Years of the Modern Electoral System', in *Towards 1990* (Wellington 1989). Dalziel does not believe that progress to full manhood suffrage was particularly rapid in New Zealand. I cannot agree.

6   ibid p.56 and from the Rolleston Papers in the ATL. This curious dismissive reference to 'the pothouse' when working men were meant was in use in New Zealand as late as the 1890s.

7   See W.B. Sutch, *The Quest for Security in New Zealand, 1845–1966* (Wellington 1966), p.67.

8   For a comprehensive account of this, see M. Tennant, *Paupers and Providers: Charitable Aid in New Zealand* (Wellington 1989).

9   This pervasive Arcadian myth has been explored in particular by Miles Fairburn in *The Ideal Society and its Enemies* (Auckland 1989). The town versus country debate is also covered in D. Hamer, *New Towns in the New World* (New York 1990). Its persistence is canvassed in M. Chase, 'This is no claptrap, this is our heritage', in Shaw and M. Chase (eds), *The Imagined Past: History and Nostalgia* (Manchester 1989).

10   For the development of Ballance's thinking, see T. McIvor, *The Rainmaker* (Auckland 1989), and in particular chapter 6, and D. Hamer, *The New Zealand Liberals* (Auckland 1988); for Stout, see D. Hamer, 'Sir Robert Stout and the Labour Question' in R. Chapman and K. Sinclair (eds), *Studies of a Small Democracy* (Auckland 1963).

11   Cited by Hamer, ibid. p.87, without attribution.

12   Cited by Sutch, op.cit. p.69.

13   Hamer, op.cit. (1963) p.92.

14   There are many exegeses of George's work. This is based in particular on Ursula Vogel, 'The Land Question: A Liberal Theory of Communal Property' in *History Workshop Journal* 27, Spring 1989, pp.106–35.

15   See chapter 1, 'Stopping the Pothouse Larrikins' in my *Shame and Disgrace* (Auckland 1991).

16   For example, by Eric Olssen in his brilliant study of the Caversham working-class community, *Building the New World* (Auckland 1995).

17   See, for instance, the comprehensive attitude survey carried out for the Royal Commission on Social Policy (1986), or the even more recent study by J. Vowles, P. Aimer et al, *Towards Consensus* (Auckland 1995), a very detailed exploration of the attitudes brought to bear by voters in determining the outcome of the 1993 general election.

18   Certainly there have been Australian essays in the same direction. Of particular note have been H. McQueen, *A New Britannia* (Ringwood, Victoria 1970) and more recently Grimshaw, Lake, McGrath, Quartly, *Creating a Nation* (Ringwood, Victoria 1994).

INDEX